THE U.S. POSTAL SERVICE

THE U.S. POSTAL SERVICE

Status and Prospects of a Public Enterprise

JOHN T. TIERNEY

Boston College

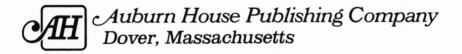 *Auburn House Publishing Company*
Dover, Massachusetts

HE
6371
.T54
1988
148239
Feb. 1990

Library of Congress Cataloging in Publication Data

Tierney, John T., 1951–
  The U.S. Postal Service.

  Bibliography: p.
  Includes index.
  1. United States Postal Service—Management.
2. Postal service—United States. I. Title.
II. Title: US Postal Service.
HE6371.T54   1988   383'.4973   88-6274
ISBN 0-86569-181-9

Printed in the United States of America

For Sue, Jamie, and Tom

PREFACE

This is a study of the nation's oldest and largest public enterprise—the U.S. postal system. The book aims primarily to examine the major elements and issues in American postal policy. My objective is to convey a sense of the complexity of postal administration and policy and, more particularly, to identify and explain what features of the Postal Service's task and environment make it difficult for the organization's executives to rationalize the mail system through the implementation of "businesslike" solutions. It is my hope that this study will clear away some of the misunderstanding that surrounds the Postal Service—and perhaps, by extension, public bureaucracies in general.

This book is my second on the U.S. postal system. The first, *Postal Reorganization*, published in 1981 (also by Auburn House), examined the 1971 corporate transformation of the Post Office Department and analyzed what difference it seemed to have made in how the huge mail delivery organization was managed. The reorganization presented an unusual research opportunity, the chance to investigate what effect substantial changes in the political and administrative structures governing an agency would have on its behavior. Here was a significant alteration in the managerial environment of an important governmental enterprise—a reorganization carried out with immodest expectations for its eventual success. When I began the research for that book in 1977, the dominant view at the time was that the reorganization had failed miserably to meet the expectations of its architects. I was interested in determining whether this interpretation was true and, if so, what might account for the alleged failures. I discovered successes as well as failures, some predictable, some not.

Though I continued to keep abreast of developments in postal policy and politics in the years following the publication of that book, I had no expectation of ever returning to the Postal Service as a subject for still more research and writing—and certainly not for another book-length project.

But I was drawn back to this topic nevertheless, chiefly by the many interesting developments in the postal policy arena in the 1980s. For one thing, the organization had reversed its financial fortunes. After enduring repeated deficits throughout the 1970s, the Postal Service had surpluses four out of the five years from 1982 through 1986, and net income exceeded net losses by $1.6 billion. Moreover, the disastrous declines in mail volume that assorted Cassandras had been predicting since the mid-1970s never materialized; indeed, mail volume has been increasing in the 1980s at the fastest rate in the postal system's history, growing by almost 50 percent (or 50 billion pieces) between 1979 and 1986 (up almost 11 percent in 1983 alone). That was not supposed to happen at the dawning of the age of "electronic mail."

Interesting developments also had occurred in the area of postal rates and rate-making. In 1983 the Supreme Court handed down an important decision resolving a dispute between two appellate courts and ruling that the actual costs of delivering a letter, magazine, or package should form the base for postal rates, but that the Postal Rate Commission should have flexibility to decide how to distribute other costs. The Supreme Court's ruling was a defeat for the National Association of Greeting Card Publishers and the United Parcel Service, each of which had claimed over the years that users of first-class mail for too long had paid too high a rate, while fees for other classes of mail (such as parcel post) had been artificially low.

Finally, the internal organizational management of the Postal Service also was undergoing changes: the Board of Governors, long perceived to be merely a rubber stamp to the decisions of top management, became conspicuously more assertive in its assorted roles—until one of its members was sent to federal prison after pleading guilty to having tried to defraud the Postal Service in a contract steering scheme; there had been four new postmasters general within three years (by the time this book went to press, there had been five within five); and a far-reaching internal reorganization had been carried out aimed at streamlining the management structure, delegating more managerial authority to the field, and encouraging managerial innovation.

Most of these developments would not have made normal people sit up straight. But as someone already generally informed about and attentive to postal policy and politics, I found most of what had been happening in the postal policy arena quite remarkable. And I found myself for many reasons increasingly tempted to write again about the Postal Service and postal policy.

For one thing, despite its seemingly prosaic nature, this subject offers those of us who are students of governmental policy and administration an unexpectedly rich tapestry to examine, for woven through it are many of the larger elements and issues that typically attract our attention: the role of organized interests in shaping public policy, the effect of legislators' electoral pressures on their policy decisions, the conflicts among government agencies that share jurisdiction in a policy arena, the increasing role of the federal courts in fashioning public policy, the difficulties of managing in a governmental context, and the challenges of making sure that governmental organizations are responsive and accountable to the public through their elected representatives—but not so responsive that their effectiveness is completely undermined.

I had another reason as well for taking up this subject once again. That is, although a few students of public policy and administration have devoted more attention to government corporations in recent years, still relatively little is known about the hows and whys of their creation and operation. But if government corporations (or similarly designed government-sponsored enterprises) are to be permanent and increasingly conspicuous features in the constellation of government organizations (as seems to be the case), more should be known about what to expect of them. If realistic and informed expectations about these organizations can be established, it may be possible to minimize problems of implementation and to avoid gross deviations from intended policy outcomes. This is important, especially if we want to avoid contributing to citizens' apparently declining confidence in the government's ability to manage the public's business.

Yet another important impetus to my taking up this subject once again is this: I believe that the conventional and popular wisdom about the Postal Service—that it is poorly managed and, overall, bumblingly incompetent—is simply wrong. This is an organization that works quite well, especially considering the constraints we impose upon it. And it is run by intelligent executives and managers—people of generally impressive business and political acumen—who operate a system of coordinated activities far more complex than most outsiders would imagine. Thinking what a shame it is that editorial cartoonists and cheap-shot artists of various occupational stripes are almost alone in getting their views of the Postal Service into print, I decided to resume my examinations of postal policy and management. And at the urging of John Harney and Gene Bailey, I have written this, my second—and, I hope, my last—book on the Postal Service.

My friends and students and family members often wonder how I can spend months upon end poring over information about something as mundane as the postal system. Their question, not always left implicit, is: Why not look at something more interesting or exciting? My only response is this. Covering the postman-bites-dog story (or its equivalent in the annals of governmental organization) is the job of journalists. The task of social scientists, by contrast, is to discern the general truths that lie in the ordinary, the everyday, the commonplace. This is, to most tastes, a much less inviting task. But my interest as a student of government is, at least in part, to understand the difficulties that confront those who try to supply a service under governmental auspices. Where better to focus for such an understanding than on the Postal Service, the nation's oldest and largest (and most extraordinarily ordinary) public service organization?

I approach this study as a political scientist, trained in the study of government institutions—not as an investigative reporter, an economist, or a management analyst. My method of inquiry was eclectic. It included reading histories, scrutinizing statutes, examining administrative structures, compiling and interpreting statements of postal policy, ferreting out internal memoranda and reports, perusing manuals and hearing records, surveying mailers' association and postal union newsletters, gathering outside evaluations and criticisms of organizational performance, visiting postal facilities, and conducting personal interviews with persons inside the Postal Service and the Postal Rate Commission, on Capitol Hill, and in the broader community of organized interests attentive to postal policy.

Many people were generous in granting me interviews or assisting me in gathering data. To all of them I extend my thanks. But there are four people in the Postal Service to whom I am especially indebted for their insights or help at various times over the long life of my interest in this subject: Bill Cummings, Jane Kennedy, Julie Rios, and Dick Strasser.

I appreciate the financial assistance of Boston College in making a small research grant available to me for this project. And I want to thank Fran Sceppa, who made life easier for me in varied ways while I worked on this book.

Finally, to Frank Rourke and Jim Wilson I owe special and enduring thanks. Each of them has profoundly shaped my thinking about the limits and possibilities of governmental administration and about the politics of public policymaking. And each has extended valued guidance and help and opportunities at various stages in my career—and friendship throughout.

JOHN T. TIERNEY

CONTENTS

List of Acronyms

ACH	automated clearinghouses
ATM	automated teller machines
APWU	American Postal Workers Union
BCS	bar code sorter
CCPR	Citizens Committee for Postal Reform
ECA	ElectroCom Automation Incorporated
E-COM	Electronic Computer Originated Mail
EFT	electronic funds transfers
EI/QWL	employee involvement/quality of work life
GAI	Gnau and Associates, Inc.
GAO	General Accounting Office (U.S. Congress)
IER	inverse elasticity rule
IRT	integrated retail terminal
MSC	management sectional center
NAGCP	National Association of Greeting Card Publishers
NALC	National Association of Letter Carriers
NDCBU	Neighborhood Delivery and Collection Box Unit
NRLCA	National Rural Letter Carriers Association
OCR	optical character reader
OOC	Officer of the Commission (Postal Rate Commission)
OTA	Office of Technology Assessment (U.S. Congress)
PES	Private Express Statutes
PMG	Postmaster General
POS	point-of-sale terminals
PRA	Postal Reorganization Act
PRC	Postal Rate Commission
REI	Recognition Equipment, Inc.
STS	Supervisory Training System
TVA	Tennessee Valley Authority
UPS	United Parcel Service
USPS	United States Postal Service
Zip + 4	nine-digit ZIP Code

INTRODUCTION

The United States Postal Service is one of the largest organizations in the world, with 800,000 employees and an annual budget over $31 billion. It now moves over 150 billion pieces of mail each year through an extraordinarily complex system of carefully coordinated activities. It is one of the few governmental organizations in the United States to touch directly the lives of most of us on an almost daily basis. Most of us, however, know very little about this organization. Unless our work brings us into contact with the Postal Service in a more extensive way than normal, our familiarity with it is slight: Most of us probably are friendly with our letter carrier, impatient with the clerks at the post office (who we think are too slow), and conversant with at least a few mail classes and rates—clear, at least, on the cost of a first-class stamp. Beyond that, most of us do not know much.

If we hear or read anything about this huge enterprise, it tends to be of a quite conventional viewpoint: the Postal Service is the epitome of inefficiency and bad management, the very paradigm of unresponsive and unaccountable governmental bureaucracies. The world is full of exponents of that view—journalists looking for instances of governmental bungling or excesses; editorial cartoonists given more to clichés than to cleverness; members of Congress and their aides, eager to attract press attention to their valiant efforts to tame bureaucratic dragons; other self-styled protectors of consumers' interests; free-market economists who see no reason for a governmental monopoly on the delivery of letter mail; and a host of others.

There are, in short, plenty of sources for a conventional view of the Postal Service. This book offers an unconventional view: the Postal Service is quite well managed and operates as efficiently and effectively as we have a right to expect, given the constraints we impose on it.

This argument is not going to attract the attention of the folks

1

on the Pulitzer committee. Nor—be forewarned—is this book going to provide much comfort to readers hoping to find confirmation of their view that the mail system faces problems because postal executives and managers are incompetent, unmotivated, prodigal, or stupid. They are not. If only the problems of the Postal Service and other governmental service organizations were that easily explained! The real explanations are far more complicated and less viscerally satisfying.

Without meaning to exonerate the Postal Service of responsibility or blame in those matters that it clearly *has* bungled, I conclude that the most serious long-term problems of the postal system stem from the failure of Congress to decide what kind of postal system we should have—a costly public service that meets a wide assortment of political demands or a lean and cost-effective mail delivery system, operated in a businesslike fashion. As it is now, Congress is asking the Postal Service to be both and, in the process, makes it an easy target for broadside attack.

The mail system has been operated as a government service for two centuries. Like most government agencies, the Postal Service has many constituencies it must satisfy—the general public, residents of rural areas, the organization's own large and politically powerful work force, and businesses that rely heavily on mail service in their operations (including magazine publishers, direct-mail advertisers, and mail-order companies). For years, members of Congress have accommodated the varied demands of these interests—and of their own reelection needs—and have consequently saddled the postal system with a wide variety of economically irreconcilable social and political objectives: frequent, speedy, and consistent delivery; universally available letter-mail services at reasonable and uniform rates; support of a large and well-paid work force; continuation of an expensive rural network; maintenance of numerous collection and distribution points; and also the mandate to accomplish this without a deficit.

The problem is not that "incompetent" postal executives do not know how to apply known managerial solutions to many of the mail system's problems. They *do* know what could be done to produce an efficient, cost-effective mail delivery system—one that would provide predictable and economically rational services. To operate the system in a more businesslike way, they would tailor its services to economic demands. They could easily keep rates low for those who generate most of the mail and pay the bulk of the system's costs (American businesses), while providing reliable services responsive to their needs. But they would probably do so by curtailing or eliminating traditional service structures now

maintained to meet the political demands of nonpaying constituencies. After all, Americans do not really need (though all may
agree it is nice to have) residential delivery to the door, six days a
week. Nor do we need post offices at every rural crossroads, at
least not when regular and satisfactory services can be provided
by alternative methods at lower cost.

Although Congress transformed the governing arrangements of
the postal system in the early 1970s with the objective of freeing it
to operate in a more businesslike fashion, the autonomy of postal
managers still does not extend to important decisions about the
scope of postal services. Their hands are continually stayed by
members of Congress who fear that the political costs attendant to
a streamlining of the system would be too great. So Congress
continues to insist—under the watchful eye and steady pressure of
the powerful postal unions and other assorted special interests—
that the Postal Service maintain a structure of traditional mail
services that meet the electoral needs of lawmakers but that do
not reflect economic demand.

Clearly, the postal system is not merely an economic enterprise
but an important part of the nation's social and political fabric. The
full value of, say, rural post offices cannot be assessed on a balance
sheet; it is true, after all, that they are often the social heart of
isolated communities, gathering places for the exchange of news,
and centers for the nourishment of local community identities.
Moreover, Congress obviously has the right and the obligation to
see to it that interests are represented and the public's wishes
heeded.

But Congress has created a situation in which the Postal Service
is bound to be a source of frustration both to those who think it
should be more sensitive to the needs of the public and to those
who think it should be doing more to rationalize the mail system.
Meanwhile, members of Congress want it to be both at once.
Thus, the problems of the postal system are not ones that postal
management can solve; there are no administrative panaceas that
will reconcile conflicting expectations. Only Congress can solve
this problem, and it can do so only by making difficult choices
among currently irreconcilable goals.

Popular Assessments of the Postal Service

In the scheme of things, relatively little is written about the Postal
Service and postal policy. There is a tiny academic literature.[1]
Most of the other written material about the subject emanates from

two sources: free-market advocates who see no reason for a government monopoly on the delivery of letter mail, and journalists and
other writers of various sorts who find the massive Postal Service
an easy target for broadside attack. But one of the curious things
about the American postal system is that most of what is written
about it is wholly out of sync with the public's own assessment,
which is quite favorable.

In the view of free-market advocates, with weak stomachs for
governmental provision of goods and services, the postal system
should not be operated by "the government," this monolithic
entity they see as determined to gouge the American public. One
of the economic right's more prolific (and vituperative) critics of
the postal system put it this way in 1985: "The United States Postal
Service is probably the worst managed and one of the least honest
corporations in America. . . . Like all monopolies, the postal
monopoly is abused, as the government forces people to accept
increasingly worse service at ever higher prices."[2]

And when writing about the Postal Service, journalists and free-
lance writers know that an "all-is-well-in-postal-land" approach will
find little favor among those editors and publishers who think the
only good story is one that makes the reader's blood boil. The
sluice gates thus open to a flood of commentary about the allegedly
"exorbitant" wages of postal workers, the sloppy inefficiency of
service delivery, and the isolation and high-handedness of postal
management.

Despite what most writers try to suggest, the fact is that
Americans are quite satisfied with the Postal Service. Results of a
survey conducted in 1987 by the Postal Service's Marketing Service Branch reveal that 84 percent of the sampled household
customers described their overall impressions of the Postal Service
as favorable. And some 56 percent rated the Postal Service as
excellent or very good from the viewpoint of sending mail, while
another 32 percent rated it as good. As receivers of mail, 57
percent said the Postal Service is excellent or very good, and 29
percent rated it as good.[3]

Fortunately, we need not rely on the Postal Service's own
surveys for data on this score. The University of Michigan's highly
respected Survey Research Center found in 1978 that 71.6 percent
of the respondents in one of its surveys rated the Postal Service as
either "good" or "very good"—the highest of any institution.
Conversely, only 5.3 percent of the respondents rated the Postal
Service as doing a poor job for the country as a whole. That was
the lowest "poor" rating given to any institution asked about in

that study. (The telephone company, for example, was given a "poor" rating for service by 9 percent of the respondents.)[4]

The Roper Organization also has conducted periodic surveys about the public's attitude toward service organizations of various sorts; the results of these studies also indicate generally favorable public impressions of postal services. In one relatively recent poll, the results of which were issued by the Roper Organization in mid-April 1987, Americans were asked to evaluate the quality of service they receive from twelve different institutions, professions, or companies. Respondents gave generally positive reviews to all of them, with especially high marks for the Postal Service (see Exhibit i-1). In the respondents' view, the best service is provided by supermarkets (79 percent of respondents said they get excellent or good service from them), the Postal Service (73 percent), doctors (70 percent), banks (69 percent), and electric utilities (69 percent). People also are content with the service they receive from the local telephone company (65 percent), hospitals (64 percent), department stores (63 percent), and long-distance telephone companies (61 percent). Criticism was somewhat more pronounced concerning service quality from insurance, credit card, and cable television companies.[5]

Furthermore, in polls conducted in 1983, 1984, and 1985, Roper asked citizens their opinions about twelve federal agencies. Each year the Postal Service was viewed most favorably of the twelve agencies mentioned. In 1985, for example, 70 percent of the respondents reported favorable opinions of the Postal Service (with

Supermarkets	79%
Postal Service	73%
Doctors	70%
Banks	69%
Electric company	69%
Local telephone	65%
Hospitals	64%
Department stores	63%
Long distance telephone	61%
Insurance company	52%
Credit card company	42%
Cable TV company	40%

Exhibit 1-1   Quality of Services: Percentage Excellent/Good. (Based on an April 1987 Roper Report.)

23 percent reporting a "highly favorable" opinion), whereas the
Departments of Labor, Energy, and Housing and Urban Development enjoyed the favorable opinion of only half the respondents
and a "highly favorable" opinion of only 6, 8, and 9 percent,
respectively.[6]

Still, when citizens complain to one another about governmental
service, they are more likely to complain about the Postal Service
than about other government agencies. One reason is that it is
unlike the many agencies whose "products" are largely unseen,
whose performances are not easily monitored, and whose effects
on the public are largely unnoticed. The Postal Service's performance is always and everywhere under scrutiny, its inefficiencies
and failings readily apparent. People *know* whether their mail
comes late or is misdelivered, whether the ceramic pumpkin sent
by grandma at Halloween arrives in a thousand pieces. They *see*
letter carriers taking lunch breaks and window clerks moving
slowly. Besides being able to observe the regular performance of
the postal system, citizens also find it easy to monitor the *costs* of
their mail service. That is, unlike most governmental services,
mail delivery is purchased by individuals, as needed, at retail
counters through simple business transactions. The individual
mailer, and not the general taxpayer, shoulders the bulk of the
costs. This means that citizens are aware of postal expenses (or at
least, of increases in postage prices) in a way that they are not
particularly alert when it comes to their increased tax outlays for
the activities of, say, the Federal Trade Commission or the Drug
Enforcement Administration.

Moreover, citizens have less difficulty understanding the activities of the Postal Service than those of agencies that deal with
highly technical bodies of knowledge and use esoteric jargon and
formulas. Many governmental agencies—for example, the National
Institutes of Health—perform complicated tasks that are not only
generally closed to the public's routine observation but outside the
general public's realm of understanding. Thus, even if these agencies are inefficient or ineffective, the public is not aware of it. But
citizens *are* aware of the postal system's having smashed a package
or delayed an important letter.

And citizens who see the government accomplish highly technical missions in less than a decade, like the moon landing, may have
trouble understanding why a postal organization that has been
operating for nearly two centuries is not a more finely tuned
instrument. This is all the more confounding since the mail operation seems reasonably straightforward: a raw material (mail) moves
through successive processing stages and emerges as a product

(mail items sorted to individual addresses), delivery of which is provided as a service to the sender who has paid a fee (postage). These processes appear to differ only in kind from industrial processes in many private sector businesses and appear to be much easier than most tasks undertaken by government.

Of course, the Postal Service is not alone among government agencies in having these features. For example, states and localities operate a variety of "businesslike" enterprises, from municipally owned electric companies to state-owned liquor stores. The federal government also is engaged in a host of businesslike enterprises. Examples include maintaining balanced and adequate supplies of agricultural commodities and products (Commodity Credit Corporation); providing insurance coverage for bank deposits (Federal Deposit Insurance Corporation); providing electric power (Tennessee Valley Authority); maintaining industrial operations in federal prisons to produce goods and services for sale to federal agencies (Federal Prison Industries, Inc.); developing, operating, and maintaining an effective water artery for maritime commerce (Saint Lawrence Seaway Development Corporation); and guaranteeing basic pension benefits in the event that covered plans terminate with insufficient assets (Pension Benefit Guaranty Corporation).

It was the apparently successful organizational form of these government corporations that postal reformers in the late 1960s imitated in hope of solving some of the persistent problems of the nation's oldest public service—high labor costs, an irrational rate structure, and growing deficits. Postal reformers believed that these and other problems of the mail system derived from defects in organizational design, primarily insufficient managerial autonomy and flexibility. Advocates of a corporate transformation of the postal system believed that a better design would produce a more effective postal organization—one that could control costs, provide service of high quality, charge reasonable rates, and be financially self-sustaining.

Chapter 1 focuses in detail on the purposes and scope of that corporate transformation and on the politics of its enactment. It also addresses general questions as to why government corporations are created and how they actually operate. Chapters 2 through 7 examine processes and problems fundamental to the operation of the postal system: devising appropriate internal managerial structures and processes, pursuing operational efficiencies in the system (especially in mail processing and delivery), negotiating fair wages for 800,000 postal workers and maintaining a work environment that elicits greater commitment by them to the organization, determining the prices of mail services, and dealing with the challenges of competition in various service lines.

Endnotes

1. See, for example, Roger Sherman, ed., *Perspectives on Postal Service Issues* (Washington: American Enterprise Institute, 1980); John Tierney, *Postal Reorganization: Managing the Public's Business* (Boston: Auburn House, 1981); Paul C. Browne, "The Roles of Top Management in Shaping Organization Design: Evidence from the United States Postal Service" (D.B.A. diss., Harvard University School of Business Administration, 1981); National Academy of Public Administration, *Evaluation of the United States Postal Service* (Washington: The National Academy of Public Administration, 1982); and (for what is probably the best volume in recent years on postal policy) Joel L. Fleishman, ed., *The Future of the Postal Service* (New York: Praeger, 1983).
2. James Bovard, "The U.S. Postal Service—The Last Dinosaur," A Cato Institute Policy Analysis, 1985, p. 1.
3. *Postal Leader,* March 3, 1987, p. 1.
4. Joel L. Fleishman reports these data in "Postal Policy and Public Accountability: Is the 1970 Bargain Coming Unglued?" in Fleishman, ed., *The Future of the Postal Service,* p. 98, n1.
5. The Roper Organization, *Roper Reports,* No. 87-2, 1987, pp. 8–9.
6. The Roper Organization, *Roper Reports,* No. 85-5, 1985, pp. 10–11; 18–19.

Chapter 1

THE CORPORATE TRANSFORMATION OF THE POSTAL SYSTEM

The United States Postal Service, created in 1971 out of the ribs of the old Post Office Department, is a monument to the capacity of the American government to change. The Postal Reorganization Act of 1970 produced the most thorough reconstruction of postal administration in nearly two centuries. It removed the postal department from the President's cabinet, ended the authority of Congress and the White House to set employee wages and postage rates, bestowed on the new Postal Service its own personnel system, and granted the new organization substantial fiscal autonomy. The architects of the reconstituted mail agency hoped to make postal management more "businesslike" by giving postal executives far greater autonomy in controlling the organization's affairs. Save for the organizational redesign that led to the creation of the Department of Defense in 1949, it is difficult to think of any other agency of the government that has undergone more comprehensive change.

The transformation occurred at the urging of policymakers who believed that the ills of the mail delivery system could only be remedied by a "fundamental change in the anachronistic relationship between the Post Office and the rest of the government."[1] They believed that the postal system was essentially a business operation that could be managed more efficiently and effectively if it were lifted from under the dead hand of partisan politics and freed from long-standing policymaking arrangements that restricted managerial flexibility and stifled innovation, discouraged

9

cost-consciousness, stunted the system's industrial development, and catered to the political needs of members of Congress and the articulated demands of special interests.

Problems with Congressional Control of the Post Office

To a degree unmatched in any other executive agency or department, Congress managed the Post Office Department. For example, the wages and working conditions of postal employees and most of the rates of postage and classes of mail were fixed by Congress; decisions on the level of capital spending and the location of postal facilities were made by Congress. Members of Congress selected the persons to fill local postmasterships; appointments to the top management positions at postal headquarters also were subject to Senate confirmation; and many other decisions, including decisions on individual personnel matters, were from time to time strongly influenced by the desires of one or more members of Congress.

The extraordinary extent to which Post Office Department officials lacked managerial authority and autonomous jurisdiction over postal operations was articulated in an exchange that occurred in 1967 between Congressman Tom Steed (D-Okla.), chairman of the House Appropriations postal subcommittee, and Lawrence O'Brien, who was then Postmaster General:[2]

> MR. STEED: *Would this be a fair summary: that at the present time, as the manager of the Post Office Department, you have no control over your workload, you have no control over the rates of revenue, you have no control over the pay rates of the employees that you employ, you have very little control over the conditions of the service of these employees, you have virtually no control, by the nature of it, of your physical facilities, and you have only a limited control, at best, over the transportation facilities that you are compelled to use—all of which adds up to a staggering amount of "no control" in terms of the duties you have to perform?*

> MR. O'BRIEN: *Mr. Chairman, I would have to generally agree with your premise . . . that is a staggering list of "no control." I don't know whether it has ever been put that succinctly to me. If it had been at an appropriate time, perhaps I wouldn't be sitting here.*

Of course, there is nothing intrinsically wrong with having Congress make postal policy except that Congress did not take the task seriously. For example, setting postal rates is one of the most important elements of postal policymaking, but Congress regularly accorded these decisions low priority, delaying rate bills for months, even years. In addition to not wanting to face up to these unpleasant decisions on rate increases, members of Congress were not particularly well equipped to deal with the complex economic and regulatory issues raised by rate bills. The multiple and conflicting duties of legislators denied committee members an opportunity to learn about the intricacies of postal rate matters. This problem was aggravated by the relatively rapid turnover of membership on postal subcommittees, caused at least partly by the low prestige legislators attached to such committee assignments. Moreover, committee staff members were not even in a position to pick up the slack; though competent, staff support was too limited to do proper justice to the task.

As a consequence of all this, Congress dealt with postal rate issues in a relatively perfunctory manner. In the usual format of legislative hearings, representatives of powerful mailing interests—publishers, greeting-card manufacturers, direct-mail advertisers, and the like—would parade before the committees, cost accountants in tow, hoping to demonstrate that the proposed rate changes would impose on them an undue share of the total adjusted rate burden, having a devastatingly adverse effect on their operations. As the mailers pleaded for congressional restraint in raising rates, the legislators would adopt their best hail-fellow-well-met posture and express their heartfelt concern for the plight of the politically powerful mailers. When compared to the painstakingly rigorous fact-finding processes typically involved in public utility rate regulation, legislative rate-making for the Post Office was, as *Reader's Digest* put it in 1968, "a circus sideshow."[3]

In other respects as well, Congress paid attention to the postal system when it was politically expedient to do so, but otherwise let the system suffer from benign neglect, the effects of which were increasingly apparent in the 1960s. Although a disregard for businesslike operation of the mail system was nothing new in Washington (between 1840 and 1969 the Post Office had run an annual deficit 113 times), the gravity of the situation was illuminated by a near doubling in the Post Office operating deficit between 1964 ($651.7 million) and 1967 ($1.1 billion). Two concurrent developments had contributed to the deepening financial crisis.

The first factor was a tremendous expansion in the work load of the Post Office. In the period of great national economic growth between 1945 and the start of the postal reform movement in 1967, the annual torrent of mail pouring into the postal system swelled from 38 billion pieces to 78 billion and was projected at the time to reach 100 billion by 1977. At the same time, extraordinary growth in the number of delivery points overburdened the system's delivery force. With the rapid postwar construction of new residential and office buildings, and especially with the acceleration of suburban sprawl, the number of daily delivery stops increased in that period by 1.5 to 2 million a year.

This enormous increase in the system's work load might have posed no problem were it not for a second factor: it was not matched by proportionate increases in the Post Office's budget. Congress and the White House accorded the postal system low funding priority in the 1960s as the financial demands of the Vietnam War and Lyndon Johnson's Great Society programs crowded the political agenda. Capital expenditures for the postal system were particularly vulnerable since cutbacks in that area were less noticeable to the public than cutbacks in operating funds. While other industries devoted 20 to 30 percent of their annual capital inventory to research and development, the Post Office devoted 2 to 3 percent. The Post Office did not even have a research and development program of its own until after World War II. Congressional penny-pinching in the R & D program stunted the development of new machinery, equipment, and physical plants. This industrial retardation was most apparent inside post offices, where mail-handling methods remained much the same as they had been a century earlier. Clerks still stood before the familiar pigeonhole cases, sorting letters by hand at the rate of about thirty a minute. Antiquated facilities hindered mechanization: weak floors would not support heavy machinery, low ceilings ruled out overhead conveyor systems, and vertical building layouts defied any attempt at instituting more efficient horizontal mail-flow systems.

The collective stress of rising volumes and outmoded processing capacities presented the Post Office with little choice but to hire more employees. "The idea," one postal official conceded, "is that if you have a mass of bodies you can *smother* the mail, and get it delivered by sheer weight of numbers."[4] Such was the philosophy underlying the mushrooming of the department's payroll by 1969 to 739,000 persons. Productivity was poor, and labor costs were becoming a rapidly increasing part of the total postal operating budget.

The efficiency of postal operations in the 1960s also suffered from another problem largely beyond the control of government policymakers. Revolutionary changes were occurring in the nation's transportation modes and patterns. For decades, most of the nation's mail had moved by train. This was a reliable and speedy means of moving mail, since in railway mail cars the mail could be sorted en route. The whole physical plant of the postal system had been built around this dependence on trains. Seventy-five of the nation's largest post offices, which handled over 50 percent of all the mail, stood in central cities near railroad terminals. But in the 1950s, the nation's transportation system began to undergo tremendous changes. Trucks and airplanes began to replace trains as the principal means of transport. Thus, by the mid-1960s, with only 900 trains in daily general use (down from 10,000 a decade earlier), movement of mail depended primarily on trucks that had to go through traffic-choked cities to reach the big postal facilities; there they often had to line up for hours, awaiting access to inadequate loading docks built long before the huge tractor-trailer was designed.[5]

It was probably inevitable that the cumulative stress of all these diverse trends—rising mail volumes, retarded industrial development, population shifts, changing transportation patterns—would someday cripple the system or a major part of it. The collapse occurred in October 1966 when Chicago's massive main post office—at 13 stories and 60 acres of workspace, one of the largest postal facilities in the world—broke down. For three weeks the facility was paralyzed by a backlog of mail exceeding 10 million pieces. Railroad cars and trailer trucks full of mail choked approaches to the post office, complicating the efforts of rattled Washington officials to divert to other cities much of the mail usually processed in Chicago.[6] Close observers of the postal system's condition in the 1960s had long recognized that its inadequacies and accumulating stresses portended chaos. But this highly visible breakdown in the system alerted the public and government policymakers to the gravity and urgency of the agency's problems.

The Postal "Subgovernment"—An Obstacle to Reform

In view of the deep disarray in the postal system, it may seem surprising that proposals to reform the Post Office were thought to have little prospect of success. Though even cursory analysis of the system's troubles could correctly trace them to badly flawed institutional arrangements in which a huge industrial enterprise was being governed according to the dictates of political expediency, those arrangements served well the interests of three powerful groups—postal employees, Congress, and the organized mailers—

that together constituted a classic "subgovernment" or "iron triangle." A *subgovernment* is said to exist when routine policymaking within an individual substantive policy area, such as postal policy, is dominated by relatively narrow, circumscribed sets of actors who work together to dominate policymaking within their realm and to formulate policies that meet the needs of parties to the arrangement. Subgovernments have been said to exist at one time or another in many policy areas characterized by the distribution of benefits—for example, weapons procurement, veterans' benefits, agricultural subsidies, merchant shipping, and water resources.[7]

In these sorts of "distributive" policy areas, where the benefits of a policy or program are concentrated on identifiable interests in society (sugar farmers, inland waterways operators, veterans, postal workers, large business mailers, etc.) but the costs are to be borne by everybody, or at least by a substantial portion of society, organizations representing the beneficiaries are vigorous in their political efforts to maintain their benefits. However, since the costs are distributed at a low per capita rate over a large number of people (through price increases or generally higher taxes), the public in general has little economic or political incentive to organize in an effort to alter the arrangement. Such policies tend to produce close, symbiotic relationships between the legislators who make the policy decisions and the beneficiaries who work hard to maintain and expand their benefits.[8]

Congress and Postal Employees

The strongest linkage in the postal subgovernment was the symbiotic relationship between postal employees and Congress. Over the years, cozy relationships had been built, both between postmasters and Congress, and between the unions and Congress. Postmasters at the time were selected under a "political adviser system," which was neither sanctioned nor recognized in law but which governed the process nonetheless. Under this system, each postal district in the country had a congressman (sometimes a senator and, more rarely, a local party chairman) as its "political adviser," a position that conferred the right to choose local postmasters when vacancies arose within that district. Although the Civil Service Commission routinely held competitive examinations for postmaster positions and submitted the top three names to the postmaster general for a choice, the new postmaster actually was not chosen by the postmaster general; the appropriate congressman made the decision. Conducting examinations and drawing up a civil service register was important only for its obstructive or dilatory capacity, for if the politically desired candidate was not among the top three qualifiers on the exam, the adviser could refuse to name anyone, preferring instead to wait until a favored candidate finally scored high enough to make the top three. Thus, some post offices went for years without a postmaster, while the examinations were given over and over until the "right" candidate appeared.[9] But once the Senate confirmed the appointment of a new postmaster, that person, regardless of actual qualification, automatically achieved full civil service status, receiving all the fringe benefits, retirement protections, and job securities.

From the perspective of postal officials, the problem with this arrangement was that many postmasters naturally felt more allegiance to the legislators who had helped secure their appointments than to their nominal superiors in the agency. The political nature of the appointment made local postmasters quite autonomous. They could decide when, if at all, they would let their actions be guided by regional or headquarters "superiors."[10] Moreover, they felt free to devote large amounts of time, money and effort to ensuring that their political patron in Congress got reelected. In return, members of Congress watched out for the interests of postmasters.

Even more closely tied to Congress were the unions representing rank-and-file postal workers. All important decisions concerning postal workers—wage schedules, classification of positions, conditions of job security, and even the details of work assignments—were determined by Congress (the House Post Office and Civil Service Committee, in particular) through prolonged tripartite bargaining with the Post Office Department and the postal unions. In order to get the most out of these political negotiations, the postal unions over time became expert at lobbying Congress. The unions enjoyed unusual political influence, derived from a combination of resources and advantages.

First, the unions enjoyed the advantage of large size and high membership density (the proportion of their potential constituency that was mobilized). The Post Office was the most highly unionized federal agency. Among letter carriers, for example, 98 percent of those on active duty in 1967 belonged to the National Association of Letter Carriers, and 92 percent of rural carriers belonged to their union. In all, 90 percent of postal employees belonged to a union, compared with only 21 percent of employees in other federal agencies.[11] These remarkably high membership rates provided union leaders not only with substantial resources but with enhanced legitimacy. Policymakers are more likely to be persuaded by a group that represents a substantial portion of its potential membership than by one that mobilizes a smaller share of its possible supporters.

Second, the postal unions had the advantage of being able to pursue their interests in Washington without any organized opponents. The other powerful interest groups in the postal policy arena were the organizations representing the large mailing industries—such as magazine publishers, direct-mail advertisers, and large mail-order companies. But in the years prior to 1970, there was no basic policy conflict between these two chief blocs. Since the Post Office Department's funding came through appropriations rather than its own revenues, postal costs and revenues were not directly linked. Therefore, an increase in postal employee wages did not necessarily mean an increase in postage rates. Consequently, the unions and the large mailers' interests were seldom inclined to assume antagonistic positions. Indeed, so muted were the policy conflicts between the postal employee unions and the mailers' organizations that for many years, one man, J. Don Kerlin, served both as a lobbyist for a powerful magazine group (Time, Inc.) and as a paid consultant for the National Association of Letter Carriers.[12] If the postal unions can be said to have had any organized and attentive adversary at all, it was the executive branch, which normally opposed pay raises or proposed smaller increases than the employee groups wanted.

Third, the postal unions were the oldest and strongest of federal employee organizations. The postal unions—in particular the two big AFL-CIO affiliates, the National Association of Letter Carriers (NALC) (190,000 members) and the United Federation of Postal Clerks (UFPC) (145,000 members)—had become highly skilled over the years at the gentle art of lobbying. They had constructed formidable political organizations in Washington, with large full-time staffs to refine and express their policy positions, monitor evolving policy issues that might impinge on postal workers' interests, marshal information, and keep tabs on supporters and opponents. In 1966, 1967, and 1968, the UFPC reported higher lobbying expenditures than any other organized interest in Washington—a distinction that passed to the NALC the next year.[13]

Nowhere was the postal unions' political prowess more apparent than in the electoral arena, where the postal workers constituted a formidable electoral presence, especially in urban districts with high concentrations of postal employees. The unions placed their organizational strength and financial resources at the disposal of congressional friends and withheld it from (or used it to the detriment of) legislators who proved unsupportive. The aim was to defeat hostile candidates, to elect ideologically compatible ones, and to create a sufficiently strong sense of indebtedness on the part of the eventual winner so that, once in office, he or she would be responsive to postal workers' political needs and policy preferences. In pursuing this aim, the postal unions gave millions of dollars in congressional campaign contributions.

Because the resources of the postal unions paved a two-way political street, members of Congress traditionally were eager to keep the postal unions happy. The postal unions enjoyed such influence among members of the House Post Office and Civil Service Committee that the committee adopted a standard pattern of response to union demands. As Richard Fenno has described it, that response was "to support maximum pay increases and improvements in benefits for employee groups and . . . to accede to executive branch wishes [only] when, in the judgment of committee members and employee groups, to do otherwise would net employee groups nothing in that Congress."[14]

This committee strategy, along with cultivation by the unions of other loyal congressional allies, helped to secure numerous spectacular victories for postal employees in the 1950s and 1960s. When, for instance, House Post Office and Civil Service Committee Chairman Thomas Murray (who, almost alone among committee members, openly decried the strength of the postal unions and regularly supported the executive branch position on pay bills) refused to act on a pay measure in 1960, the union supporters on the committee saved the bill by acquiring the 218 signatures needed to discharge it from committee. They then pushed the bill through the House (even under the threat of a presidential veto), and led a successful fight to override the veto—one of only two overrides during the entire Eisenhower administration. This impressive victory resulted from effective legislative maneuvering by friendly members of Congress and from the prodigious lobbying efforts of the postal employee unions in face-to-face contact with individual members of the House. A Post Office Department executive who observed the unions at work on this bill (and others like it) said of their effectiveness: "The pressure from the postal employee groups is terrific—just terrific. They are the best-organized union in the world. When they want to turn on the heat they are almost unbearable."[15] And these efforts by the unions produced impressive though not surprising results; only one postal pay bill was defeated on any kind of vote in the House during the twelve years from 1955 to 1967.

Congress and the Organized Mailers

The other partner to the cozy political triangle that governed postal policy until 1970 was the community of organized mailers, consisting largely of trade associations (the National Newspaper Association, the Direct Mail Advertising Association, the Magazine Publishers Association, and so on), as well as large mailers themselves—companies like *Time, Newsweek*, and Sears. The concerted political power of these formidable organizations was manifest in their consistent success at keeping rates disproportionately low for second- and third-class mail, subsidized by increased first-class mail rates, by larger appropriations, or both.

So great was the influence organized mailers enjoyed on Capitol Hill that in the early stages of drafting a proposal for new rates, postal and budget officials would take informal soundings from the heavy users of specific classes of mail—magazine publishers, direct-mail advertisers, mail-order companies, and the like. For example, after the Office of Postal Economics had completed the staff paper on possible rate proposals in anticipation of the 1967 rate bill, postal officials held discussions on an informal, off-the-record basis with numerous large mailers. About twenty to thirty different groups and associations were informed of the planned rate increases, and their comments were taken as a measure of "what the traffic would bear."[16]

The dominance of political expediency over economic considerations was even more apparent once a rate measure had been submitted to Congress and was under deliberation. Congressional hearings on a rate bill (usually held first before the Subcommittee on Postal Rates of the House Committee on Post Office and Civil Service) provided a forum in which organized mail users could present their case to elected officials. A parade of organized mail users, from the largest publishers to small church groups, would argue for leaving the rates undisturbed or reducing the increases requested by the administration. The hearings were filled with visions of magazines having to cease publication, direct-mail advertising companies going bankrupt, and the nation's intellectual and commercial exchange breaking down.

After the hearings, the subcommittee would go into executive session to review them and mark up the bill, a process that frequently caused dramatic changes in the proposal. During consideration of the 1967 rate bill, for example, the House subcommittee substantially altered all 27 points in the measure.[17] Rate bills were open to still further amendment after submission to the full committee and again after debate began on the House floor.

Through these stages, the initial form of the legislation as introduced by the executive branch usually changed considerably when the legislators began to accommodate the wishes of the mailing industries. The main changes usually came in the committee; its members dealt with the intense pressure from the mailer's organizations by adopting a decision rule politically similar to the one they followed on postal pay bills: "oppose all rate increases for mail users."[18] If Senate hearings were held, the arguments presented there tended to duplicate those presented during the House hearings. Senate deliberations and, if necessary, conference committee reconciliations provided further opportunities for changes in the rate proposals.

Several features of this extended legislative process worked to the relative advantage of organized mail users. First, the process was highly permeable, affording interested organizations many opportunities to shape the course of rate legislation. Indeed, the process may have been *too* permeable, as suggested by several bribery scandals that occurred in the 1960s; direct mailers were held to be buying the votes of influential members of the post office committees.[19]

Second, legislative rate-making had little in common with more rigorous forms of public utility rate regulation, characterized by sophisticated economic presentations and careful cross-examinations and rebuttals. Instead, they were largely characterized by relatively simple and repetitive expressions of self-interest on the part of organized mailers. This pattern was attractive to the organized mailers not least because it saved them the expense of retaining professional help to prepare rigorous, carefully documented arguments.

Finally, time was on the side of the mailing interests. The legislative process provided them with both the opportunity and the incentive to prolong the proceedings, the objective being to delay enactment; each day that passed without higher rates represented a significant "savings" to the mailers. During the lengthy proceedings surrounding the 1967 rate bill, for example, each week's delay meant the loss of close to $15 million in expected federal revenue, and that much saved by the mailers collectively.[20]

The Push Toward Reorganization

Clearly, the institutional and political arrangements governing postal policy permitted the postal employee organizations and the organized mailing interests to shape postal policies to their liking.

The inattentive partner to this whole arrangement was, of course, the U.S. taxpayer. But except in unusual circumstances (such as the temporary breakdown of Chicago's postal operations), the public paid relatively little attention to the decisions of Congress on postal policy. As long as their mail got delivered and the cost did not seem exorbitant, most citizens were content with the postal system. Moreover, the relatively prosaic mission of the Post Office did not exactly accord it a high place on the public's agenda of important issues—especially not in a decade that featured much more prominent causes for concern such as the Vietnam War, urban disorders, and rapidly rising health care costs. But the simple fact that Congress and the organized interests found the existing arrangements congenial did not mean that they would necessarily persist.

Cozy policymaking systems of the sort that prevailed for decades in the postal policy arena are not impervious to change. For example, one of Washington's most famous long-standing subgovernments dictated tobacco policy for decades. That subgovernment—consisting of the legislators on committees that handled tobacco legislation and related appropriations, certain officials inside the Department of Agriculture involved with the various tobacco programs of that agency, and representatives of tobacco growers and cigarette manufacturers—quietly conducted important and complex tobacco programs, like price supports and export promotion, without interference from political forces outside the subgovernment. But the subgovernment changed completely in the years from 1964 to 1972. The small group of people who for so long dominated tobacco policy under their mutual self-help arrangement lost control of the policymaking processes as other political actors in Washington—especially the Federal Trade Commission, the Federal Communications Commission, the Public Health Service, and assorted health interest groups—entered the fray and forced dramatic changes in public policy. The breakdown of the tobacco subgovernment was testimony to the awesome political power of executive branch agencies.[21]

In American government, Congress and interest groups are by no means sovereign. The executive branch also is a formidable policymaker with powerful interests and preferences of its own, and with the resources to pursue them. Just as in the case of the tobacco subgovernment, the prevailing power arrangement in the postal policy arena collapsed in the face of persistent and skillful maneuvering by the executive branch—in particular by the Post Office Department itself.

The department's drive toward self-determination started in late

1966 under the initiative of Postmaster General Lawrence O'Brien. Months earlier, when President Lyndon Johnson first appointed O'Brien, formerly the President's special assistant for congressional relations, to become postmaster general, persons who cared about the postal system's problems despaired. The appointment appeared to be in line with the long-standing practice of giving the top job to a trusted political ally who could serve the President as a kind of minister without portfolio, dealing with a wide range of matters not related to postal affairs. As a result of this traditional practice, the postmaster general's chair had seldom been occupied by persons who were at once concerned about increasing the effectiveness of the postal system and skilled at such a job. But O'Brien surprised those worried about his commitment to the job by making a serious effort at managing the postal system.

The new postmaster general had been in office only a few months in 1966 before he fully appreciated what a hard task he had set for himself. He was nominally the chief executive of the largest civilian agency in the government. Indeed, with 740,000 employees the Post Office employed more people than any business in the country, with the exception of AT&T and General Motors, and its revenues exceeded those of companies like U.S. Steel, Texaco, IBM, and Du Pont.[22] And yet, as O'Brien complained to Congressman Steed in the exchange cited earlier, the Post Office had no managerial autonomy whatsoever. Congress, influenced by organized interests, dictated virtually all of the important decisions on postal operations, finances, rates, and wages. Other Washington institutions—the White House, the Civil Service Commission, the General Services Administration, the General Accounting Office, the Treasury Department, the Civil Aeronautics Board, and the Interstate Commerce Commission— also had a say in certain elements of postal policy.

In O'Brien's view, subjecting postal policy to this fragmentation and dispersion of control was absurd. He believed the postal service was essentially a business operation that could be managed much more efficiently and effectively if its executives had greater managerial autonomy—that is, independent control of the organization's finances, personnel policies, service levels, and the like.

The complex and anomalous postal rate-making procedures, the backwardness of postal facilities and equipment, the restrictions of the budgetary process, the inflexibility of the civil service system—all these also startled O'Brien by their apparent intractability. The new postmaster general began to regard as futile any attempt to make isolated improvements and was moved to try for drastic changes in the organizational and political status of the Post

Office Department. Accordingly, he created a small, highly confidential task force inside the Post Office Department and charged it with developing a reform plan that would provide postal management with much greater autonomy in its policymaking.

Early in 1967, the task force brought O'Brien what he wanted— a formal, presentable proposal to convert the Post Office Department into a more businesslike, corporate form of organization. And in April 1967, the postmaster general stunned an audience at a Washington convention of the Magazine Publishers Association by proposing that the Post Office Department be removed from the President's cabinet and converted to a government corporation. O'Brien referred in his speech to the "restrictive jungle of legislation and custom" that had grown up around the Post Office Department over the years, leaving postal executives almost "no control" over the system. O'Brien told his audience: "The only effective action I foresee is sweeping it away entirely."[23]

Within a week of the postmaster general's address, President Lyndon Johnson appointed Frederick Kappel, the retired chairman of AT&T, to head a commission to review the status of the Post Office and make recommendations for its future. The "Kappel Commission," as it came to be called, was composed of some of the nation's most prestigious business leaders. In approaching its task, the commission decided to assemble a small professional staff and to engage some of the nation's top management consulting firms to prepare a more polished rationale for the organizational change.

The consultants from Arthur D. Little, Inc., noting that certain dominant principles of organizational and managerial thought in the United States had strongly influenced their concepts of what is "natural, obvious, inevitable, and proper in organizational behavior," recorded some of those principles:[24]

> *An organization is a* container *which must hold all essential elements and no superfluous ones. Its* boundaries are the key to its manageability. *Such functions as budgeting and labor relations, for example, must not spill out of the container, and such elements as patronage politics should not wash into it.*

The consultants found that the organization and management of the Post Office Department conformed not to this "contained" mode of organization but to a "fragmented," or "politically oriented" design with different characteristics:[25]

> *This organization does not have all its elements in one managerial container. It occupies ground which is simultaneously occupied by other systems and is itself an aspect of a larger system. . . . A*

> *fragmented organization is designed to reduce the need for reliance
> on top-level authority. Its many bits of limited discretion, limited
> authority, limited mobility, limited opportunity, limited incentive
> and limited responsibility are controlled by highly specific and
> comprehensive legislative prescriptions built into rule books, proce-
> dural manuals and administrative directives. . . . It progresses by
> means of incremental improvisation, as opposed to sweeping sys-
> temic design. Coalitions have to be built and rebuilt to support each
> bargained "set" of incremental changes.*

Though the consultants acknowledged that both kinds of organization and management—the contained mode and the fragmented, politically oriented mode—are "rational, effective, and
legitimate approaches in our society," they argued that the businesslike boundaries of a contained organization would provide a
more promising organizational form for the Post Office.[26]

In June 1968, the President's Commission on Postal Organization
issued its final report, identifying in clear terms what it considered
the fundamental problem of the postal system:[27]

> *The organization of the Post Office as an ordinary Cabinet depart-
> ment guarantees that* the nominal managers of the postal service do
> not have the authority to run the postal service. *The important
> management decisions of the Post Office are beyond their control
> and therefore cannot be made on the basis of business judgment.*

Accordingly, the commission formally recommended transforming
the Post Office Department into a government corporation.

This endorsement of the postal corporation idea by a blue-
ribbon commission of luminaries from the American business
community was widely publicized by the American press and
received strong editorial support. But perhaps more important, it
stimulated a change of sympathies among the organized mailers,
who began to see that despite the steady stream of benefits they
enjoyed over the years as a consequence of their cozy relationships
with Congress, the proposal to transform the system had merit.
The mailers' support of the proposal was based on the belief that
although rates might rise more precipitously under corporate
managers than under Congress, in the long run entrusting additional authority and managerial freedom to postal executives was
the best way to ensure a more stable, modern, and predictable
postal system. To many in the business community, it only made
sense that, as a spokesperson for the National Association of
Manufacturers put it, "our society should employ the know-how
developed in our commercial and industrial life to manage this
function that so closely resembles a commercial or industrial
enterprise."[28] A corporate transformation of the system seemed to

hold the promise of improved service, lowered costs, and steadier
rates. It was this last prospect that chiefly accounted for the
support of the large publishers. Stephen Kelly, the president of
the Magazine Publishers Association, told a congressional committee:[29]

> *In addition to the higher postage costs resulting from eight legislated*
> *increases by the Congress in the past 11 years, this frequent*
> *recurrence of rate bills . . . keeps the industry constantly off balance*
> *in long-range planning.*
>   *Magazines have encouraged the long-term subscription—2, 3, 5*
> *years. These rates cannot be changed without substantial lead time.*
> *Magazines are locked into them, at a minimum usually, for 18*
> *months. Increases in postal rates simply cannot be passed along*
> *speedily to any of our customers—readers or advertisers. And, as*
> *an industry, we do not have the profits to absorb them. . . . The*
> *Post Office is the major mode of distribution for magazines. We*
> *have, therefore, an enlightened self-interest in proposals to reorga-*
> *nize the Post Office as well as a commitment to our reading public*
> *to support sound programs that strengthen and improve service, at*
> *reasonable cost.*

Even though there seemed to be growing support in the business community for a corporate reform of the postal system, the
modest momentum in that direction flagged in the waning days of
the Johnson administration. This happened because President
Johnson had removed himself from the 1968 presidential race, and
Postmaster General O'Brien had relinquished his post to work on
the presidential campaign of Senator Robert F. Kennedy. O'Brien
was succeeded by one of Johnson's chief troubleshooters from the
White House, Marvin Watson. Watson did not share O'Brien's
enthusiasm for the postal corporation idea and made no effort to
advance it in Congress.

Thus, not until early 1969, with the inauguration of President
Richard M. Nixon, were efforts to build a coalition in support of
the proposal rekindled. President Nixon and his first postmaster
general, Winton M. Blount, a successful Alabama contractor and
former chairman of the U.S. Chamber of Commerce, indicated
early in 1969 that they were committed to the wholesale restructuring of the postal system. Under the Nixon-Blount administration, the Post Office Department launched an intense and skillful
campaign for the agency's overhaul.

Marketing the Reorganization

When top postal officials began in early 1969 to map a strategy to
secure passage of the reorganization plan, they anticipated several

hurdles. First was the potential reluctance of congressmen, especially members of the House Post Office and Civil Service Committee, to relinquish the control they exercised over the postal system, or to lose the attentions of the powerful interest groups in the postal community. Second, postal officials worried about generating sufficient public support for the reorganization, especially since the proposed changes held no promise of immediate benefits and could even appear threatening to services the public expected. Third was the opposition of the department's own rank-and-file employees. The unions worried aloud about the possible loss of their influence in the event of a reorganization. Their resistance to the plan loomed as perhaps the most formidable obstacle.

Thus, the Post Office Department's top officials set about trying to quiet the anxieties of these various constituencies and to find ways of reducing resistance and building a solid coalition in support of the reorganization. In early 1969, Postmaster General Blount assembled a team of high-level postal executives, under the direction of his general counsel, David Nelson. The task of this group was to smooth the political path for postal reorganization legislation and to think seriously about the public relations aspects of the legislation.

The group developed an intricate "marketing plan," the ultimate objective of which was to win the support of enough representatives and senators to ensure that the measure was passed in Congress. To help sell the proposal to skeptical members of Congress, the Congressional Liaison Office in the Post Office Department enlisted the efforts of large corporations and trade associations. Some of these organizations included General Electric, Procter & Gamble, J. C. Penney, the Chamber of Commerce, and the Magazine Publishers Association.[30]

But postal officials recognized that even this lobbying blitz would not be enough. In an April 7 memo to Nelson, Jim Henderson, Blount's special assistant for public information, wrote:[31]

It should be accepted that a massive "selling" job will be required for any plan that will result in Congress relinquishing control over the bulk of postal operations. By law we are debarred from this kind of "selling" job, although of course the public pronouncements of the Postmaster General do not fall within that limitation. We can, however, try to engineer some form of separate organization designed to further improving postal service. Perhaps the U.S. Chamber of Commerce might designate this as "improved postal service year" and provide an ongoing organization to press for reform; or, failing that, a foundation might be enlisted to establish a working group for reorganization.

Blount and his advisers agreed with Henderson's conclusion about the need for a "massive selling job." Consensus also reigned on the advisability of setting up a separate organization—bluntly referred to in Post Office Department memos as the "front organization"—to push the reform idea. One advantage to establishing such a group, as Henderson had indicated in his memo, was that it provided a way of circumventing restrictions on lobbying. Under federal law (18 U.S.C. 1913) it was a criminal offense for a department to use appropriated funds directly or indirectly to pay for advertisements, telephone calls, letters, and printed or written matter designed to influence a member of Congress on pending legislation. Agencies also were barred from using appropriated funds for publicity or propaganda designed to support or defend pending legislation. But, of course, organizations outside the government could pursue all these activities. Moreover, a front organization also had the advantage of disguising the business community's heavy spending in support of postal reform. It was far better politically that the support appear to be coming from a "good government" group.

Thus, the Post Office Department supplemented its own internally directed push for a postal reorganization by sanctioning and helping to establish an organization known as the Citizens Committee for Postal Reform (CCPR) and headed by Lawrence O'Brien and former U.S. Senator Thruston B. Morton. The organization was structured along consciously bipartisan lines, for the specific purpose of trying to elicit Democratic support. O'Brien, in addition to having once served as postmaster general, had also served as national chairman of the Democratic party, and Morton similarly had served as national chairman of the Republican party. Having the two former party heads serve as co-chairmen of the lobby organization gave the organization a desired bipartisan cast, but inducing O'Brien to serve was especially important, since he could do things on the Democratic side of the congressional aisles that Nixon administration Republicans could not. CCPR had the financial backing of some of the nation's largest business firms. The committee emerged as the seventeenth heaviest spender among the nation's lobbying organizations in 1969, the tenth largest in 1970.[32]

Relying in part on the aid of CCPR, Post Office strategists ran supportive advertisements in newspapers and arranged for a continuous flow of supportive news and feature stories. They also launched a campaign to flood newspaper editors with letters expressing support for the reorganization, distributed brochures to voluntary associations and schools, arranged for the postmaster general to appear on national and regional television and radio programs, and formed a national speakers' bureau with branch operations in each region to make speakers available for public functions, including convention panels, Rotary Club meetings, and the like. The list of such activities is extensive.[33]

In these pitches to the public, the reorganization's advocates repeatedly portrayed a postal system on the verge of collapse and claimed that the best way to save it was to "take politics out of the postal system" and infuse it with private business management techniques. The argument was clear: postal reform would bring faster and more reliable service, would reduce the postal deficit that burdened the taxpayer, and would slow the rise in postage rates.

In its appeals to members of Congress for support, the Post Office Department sought to persuade the legislators that they had an obligation to provide the public with a revitalized postal system. The department tried to convince the legislators that postal reform was what the voters wanted and that support of the reorganization measure would be to the members' advantage when they were campaigning for reelection. Reform strategists also tried to persuade the legislators of other advantages they would reap from the reorganization: they would no longer be bothered by postal job seekers, pressed by the unions for wage increases and improved benefits, pestered by the organized mailers for subsidized postal rates, or plagued by constituent complaints about postal service.

In sum, the Post Office Department initiated a massive effort in 1969 and 1970 to achieve the reorganization that seemed to hold the promise of managerial autonomy. As time passed, the groups that proved most resistant to the department's active solicitations for support were the labor unions representing the department's own rank-and-file employees. As already indicated, the unions were not convinced that the reorganization held any advantages for them or their members. Equally important, the unions believed that the whole question of reorganization was obscuring an issue they felt merited more immediate attention—a pay raise for postal workers.

Victory for the Reformers

The political struggle over the reorganization plan lasted more than a year and was eclipsed for much of that time by the controversy over postal wages. After an eight-day strike in March of 1970 that crippled business activities and severely disrupted commerce nationwide, postal workers won not only a two-step, 14 percent pay increase but also the chance to participate formally in formulating the details of a reorganization plan. The agreement finally reached included most of the same features the Post Office had been pushing all along, but there was one important change intended to secure beyond doubt the support of the unions. The proposal provided for third-party binding arbitration, a provision the unions had sought as compensation for the reduction in Congress's role in making postal policy and the consequent severing of the unions' principal line of influence over postal labor policies.

The measure passed through the House of Representatives without any important changes, but it faced a more tortuous path in the Senate, where some important changes were made in the postal rate-making machinery. In a ceremony held in the postmaster general's reception room on August 12, 1970, President Nixon signed the Postal Reorganization Act. Less than eleven months later, on July 1, 1971, the new United States Postal Service officially became an independent establishment of the federal government.

The Postal Reorganization Act made many important changes in the institutional and procedural arrangements for postal management. The act, among other things, did the following:

- Vested direction of the Postal Service in an eleven-member board of governors, nine members of the board being appointed by the President on a bipartisan basis with the advice and consent of the Senate. These members in turn appoint a tenth member of the board, the postmaster general, who serves as the chief executive officer of the Postal Service. These ten appoint a deputy postmaster general, who serves as the eleventh member of the board.
- Established the independent Postal Rate Commission to recommend postal rates and classifications for adoption by the board of governors.
- Established an independent personnel system for the Postal Service, with provisions for direct collective bargaining between postal management and the unions.
- Authorized appropriations for a general "public service" subsidy through fiscal year 1979 in an amount equal to 10 percent ($920 million) of the fiscal 1971 appropriations to the Post Office Department. After 1979, this annual authorization was to decline by 1 percent a year through fiscal 1984, by which time the Postal Service was expected to be self-sustaining.

- Provided for the gradual phasing out of preferential rates for certain categories of mail and required that rates for each class of mail cover those costs directly and indirectly attributable to it plus some "reasonably assignable" portion of the system's institutional costs.
- Authorized the Postal Service to borrow money and issue public bonds (up to $10 billion) to finance postal buildings and mechanization.

All these and many other provisions of the Postal Reorganization Act made the law both the most controversial and the most comprehensive postal legislation in the mail system's 200-year history.

Factors Conducive to Victory

It is remarkable that the proponents of this massive overhaul of the mail agency were able to overcome both the opposition of powerful and well-organized interests and the procedural bias in the American political system against those who try to reorganize the structure or redirect the activities of government. Because of the extraordinary advantages built into the political system favoring those who oppose changes, it is cause for wonder that this set of extensive changes reached enactment. The proponents of postal reorganization achieved their goal largely because the timing was right for their initiative and because they orchestrated a brilliant campaign to persuade both the public and policymakers that the plan was meritorious. But this particular reorganization (and the policy arena in which it took place) possessed several distinctive features that increased the likelihood of success for those who promoted its passage.

First, the reorganization effort did not find postal officials in the position of protective bureaucrats looking with fear on outside calls for changes in their domain. Rather, the whole postal reform movement was essentially an attempt to secure managerial autonomy—independent authority to decide about financing, personnel, services, and other basic policy matters. Thus, from the time of its earliest conception within the department itself, the reorganization plan was vigorously supported by the highest reaches of the postal bureaucracy—a prominent vantage point from which the basic outlines of the reorganization idea were drafted and coalitions built supporting it.

Second, the push for the reorganization's enactment required no enormous expenditure of political capital by any individual or organization except the Post Office Department itself (and it really had nothing to lose by its efforts). Many significant reorganization proposals fail to receive adequate political support partly because building a sufficiently strong coalition requires too great an outlay of political capital, usually by the President, with no guarantee of success. But in this case, President Nixon did not have to spend precious political resources, partly since there were no substantial disputes over the plan from within the executive branch, and partly since the reorganization would disrupt congressional committee structures to only a limited extent. Moreover, proponents of the plan were able to offer members of Congress the appealing prospect of being freed from the responsibility of having to make politically uncomfortable decisions about patronage, rates, and wages. And although the reorganization plan drew some sustained opposition from the unions, it enjoyed strong support from other constituencies—large publishers and the general business community.

Third, throughout much of its legislative history, the controversial reorganization proposal was overshadowed by the even more volatile issue of a pay increase for postal employees. This concurrence of events had the dual effect of shielding the reform plan from some of the dilution that fuller scrutiny and wider debate might have brought it and of giving the measure's proponents the opportunity to enlist the support of the postal unions.

Fourth, unlike the situation facing those who might promote reorganization in, for example, federal health or education policy, the postal policy setting was relatively isolated and free-standing. That is, there were no other federal agencies charged with performing even remotely similar tasks. Thus, no agencies rose in alarm over the reorganization's potential effects on their activities—a common occurrence in policy areas when several agencies have like missions.[34] Moreover, unlike many other federal agencies, the Post Office Department did not operate through state or local agencies or depend on them; therefore, advocates of the reorganization did not have the additional problem of having to satisfy the demands of state or local officials who might have felt threatened. Also, the postal reorganization measure did not try to elevate the organizational status of the department or its functions at the expense, explicit or implicit, of other federal programs.[35] Postal reformers were not threatening other programs and priorities with arguments that the increasing severity of the postal problem required that the agency receive more federal money or increased attention from the President and Congress. Rather, the postal reformers explicitly sought to remove the department from the President's cabinet, to reduce the number of tax dollars devoted to postal activities, and to decrease the demands of postal issues on the attentions of legislators.

Finally, the advocates of postal reorganization had more than sterile, unemotional arguments to back their proposal. Though dull theories of organizational management provided the chief theoretical justification for the proposal, the reorganization's proponents were able to sell it to the public as a way of ridding the postal system of "politics" and everything the pejorative sense of that word conveyed—corruption, waste, favoritism, and the like. The postal reorganization's advocates, in framing the issue to the public that way, made it difficult for members of Congress to oppose the plan.

In sum: the 1970 reorganization of the postal system transformed the legal and institutional arrangements of the postal policymaking machinery. These changes were the most extensive in the postal system's history and among the most extensive ever for any federal executive agency. The reorganization was a highly conspicuous effort by the federal government to improve the management and performance of the nation's oldest and largest public enterprise. By and large, the reconstitution of the postal system has achieved many of its objectives, but in the years since the reorganization's passage, postal executives and managers have found that the postal system is less adaptable to business management techniques than the reformers believed and that the managerial autonomy allegedly granted to the organization does not extend to many important elements of postal policy.

Government Corporations: The Model for the Postal Business

Readers with a general interest in the Postal Service, but not so much in the anatomy of government agencies' organizational forms, may want to go straight to the next chapter. What follows still in this one is meant to locate the Postal Service in its larger governmental context by addressing several rather basic questions about government corporations and similar independent establishments of the federal government: Why does the federal government sometimes use the corporate form of organization in lieu of more traditional formal-legal organizational structures? What kinds of political incentives lead to the creation of these organizations?

How independent do these organizations manage to remain in practice?

The Distinctiveness of Government Corporations

Governments in mixed economies committed to full employment and stable growth employ a variety of instruments for performing the public's business—taxing, spending, regulating, and controlling organizational form (for example, by nationalizing industries or creating government corporations). The interesting question here is why the federal government of the United States has sometimes chosen the government corporation as its strategy of intervention rather than employing some sort of subsidy, tax expenditure, or coercive regulation. The typical answers involve three sorts of problems: *risk*, where private entrepreneurs do not see sufficient possibility of return on investment (as in the case of the Synthetic Fuels Corporation); *scope*, where the amount of capital to be raised and the area of activities to be covered are great (as in the case of large infrastructure investments such as the projects of the Tennessee Valley Authority); and *service-maintenance*, where not only are economic returns not particularly promising, but alternative sources of service are uncertain. This last category would encompass Amtrak, the Postal Service, and the like.

The most common rationale in textbooks and conventional wisdom for the establishment of government corporations is that they provide for the efficient and effective operation of "businesslike" enterprises, either owned or sponsored by the federal government. The general criteria governing the establishment of government corporations were most clearly enunciated by President Harry Truman in his 1948 budget message:[36]

> *Experience indicates that the corporate form of organization is peculiarly adapted to the administration of government programs which are predominantly of commercial character—those which are revenue producing, are at least potentially self-sustaining, and involve a large number of business-type transactions with the public. In their business operations, such programs require greater flexibility than the customary type of appropriation budget normally permits. As a rule, the usefulness of a corporation lies in its ability to deal with the public in the manner employed by private enterprise for similar work.*

Thus, the corporate form of organization is likely to be adopted in cases where government itself will be managing an economic enterprise (for whatever reason—historical accident, private sector default, high cost or technological barriers to private initiation, protection of "the public interest") and where there is a perceived need to confer on the managers and executives of the enterprise a considerable amount of flexibility or autonomy—not as much as private organizations have, but more than is common for most government agencies. These differences of degree bear elaboration.

Most public managers operate under a wide variety of constraints, especially compared to those faced by managers in private business. The managers and executives in a traditional government agency ordinarily do not have unilateral control over the organization's factors of production—inputs such as personnel, land, buildings, and capital. The various rigidities of the civil service system mean that a government agency has little flexibility in hiring and firing employees. It cannot pay any of its employees more or less than the amount set by Congress. The agency's purchase of goods and services must be authorized and paid for by appropriated funds. Its earnings (if there are any) may not be retained by the organization. A government agency must produce statements specifying the likely environmental effects of its activities, whether building a big dam or a small post office, constructing a port or widening a road. Moreover, an agency is expected to conduct most of its business in public and is thus subject to far greater visibility and scrutiny than a private business firm is. Along with this enhanced visibility come not only increased public sensitivity to the agency's fiscal integrity but also heightened public expectations that the agency will be responsive, accountable, equitable, and efficient.[37]

All these expectations mean that government agencies operate in a much more volatile environment than business organizations do. Outside groups affected by the agency's actions will use the political process to try to bring the agency's goals and activities in line with their own interests and expectations. And since the agency is likely to have more than one public to which it must pay attention, the possibly contrary demands of those groups will only further confuse the cross-signals the agency receives about the way it should behave. Business firms typically operate in a less complex environment: demands are made known to the firm through meetings of stockholders or through the workings of the marketplace, as consumers exercise economic choice.

In sum, management in government agencies is more sharply constrained than in business organizations. Public managers have far less discretion in setting goals and in planning. The goals, given to the agency by political institutions (legislatures, courts, chief executives), are not likely to be specified clearly and are likely to be multiple and possibly irreconcilable. Planning is much more difficult in public organizations, moreover, because resources and the use of these resources are determined by political institutions whose support for the agency is likely to be, as James Q. Wilson has suggested, contingent and conditional:[38]

> *[Support] is contingent in that it may be withdrawn, altered, or reduced at any time, often without recourse or appeal (a bureau chief cannot sue a budget examiner or an appropriations committee chairman for breach of contract). It is conditional in that obtaining it at all requires the executive to accept a long and growing list of constraints on his authority—civil service rules governing the hiring, assigning, and firing of personnel, accounting rules governing the uses to which money can be put, freedom of information laws designed to minimize his opportunities for acting in secret or maintaining confidential records, and so on.*

Government corporations and quasi-corporate enterprises are not all alike in their specific powers and constraints, but they commonly enjoy far more latitude than that accorded traditional agencies. For example, the corporations typically have separate personnel systems of their own, and may thus be exempted from all the civil service pay and employment restrictions. Some of the corporations are permitted to set their own employment policies and to engage in direct collective bargaining with their employees over wages, working conditions, and the like. Unlike traditional government agencies or bureaus, government corporations also typically have power, acting in their own names, to sue and be sued, and to acquire, develop, and dispose of real estate and other kinds of property.

One of the most striking differences between government corporations and traditional agencies is in the way their activities are financed.[39] Government agencies are provided with funds through regular congressional authorizations and appropriations. These are usually accompanied by detailed specifications about the purposes and methods of expenditure. If an agency has any surplus funds at the end of the fiscal year, that surplus reverts to the U.S. Treasury, and funds for the next year come through another appropriation. Government corporations, by contrast, typically derive funds from their own revenues (which typically come from user charges) or by borrowing from the Treasury or issuing public bonds and notes. This fiscal autonomy generally carries a "price" of sorts, in that most government corporations, unlike traditional agencies, generally are expected to be financially self-sustaining (though some regularly fall short of that goal).

Another important (some would say the most important) feature distinguishing government corporations from regular agencies is that the former are theoretically freed of many of the direct controls of Congress and the White House. Government corporations are supposed to be "above politics"; their management and operations are theoretically insulated from untoward political influences, especially those of a partisan variety.

The Creation of Government Corporations

More is known about the publicly stated rationales behind the creation of government corporations than about the actual processes and politics involved in creating and operating these organizations. But an examination of the circumstances surrounding the formation of five such organizations (the TVA in 1933, the U.S. Postal Service and Amtrak in 1970, Conrail in 1973, and the Synthetic Fuels Corporation in 1980) provides some useful generalizations about the formation of government corporations and about the political appeal this organizational form holds for elected officials.

First, it is clear that the establishment of a government corporation is typically an action of high political visibility. It is a conspicuous and symbolic way for elected officials to appear to be "doing something" about a problem. They appear to be taking bold and decisive action. Establishing a corporation especially appeals to politicians when there appears to be a crisis or some other alarming change in objective conditions. In the case of the Postal Service, as shown earlier, it was the collapse of the Chicago post office and the generally worsening state of the postal organization. Alarming circumstances also preceded the move to create Amtrak (the National Railroad Passenger Corporation) and the Synthetic Fuels Corporation.

Amtrak was created by Congress in 1970 (and started up on May 1, 1971) in response to a long-term decline in America's system of private passenger rail lines. In the late 1920s, the railroads had dominated the public transportation market, carrying over three-fourths of all the passengers who traveled by common carrier. By the mid-1950s, trains were eclipsed by both buses and airplanes in the intercity passenger market. And by 1970 even the handful of trains still operating were candidates for discontinuation by railroad executives, who saw the passenger services as a costly drain on their slightly more remunerative freight business. The deteriorating situation took on the dimensions of a crisis when the Penn Central Railroad went bankrupt in 1970.[40]

The creation of the Synthetic Fuels Corporation occurred under similar circumstances—important economic changes accompanied by a sense of crisis. For decades, the main obstacle to the development of alternatives to conventional fossil fuels (oil, natural gas, and coal) was the relative expense. Even as the economics of the overall energy situation changed in the 1970s, the government still refrained from adopting a synthetic fuels policy, because assorted opponents objected to the likely environmental effects and to government subsidies for huge private energy projects. But these objections diminished by 1979, when the cutoff of Iranian oil to the United States once again put Americans into gasoline lines and sent elective officials into a panic. When President Jimmy Carter then proposed that a government corporation be created to encourage the construction of synthetic fuel plants through loans, loan guarantees, price guarantees, and purchase agreements, Congress responded and had the Energy Security Act ready for the President's signature by early in the summer of 1980. [41]

Forming a government corporation to deal with critical problems such as these is attractive to elected officials because such organizations are different and newsworthy. In addition, they provide their sponsors and supporters with a welcome, well-publicized opportunity to claim credit for responding to a tough situation in a creative way. [42]

A second source of the government corporation's appeal to elected officials is that there has usually been a large reservoir of political capital to be tapped by the mere process of organization-building. Franklin Roosevelt was confident that the massive projects to be undertaken by the Tennessee Valley Authority (TVA) would eventually fire the public's imagination (as well as that region's economic development), and he let his optimism shine through when he promised that the TVA would bring a revival of the spirit and vision of American pioneers. Richard Nixon could promise that the transformation of the old Post Office Department into the new Postal Service would cure problems that had been festering for years in the postal system—knowing that the final judgment on that promise was years away and that, in the meantime, symbolic changes alone would bring some political credit as the public watched the drab old mail agency outwardly transformed by a new name, a bold new logo, and bright new colors adorning offices, equipment, and vehicles.

A third way in which the creation of a government corporation appeals to elected officials is that it provides them with the opportunity to shift the responsibility for difficult or intractable problems onto someone else's shoulders. It is no coincidence that the legislative records attached to the laws creating these organizations are filled with pointed references to the independence these organizations are to be granted. The political calculus here is not difficult to understand. If all goes well later, the politicians can share in the glory. If all goes poorly, the politicians can point the finger of blame at others who, after all, had been given independent responsibility for handling the problem. As noted above, this rationale was no small part of the thinking behind the willingness of members of Congress to divest themselves of responsibility for the postal system. And in 1980 legislators, uncertain as to the costs and benefits of a new set of allocation decisions, passed the politically difficult task of awarding government-backed loans to the Synthetic Fuels Corporation.[43]

But to be really appealing to politicians, proposals to create government corporations have to have credibility and legitimacy. Elected officials must be able to argue convincingly to their constituents (even if they do not themselves fully believe) that creation of the corporation is the best way to solve a problem or to manage a complex undertaking with efficiency and effectiveness, especially given the abbreviated decision time forced by the accompanying "crisis." The more plausibly one can present such an argument, the better the chances of legislative passage. For example, in the case of the Postal Service, it seemed perfectly reasonable that a reconstituted postal organization—infused with private business management techniques and freed from the caprices of political patronage and control—might well manage the mails better than did the administratively tangled Post Office Department. Similarly, although no one may actually have believed in 1970 that the government could do a better job than the private sector at running the freight railroads of the Northeast, permitting the Consolidated Rail Corporation (Conrail) to get into the act seemed preferable (especially in light of the failure of the private rail companies) to letting the rail systems collapse into ruin, thereby leaving much of the nation's commercial and industrial infrastructure without access to rail service.[44]

There is another dimension to this point that bears mentioning. To win enactment, a corporation's proponents must be able to argue credibly that creation of a government corporation is necessary, legitimate, and desirable. But the ability to prevail with such an argument is likely to vary over time—not just with the specifics of each proposal, but with changing attitudes toward government intervention and toward commercial and industrial vitality, as well as with changing public confidence in the government's managerial capacities.

Although the great frequency with which government corporations were established in the 1930s would suggest otherwise, there is good reason to believe that it was much more difficult for President Roosevelt and his political allies to convince Congress and the public of the need for a government corporation than it is today. After all, because Roosevelt's were among the early such proposals, he had to battle the specter of "creeping socialism." He gamely promised that the TVA would be "a corporation clothed with the power of Government but possessing the flexibility and initiative of a private enterprise," and concerned with the Tennessee River but working "for the general social and economic welfare of the Nation."[45] But in fact, as James Branscom has pointed out:[46]

> *For all the comfort these words gave the private power interests, Roosevelt might as well have said that he was creating a socialist river-damming project that would be used to barge children to integrated schools and supply electric power to the Kremlin.*

As decades passed and as people saw that the creation of the TVA was not the penultimate step toward a socialist society— rather, that the TVA and other government corporations were actually doing a lot of good—the government corporation shed some of its "bogeyman" image. One finds little earnest reference to "creeping socialism" in more recent legislative or public debates over government corporations.

The Politics of Government Corporations

As has been shown, the basic rationale offered for the creation of most government corporations is that these organizations are to perform certain businesslike functions that require managerial autonomy—that is, freedom to make policy decisions without politically motivated intervention by Congress and the White House. In other words, these organizations are to be "above politics," so that their managers and executives base their decisions on considerations of cost-effectiveness, efficiency, and the like— not on considerations of political expediency.

In practice, of course, the government corporation with unassailable autonomy does not exist, yet it persists in the mythology of governmental organization. The misconceptions surrounding government corporations encourage all sorts of misguided and unrealistic expectations of how these organizations will operate and what they can accomplish. Even people who should know better seem willing to believe that elected officials will be unable or unlikely to interfere in decisions about an organization's policies and practices if that organization formally enjoys the status of a government corporation.[47]

However, as the whole history of "independent" regulatory agencies shows, the President and members of Congress can find ways of making their preferences influential. Their latent powers alone, which even include the ability to alter the statutory independence of a government corporation, are often more than sufficient to influence successfully the affairs or direction of a government corporation. Moreover, there is certainly nothing inherent in the corporate form of organization that isolates those entities from effective intervention by elected officials or that otherwise prevents internal decisions from being made on the basis of political or organizational maintenance considerations, in addition to economic considerations.

It is nevertheless true that much of what people normally associate with "politics," such as nepotism, can be kept out of these organizations. The TVA, for example, has historically been highly successful at making sure that its engineers, land buyers and other employees are not appointed simply because they (or their relatives or friends) helped elect certain candidates to public office. Professionalism and merit are clearly the standards at the TVA.[48] But to think of "politics" merely in terms of patronage, favors, and the like, is to think of it too narrowly. If the concept is expanded to mean disagreement or conflict over the authoritative allocation of resources, then it becomes clearer why it is difficult to take "politics" out of these organizations, or to take their activities out of the purview of elected officials or other interested political actors. After all, as Harold Seidman has noted:[49]

> *Government corporations are organized to achieve a public purpose authorized by law. This fact is often forgotten. So far as purpose is concerned, a corporation cannot be distinguished from any other government agency. This view was vigorously stated by the United States Supreme Court in the case of* Cherry Cotton Mills v. U.S. *(327 U.S. 561) when it held that the fact "that the Congress chose to call it a corporation does not alter its character so as to make it something other than what it actually is, an agency selected by the government to accomplish purely governmental purposes."*

Thus, it is no surprise that "politics" is every bit as much a part of the government corporation's working environment as it is for a traditional agency. The actions and decisions of government corporations may affect the lives of citizens every bit as much as do the actions and decisions of other agencies. In some corporations, such as the Postal Service, the relationship may even be far more frequent, direct, and conspicuous than is found with most traditional agencies. But even if a corporation's activities are neither conspicuous nor of direct interest to large numbers of citizens, its functions are still likely to be important to some organized special interest. In either case, elected officials will keep themselves aware (or they will be made aware) of the corporation's actions and will step in to protect their constituents' interests if the electoral incentive is sufficiently strong. It is fallacious to establish government corporations with the expectation or hope that these organizations will be above the political fray and that they will operate as would a private firm.[50]

Endnotes

1. President's Commission on Postal Organization, Report of the Commission, *Towards Postal Excellence* (Washington: U.S. Government Printing Office, 1968), p. 53.
2. U.S., Congress, House, Committee on Appropriations, *Postal Appropriations, Hearings before a Subcommittee of the House Committee on Appropriations*, 90th Cong., 2d Sess., 1967, pp. 27–28.
3. James N. Miller, "The Awful Truth About the U.S. Post Office," *Reader's Digest*, November 1968.
4. Maurice B. Feimster, quoted in *Newsweek*, July 13, 1959, p. 23.
5. Dan Cordtz, "It's Now or Never for the Post Office," *Fortune*, March 1967, p. 136.
6. President's Commission on Postal Organization, *Towards Postal Excellence*, p. 11. For a full description of the Chicago collapse, see Charles Remsberg, "The Day the Mails Stopped," *Saturday Review*, December 17, 1968, pp. 21–24.
7. The concept of "subgovernments" is discussed in many places. See, for example, Randall B. Ripley and Grace A. Franklin, *Congress, the Bureaucracy, and Public Policy*, 4th ed. (Homewood, Ill.: Dorsey Press, 1987).
8. The analysis in this paragraph draws on the approach of James Q. Wilson, presented by him in multiple writings with varying degrees of elaboration. See, for example, *Political Organizations* (New York: Basic Books, 1973), chap. 15; and "The Politics of Regulation," in *The Politics of Regulation*, ed. James Q. Wilson (New York: Basic Books, 1980), pp. 357–94.
9. "New Era Favors Career Postmasters," *Postal Life* (May 1969), pp. 8–11.
10. President's Commission on Postal Organization, *Towards Postal Excellence*, Annex, vol. 3, part 4, p. 25.
11. Ibid., vol. 4, part 7, p. 44.
12. *Washington Post*, July 23, 1967, p. A22; cited in Richard F. Fenno, Jr., *Congressmen in Committees* (Boston: Little, Brown, 1973), p. 37.
13. Cited in Frank S. Joseph, "Pressures Come from Many Directions to Set Postal Reform's Eventual Course," *National Journal*, December 13, 1969, p. 326.

14. Fenno, *Congressmen in Committees*, pp. 64, 66.
15. Quoted in ibid., p. 246. The information in this paragraph is also from Fenno, pp. 246–47.
16. Arthur D. Little, Inc., "Procedural Matters Related to Establishing Postal Classifications and Setting Postal Rates," Working Memorandum FLA/CM-3, September 1967, p. 5.
17. For a good account of the compromises and amendments, see *Congressional Quarterly Almanac*, col. 33, (1967), pp. 541–58.
18. Fenno, *Congressmen in Committees*, p. 64.
19. In late 1969, for example, a federal grand jury indicted Spiegel, Inc. (a major user of third-class mail) and former U.S. Senator Daniel B. Brewster (D., Md., 1963–1968) on charges that Brewster had accepted $24,500 from Spiegel to influence his vote on postal rate legislation. See *Congressional Quarterly Weekly Report*, December 12, 1969, pp. 2548–49.
20. *Wall Street Journal*, September 20, 1967, p. 3.
21. See A. Lee Fritschler, *Smoking and Politics: Policymaking and the Federal Bureaucracy*, 3d ed. (Englewood Cliffs, N.J.: Prentice-Hall, 1983).
22. Gerald Cullinan, *The Post Office Department* (New York: Praeger, 1968), p. xi.
23. Lawrence F. O'Brien, "A New Design for the Postal Service," address presented at meeting of the Magazine Publishers Association and the American Society of Magazine Editors, Washington, April 3, 1967.
24. President's Commission on Postal Organization, *Towards Postal Excellence*, Annex, vol. 1, part 1, p. 122.
25. Ibid., pp. 123–24.
26. Ibid., p. 125.
27. President's Commission on Postal Organization, *Towards Postal Excellence*, p. 33. (Emphasis as in original.)
28. U.S., Congress, House, Committee on Post Office and Civil Service, *Post Office Reorganization, Hearings before the Committee on Post Office and Civil Service*, 91st Cong., 1st Sess., 1969, p. 705.
29. Ibid., pp. 796–97.
30. Confidential internal memorandum from Post Office Department's Congressional Liaison Office to Postmaster General Winton Blount, August 27, 1969; files of the postmasters general, U.S. Postal Service, Washington.
31. Jim Henderson, memorandum to the General Counsel (David A. Nelson), "Reorganization of Postal Service, Suggestions For," dated April 7, 1969, typewritten.
32. *Congressional Quarterly Weekly Report*, July 31, 1970, p. 1967; August 6, 1971, p. 1681.
33. U.S. Post Office Department, "Marketing Plan," pp. 15–20.
34. For interesting examples of interagency conflicts over reorganization proposals, see *New York Times*, January 23, 1978, pp. 1, 13. And for the best detailed study of such a conflict, see Patricia Rachal, *Federal Narcotics Enforcement: Reorganization and Reform* (Boston: Auburn House, 1982).
35. Rufus E. Miles, Jr. suggests that efforts to elevate the organizational status of an agency through reorganization may elicit opposition to the measure from other agencies and interests. Miles, "Considerations for a President Bent on

Reorganization," *Public Administration Review*, 37 (March/April, 1977), p. 156.

36. *House Document 19*, 80th Cong., pp. M57–M62, quoted in Harold Seidman, *Politics, Position, and Power*, 3rd ed. (New York: Oxford University Press, 1980), p. 276.

37. James Q. Wilson, "The Bureaucracy Problem," *Public Interest*, no. 6 (Winter 1967), pp. 3–9.

38. James Q. Wilson, *The Investigators: Managing FBI and Narcotics Agents* (New York: Basic Books, 1978), p. 164.

39. By noting this and other distinctions between government corporations and traditional agencies, I do not want to imply that all the organizations within each category are alike. In fact, corporate enterprises differ along so many dimensions that observers seldom agree as to which enterprises actually merit the label "government corporation" and which do not. Listings of government corporations therefore vary substantially, depending on whose definition is used. Perhaps the clearest definitions and listings are those set forth in National Academy of Public Administration, *Report on Government Corporations* (Washington, D.C.: National Academy of Public Administration, 1981), vol. 2.

40. See Joseph R. Daughen and Peter Binzen, *The Wreck of the Penn Central* (Boston: Little, Brown, 1971); John Harr, *The Great Railway Crisis: An Administrative History of the United States Railway Association* (Washington, D.C.: National Academy of Public Administration, 1978).

41. See Christopher Madison, "You Know That Synfuels Are for Real When the Big Boys Enter the Picture," *National Journal*, September 13, 1980, pp. 1508–09; and Eric M. Uslaner, "Energy, Issue Agendas, and Policy Typologies" (Paper presented at the 1982 Annual Meeting of the American Political Science Association, Denver, Colorado, September 2–5, 1982), esp. pp. 32–33.

42. On the potential electoral advantages of "credit-claiming," see David R. Mayhew, *Congress: The Electoral Connection* (New Haven: Yale University Press, 1974).

43. See Uslaner, "Energy, Issue Agendas, and Policy Typologies," pp. 32–33.

44. The total collapse of the freight railroads of the Northeast seemed a distinct possibility in the late 1960s and early 1970s. As rail earnings dropped and one road after another collapsed, railroad executives predicted a financial crisis and the total collapse of the Northeast's rail system. Under the pall of this imminent crisis, Congress produced the Regional Rail Reorganization Act of 1973 (P.L. 93-236) which, among other things, created the Consolidated Rail Corporation, popularly known as "Conrail."

45. Franklin D. Roosevelt, "Muscle Shoals Development: Message from the President of the United States Transmitting a Request for Legislation to Create a Tennessee Valley Authority," 73d Cong., 1st sess., House Doc. 15, 1.

46. James Branscom, "The TVA: It Ain't What It Used to Be," *American Heritage* 28 (1977): 70.

47. See, for example, Amitai Etzioni's argument advocating the transformation of the U.S. Food and Drug Administration into a Food and Drug Testing

Corporation, in the hope that the "new organization would be removed from the political pressures which hamper the effective operation of the FDA." See Etzioni, "The Third Sector and Domestic Missions," *Public Administration Review* 32 (1973): 319.

48. For a discussion of how an ethos of professionalism and nonpartisanship developed in the TVA during its first twenty years, see David Lilienthal, *TVA—Democracy on the March* (New York: Harper & Row, 1953).

49. Harold Seidman, "The Theory of the Autonomous Government Corporation: A Critical Appraisal," *Public Administration Review* 12 (1952): 93.

50. Much of the discussion of government corporations in the last quarter of this chapter first appeared in John T. Tierney, "Government Corporations and Managing the Public's Business," *Political Science Quarterly* 99 (Spring 1984): 73–92, and is adapted here with permission from *Political Science Quarterly*.

Chapter 2

THE MANAGERIAL APPARATUS

From the earliest days of the United States postal system, one of the primary tasks facing its executives has been developing internal organizational arrangements that strike the right balance between the system's forces of centralization and those of decentralization. Because the postal system is a complex, highly interdependent processing and distribution network, it must be coordinated and controlled from headquarters. That is, postal facilities, transportation routes, distribution schemes, and the like all must be arranged and concerted by persons with a large enough perspective on the entire network to ensure that a letter dropped in a collection box in Pleasant Valley, Montana, actually has some chance of being delivered to a house on Greenacre Road in Westwood, Massachusetts, in only a few days. The top-down control needed for this degree of coordination in operations is also clearly necessary for maintaining standard personnel practices throughout the system, for properly accounting for daily postage receipts, for controlling acquisition of equipment, for preserving the privacy of the mails, and the like.

But this need for coordination and centralized managerial control has long conflicted with strong pressures, also inherent in the system, toward decentralization and fragmentation. Perhaps the most obvious of these decentralizing forces is the sheer size and geographical distribution of the postal network. With post offices at over 30,000 sites around the country, the variations in local service requirements are great, and it is difficult, to say the least, for a centralized administration to develop sensible rules and regulations that are appropriate everywhere. The recent administrative history of the Postal Service finds postal executives still grappling with this central organizational dilemma as they implemented a major internal reorganization in 1986. This chapter examines that change and the principal organizational structures and control mechanisms through which the vast postal enterprise is managed.

The Postmaster General and the Executive Apparatus

At the apex of the Postal Service's organizational hierarchy is a small group of top executives, situated to influence the ways in which the basic elements of the Postal Service interact and function. These key individuals are the thirty-nine "officers" of the Postal Service. Chief among these officers are the postmaster general (PMG) and the deputy postmaster general, whose authority is derived from the Postal Reorganization Act. This authority is very broad, for the postmaster general's role is defined simply as that of chief executive officer to be appointed by and to serve at the pleasure of the board of governors. The deputy postmaster general is the alternate CEO. The remaining officers are appointed by and serve at the pleasure of the postmaster general. The nature and scope of their responsibilities are determined by the postmaster general with the concurrence of the board. These officers include two associate postmasters general, five senior assistant postmasters general (in charge of the major management "groups"), nineteen assistant postmasters general, six other headquarters functional heads (general counsel, chief postal inspector, deputy general counsel, treasurer, judicial officer, and consumer advocate), and five regional postmasters general.

In addition to these officers, there are roughly 800 other persons in senior management positions around the country. Most of these are divisional, regional, and headquarters general managers and office directors in charge of functional groupings, or they are managers of sectional centers (geographically defined units with responsibility for all post offices within their territory).

Together, all these officials constitute what might best be called the executive apparatus of the organization. Their functions serve to maintain the organization as a system of cooperative effort. It is not quite correct to say that the function of these persons is to "manage" the Postal Service. Rather, to use Chester Barnard's apt simile, the functions of the executive apparatus are more like those of the nervous system, including the brain, in relation to the rest of the body: "It exists to maintain the bodily system by directing those actions which are necessary more effectively to adjust to the environment, but it can hardly be said to manage the body, a large part of whose functions are independent of it and upon which it in turn depends."[1]

Most of the persons who have held the PMG's chair in the past two decades have been reasonably able executives. Some of them have realized that, as James March has put it, "what makes an organization function well is *the density of administrative competence*."[2] These leaders have concentrated on trying to enhance the capacity of long-term employees to do their jobs efficiently, adeptly, and with a sense of organizational mission and esprit de corps—a goal that has seemed to call for the redesign of organizational structures and the delegation of more managerial authority to lower levels, the granting to field managers of more responsibility and freedom to make decisions that previously had been reserved to higher levels.

For example, immediately after the corporate transformation of the postal system in 1971, Postmaster General Winton Blount restructured the functional organization at headquarters, reduced the number of regions from fifteen to five, created two new levels of management (the districts and the sectional centers), and pushed managerial responsibility for day-to-day operations out of headquarters to the field, where there was a need for greater managerial flexibility and opportunity to exercise initiative. In a letter to postmasters describing the changes, Blount wrote in 1971: "It [decentralization] will get us away from that strait jacket of the past, whereby the postal system was run by the book and the book was written in Washington. We want to give managers a chance to manage, to innovate and initiate—and even to make mistakes."[3]

Blount's successor as postmaster general, E. T. Klassen, continued the decentralizing trend through his administration. In March 1973, Klassen declared: "I am determined to decentralize the system to give our local managers the flexibility to make the thousands of individual decisions that must be made in the course of each work day."[4] In line with this philosophy, field managers and postmasters were delegated hundreds of items of authority previously exercised by headquarters.

But finding the right organizational structures and distributions of managerial authority has proven to be a continuous challenge for postal executives. Thus, in 1986, the Postal Service carried out yet another major internal reorganization affecting both headquarters and field structures. Once again, the overall purpose of the reorganization was to streamline postal management and to shift still more operating management expertise and responsibility to the field.

The initiative for this recent reshuffling came from Paul Carlin, a 16-year postal veteran who served as postmaster general for the full calendar year of 1985. Carlin's predecessor as postmaster general had been William Bolger, who led the postal system brilliantly from 1978 to 1984, successfully bringing the organization away from the brink of disaster upon which it seemed to teeter in 1976 and 1977. At the time Carlin assumed the position of postmaster general, the Postal Service was stronger than it had been in years. Mail volume had been increasing steadily in the preceding years (a dramatic 10.2 percent increase in fiscal 1984), and the organization's financial position finally had improved: fiscal 1984 was the third straight year ending in a net surplus.

Despite the apparent success of existing organizational arrangements, Carlin committed himself to trying to transform the organizational culture of the USPS. Soon after becoming postmaster general, Carlin sent roughly 12,000 copies of *In Search of Excellence* to USPS managers and announced that he wanted to shift the Postal Service "away from the negative, authoritarian patterns of the past and toward the progressive, participative patterns of the future." He stated his view with more than a trace of urgency: "These are not ideas we can take or leave. They are an organizational imperative. Without them, we will decline and fall as an enterprise."[5]

As it turned out, Carlin was fired by the Board of Governors before he could carry out his wishes. (It later became clear, as the following chapter shows, that Carlin and a handful of other senior officers were fired at the insistence of Peter Voss, a member of the postal Board of Governors. Voss felt that Carlin and the others stood in the way of a fraudulent contract-steering scheme Voss had devised, for which he was later convicted and sent to federal prison.) In his place, the Board of Governors appointed Albert V. Casey, the former chairman of American Airlines, who was well known for turning financially troubled organizations into money makers. On his merits, Casey was clearly an extraordinarily good choice to be postmaster general. (But it also became clear in the wake of disclosures surrounding the Voss scandal that the selection of Casey had been recommended to the Board of Governors by an executive recruiting firm with ties to Voss. The apparent hope was that Casey, a Texan, might help steer a desired Postal Service contract for multi-line optical character readers to the Texas firm involved with Voss in the procurement conspiracy. It is important to note, however, that Casey knew nothing of the scheme and has never been implicated in it in any way. His service as postmaster general was a model of probity.)

Casey accepted the position of postmaster general on January 7, 1986, with the intention of staying less than a year (he was committed to take a teaching post at Southern Methodist University in Texas by September 15, 1986). Casey saw it as part of his mandate to reorganize and trim the postal management structure from headquarters all the way down through the larger post offices.

Headquarters Reorganization

Casey's view was that large organizations work best under simplified corporate structures, and he believed that the activities of any large organization can be grouped in four major categories: operations, marketing, finance, and "all others."[6] Casey also had a strong preference for a limited span of control. The new organizational scheme he crafted in 1986 for Postal Service headquarters reflected these preferences.

The obvious way to reduce the number of headquarters units reporting directly to the postmaster general was to create a new top management position, the incumbent of which could help carry the burden. Casey's reorganization created the new position of associate postmaster general, a post designed to serve as the third leg of a new top management triad including the postmaster general and the deputy postmaster general. Whereas the postmaster general is seen as being responsible for maintaining the overall integrity and effectiveness of the system, and the deputy postmaster general is responsible for day-to-day operations (with the operations support group and the five regional postmasters general reporting to him), the new associate postmaster general has responsibility for overall system development. This is reflected in the kinds of organizational subunits reporting to the associate: marketing and communications, human resources, and such administrative services as procurement and supply. Exhibits 2-1 and 2-2 show pre- and post-reorganization, respectively.

In addition to creating an associate postmaster generalship for systems, Casey's headquarters reorganization also elevated the marketing function to the senior level, with a senior assistant postmaster general heading a new Marketing and Communications Group. This change underscored Casey's view—and a growing awareness in the Postal Service generally—of the crucial role that marketing plays in ensuring that the services offered meet customer needs and that potential customers are aware of available services. (Interestingly, the revised organization structure did not have the head of the new marketing group report directly to the postmaster general, despite Casey's view that marketing is one of the most important activities. Apparently, the architects of the reshuffling thought it essential that the general counsel and the chief postal inspector report directly to the postmaster general.

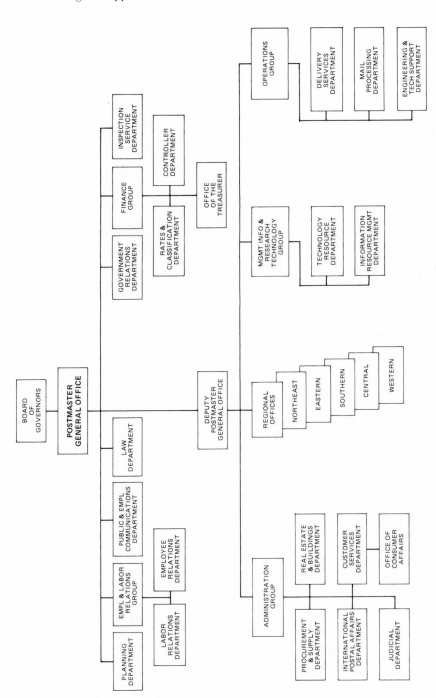

Exhibit 2-1   United States Postal Service Headquarters Organizational Structure, Pre-1986.

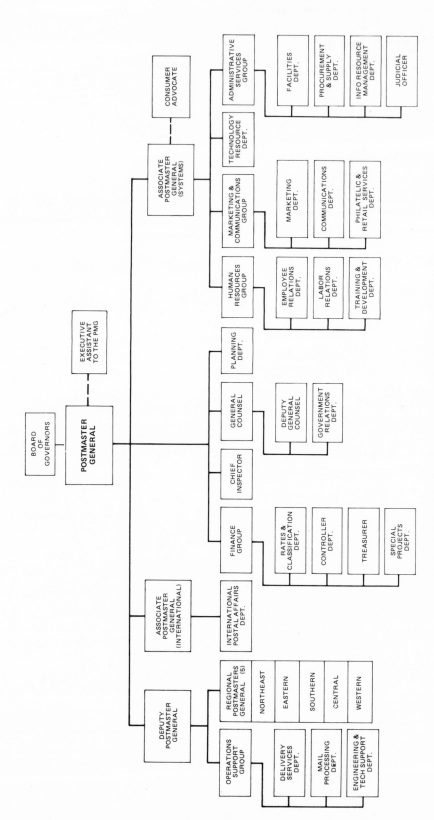

Exhibit 2-2   Headquarters Organization Structure, 1988.

Casey's ironclad insistence that his span of control be limited to five subordinates prevailed over his desire to consecrate the status of the marketing function.)

The headquarters realignment implemented under Casey's leadership was refined in May 1988 when Postmaster General Anthony M. Frank, only two months into the job (having succeeded Preston Tisch), ordered some marginal restructuring of headquarters management. Frank created a second associate postmaster generalship, this one charged with oversight of international postal matters. This new position was established to reflect the growing importance of the Postal Service's role in the international mailing community. More specifically, the postmaster general wanted to highlight the importance of international postal matters in light of the hosting by the United States of the 20th Universal Postal Union Congress, to be held in Washington, D.C., in November 1989. The 169-member UPU is an arm of the United Nations. The 20th Congress will determine the policies under which international mail will be exchanged for the following five years. The newly appointed associate postmaster general-international, Edward E. Horgan, Jr., is likely to serve as chairman of that Congress.

Postmaster General Frank's fine-tuning of the headquarters structure also elevated the organizational status of two units (technology resources and the consumer advocate) by having them report directly to the associate postmaster general-systems. The Technology Resources Department obviously has an increasingly important mission as the Postal Service struggles to find technological solutions for handling its rapidly rising mail volumes. And the responsibilities of the Postal Service's consumer advocate, which include representing individual consumers and recommending customer-related policy changes and service improvements, have been expanded to include oversight of all service measurement systems, such as the Origin-Destination Information System, described later in this chapter. The consumer advocate now is charged also with assessing the effectiveness of the measurement systems currently in place, considering additional service reporting systems, and recommending appropriate changes and adjustments to service measurement.

Moreover, rectifying one of the few flaws with Casey's 1986 restructuring, Postmaster General Frank placed the planning department in a direct reporting relationship to him, thus taking it back out of the finance group where it had been tucked two years earlier. This change seems especially important both as an indication of the fundamental importance of the strategic planning function for the Postal Service as it enters the twenty-first century and as an indication of the postmaster general's high regard for Richard J. Strasser, Jr., the assistant postmaster general for planning, who in the past half decade has become one of the most illustrious stars in the constellation of top postal executives.

Field Reorganization: Regions and Divisions

Despite all these changes in Washington, it is probably the case that the more important changes have occurred in the field organization, where the effects are still emerging. The rationale of the field reorganization was to eliminate administrative layers and put operating management expertise as close as practical to the locations where postal services are provided to the public. The idea was to shorten communications lines and give operating managers the staff and professional support they need in carrying out their activities. The reshuffling aimed at emphasizing, and taking advantage of, what postal executives considered the "least common denominator" in general management—namely, the unit that actually performs the organization's critical tasks but is large enough in its activity to support all of the professional activities necessary for operations support.[7] A key principle of the reorganization was to allow local postal managers as much scope as seems reasonable and practical for faster decision-making and to heighten job satisfaction and management development. The expectation was not only that the organization would be more focused as a consequence of these changes, but that it would be more responsive to market needs and economic realities.

The field reorganization was implemented by the line managers in the organization. The regional PMGs headed up the implementation team. In carrying out the reorganization, headquarters involved as many people as possible so as to minimize surprises and so that the changes could be hammered out against the practical knowledge and thinking of the people involved.

As the accompanying pre- and post-reorganization charts (Exhibits 2-3 and 2-4, respectively) indicate, the field reorganization refocused regional responsibilities from operations management to concentration on projects and programs to improve service, enhance productivity, reduce costs, strengthen financial performance, and develop an effective group of field managers. The regions monitor performance at subordinate levels through the use of management information reports, performance analyses, and on-site visits, but the region overview function has shrunk because new subordinate offices (field divisions, described next) now have

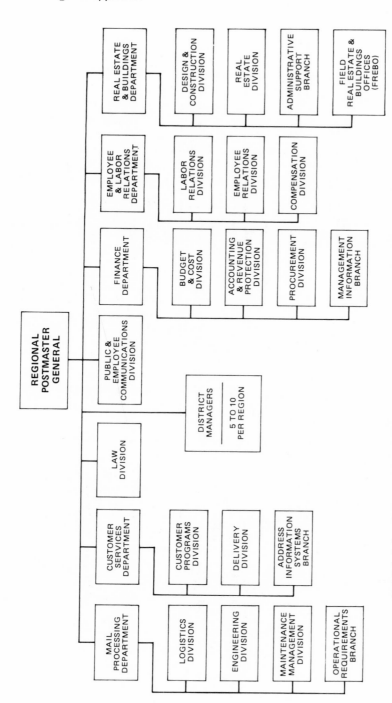

Exhibit 2-3   United States Postal Service Regional Organizational Structure, Pre-1986.

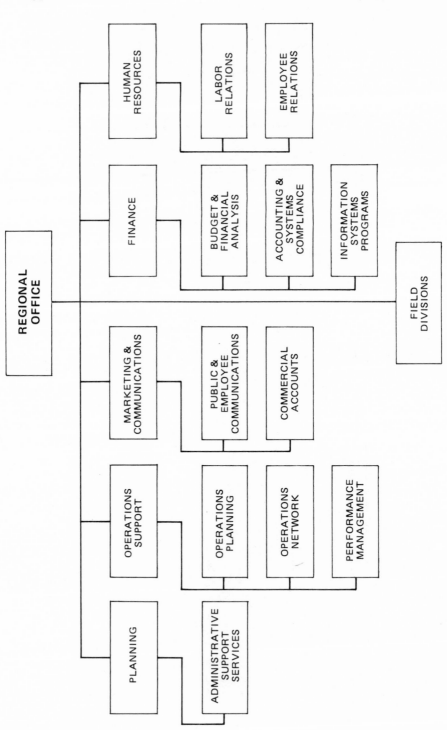

54

The U.S. Postal Service

Exhibit 2-4   United States Postal Service Regional Organizational Structure, Post-1986.

the staffs to carry out much of the performance reviews and analyses required. The regional postmasters general (RPMGs) are now seen less as directors of current field activities and more as assistant deputy postmasters general, supported by small analytical staffs, serving as catalysts for improvements in field operations.

Prior to the reorganization, each of the 5 regions had about 8 district offices (38 in all) reporting to it; each district had about 6 management sectional centers (219 in all) reporting to it; each MSC had about 133 associate offices (29,000 in all) reporting to it. With the reorganization, the district offices were eliminated completely, and their functions (as well as many others) have been moved to a new organizational entity in the Postal Service known as "field divisions." The field divisions now are regarded as the Postal Service's key organizational units, with all other local offices reporting to a division. Increased authority, responsibility, and accountability have been given to the heads of these divisions, known as field division general managers/postmasters, whose ranks are said to consist of "the best managerial talent in the Postal Service."[8] These 74 field divisions are located in key cities throughout the country at already existing management sectional centers (MSCs). (There used to be 219 of these MSCs; now there are 74 major ones, with the others reporting to them.)

The field divisions are supposed to be substantially self-sufficient and autonomous, equipped to meet the ongoing management needs within large geographic areas. For example, these units now have marketing and communications functions, equal employment opportunity functions, labor negotiation functions, and the like, as well as the obvious operations functions. Exhibit 2-5 shows the organization at the field division level.

The substantial staff resources needed for these new field divisions have been drawn largely from both the old district offices and the regional offices. That is, the staffs from the district offices have moved down to the new field division level, and most of the people formerly staffing the regions have moved down as well, leaving each of the regional offices with fewer than 100 employees, instead of the 400 to 600 they previously had. Some personnel in the marketing area also have moved up to the divisions from the management sectional centers.

The MSCs that were not made into divisions by the 1986 reorganization were temporarily left unchanged, but in early 1988 changes came to them as well when the MSCs were realigned to mirror more closely the field division structure. This rearrangement consolidated all line functions under one manager, like at the division level, thus eliminating an organizational barrier be-

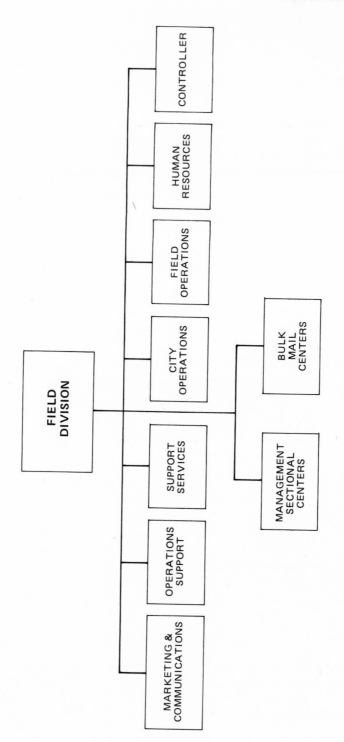

Exhibit 2-5   United States Postal Service Field Division Organizational Structure.

tween mail processing and delivery that long had existed at the MSC level and that had been an impediment to collaborative activity between the two functions.

Local Facilities Managers: Postmasters and Supervisors

All of these various hierarchical strands are visited upon the heads of local managers who operate postal facilities that vary greatly in the scope and nature of the actual tasks performed.

At one end of the spectrum is the tiny contract or community post office (roughly 5,680 of them nationwide), which uses only part of the premises of a small retail business, perhaps a general store or small market in a crossroads community. Here the postmaster is the only postal worker and devotes only part-time to postal matters. All that is required is the ability to supply space and apply a rudimentary knowledge of postal regulations. The postmaster in such a situation is often a prominent member of the local commercial community, even without reference to her or his postal position. This assignment, of course, enhances her or his stature. (The majority of persons serving as postmasters in such offices are women.) The postmasters in these operations come the closest today to what the postmasters of 200 years ago were. Then, innkeepers along the post roads were charged with providing horses for postal coaches and riders, and the inn's tavern would serve as a collection and distribution point for mail between scheduled runs.

Life is still quite simple for postmasters who run offices of the next larger size. There may be one or more clerks assisting with window service and mail sortation, a star route (i.e., a contract route) or two for rural delivery, and possibly a small work force of city or rural carriers. At this level the postmaster must oversee the work of several immediate subordinates.

As the post office gets larger, the managerial job becomes more complex. The number of employees and the functions they carry out increase. Supervisors assume responsibility for direct oversight of the work.

At the far end of the scale is the job of the postmaster who is a management sectional center manager or field division general manager/postmaster. The most complicated of these assignments may involve responsibility for anywhere from 5,000 to 40,000 employees working in highly mechanized mail processing facilities, in large carrier offices and in dozens of associate offices, branches, and stations.

The jobs held by supervisors vary in complexity almost as much as those of postmasters, from very simple oversight at the level of a small carrier station to very elaborate in a major mail processing facility. There are also variations by function. The greatest concentration of supervisors is in mail processing, where under a tour superintendent in a large facility there are supervisors and foremen in a hierarchy of two or three levels overseeing the work of employees ranging from as few as 8 to as many as 120 clerks and mailhandlers engaged in loading and unloading at the platform, culling and cancelling operations, letter sorting by machine, manual sorting of flats, small packages and rolls, optical character reading machine operations, secondary sortation, traying, bag racking, and several other utility functions. Supervisors also oversee window service units, carrier stations, administrative units, and functional support units.

Most supervisors are long-term employees with substantial experience and seniority of service. They have entered at the mail-handler, clerk, or carrier levels and worked their way up, the greatest number coming from the clerk craft. They tend to remain in one facility for most of their careers.

Prior to the reorganization in 1971, most training for supervisors was on the job and through direct observation and experience. It tended to be narrowly focused on operational requirements. Since reorganization, however, most supervisors (and most postmasters) receiving promotions have been given fairly extensive and sophisticated supervisory and management training in such subjects as problem analysis, decision-making, planning, supervision and control, and communications. Many incumbent managers also receive similar training, so these days it is unusual to find a supervisor who has not recently been involved in some formal management training experience.

As the preceding discussion makes clear, the postal system is vast and varied, consisting of postal facilities that range widely in complexity and that confront very different local circumstances. A central problem for postal management is to find ways of controlling and standardizing the activities in this system yet still reserving areas of managerial discretion and initiative for managers in the field. The balance of this chapter first examines how top management approaches this problem through the development of procedural guidelines, looking particularly at the role played by functional specialists at headquarters. Then it examines the pressures that local managers face in trying to meet performance objectives and concludes with a brief look at how the Postal Service has operationalized some performance measures for itself in the absence of meaningful external measures of success.

Distribution of Managerial Authority

The successful delegation of authority is, of course, highly complicated in any large organization. It involves three fundamental components: maintaining formal communications channels throughout the organization and nurturing informal ones; developing formal and informal means of coordinating the behavior of persons and organizational units; and developing a satisfactory scheme of organization. Each of these elements is necessary so that when the chief executive states the general purpose or direction in which he or she wishes to move (better service, better control of costs, or whatever), each subordinate level in the organization is able to see what that means for their own activities. By the time the "purpose" is communicated to the lowest subunits in the organization, its meaning must be apparent—with respect to specific jobs, specific groups, specific times, accomplished results. This requires not only that persons at higher levels understand the concrete conditions and specific kinds of decisions facing those at the operating level, but also that systems be maintained for up-and-down-the-line coordination of purposeful decisions. For the definition of purpose to be successful, it must involve persons throughout the organization—up and down, within each level—so that obstacles and difficulties (as well as accomplishments) are reported and so that purposes can be redefined and modified at each level.[9]

Through its direction of headquarters functional units, the top management of the Postal Service standardizes behavior across this vast system's multiple geographic and functional lines. This is done largely through the extensive use of detailed operating manuals and a steady stream of management instructions and guidelines. As noted earlier, this kind of approach is necessary in part because of the critical interdependencies among the dispersed operational facilities and interwoven parts of the mail processing network. It also is desirable inasmuch as it helps to achieve economies of scale and operational efficiencies derivable from standardization.

As we shall see below, the actual development of the specific procedural guidelines in each functional area is in the hands of specialists at headquarters, well below the level of top management. Nonetheless, top management orients the work of functional specialists, influencing the general nature of the formal rules for the designing of jobs, the grouping of activities, the setting of work standards, and the development and implementation of systems for monitoring, evaluation, and control.

Top management also delegates authority through the regional structure to divisional, sectional center, and postal facility managers. The interactions of the postmaster general and other headquarters officials with the regional postmasters general (and now with divisional managers, too) determine how well this delegation works. The selection, training, direction, evaluation, and rewarding of the middle-level managers also are important. As noted earlier, the tendency since 1971, particularly, has been to seek an increase in the managerial competence of middle-level managers, widen the scope of their responsibility for operating decisions, especially on matters that are affected in important ways by local conditions, while strengthening the influence of the central functional units in providing the guidelines within which local operations will be managed.

For example, the 1986 reorganization transferred the authority for a major portion of the facilities program to field organizations. Division managers now have approval responsibility for capital investment projects up to $2.5 million. Division offices also have been given responsibility for making recommendations concerning closings or consolidations of small post offices and preparing the case for action. The senior assistant postmaster general in charge of the Operations Support Group at headquarters still has final decision-making responsibility on such matters, but two layers of review have been eliminated.

Marketing is another function that has been accentuated at the divisional level as well as at headquarters. There are some 200 new marketing managers and 1,800 new marketing staff persons—commercial accounts representatives—assigned to the divisions. Their job is to sell postal products and services and coordinate service for major business mailers within assigned territories.

As part of the new attention to marketing and customer service, division managers have been given discretion to adjust window hours in local postal facilities beyond the traditional 8-to-5 workday in order to meet local community needs. The aim is simply to make it more convenient for customers to do business with the Postal Service, while also helping to eliminate long lobby lines and reduce traffic congestion around post offices. The system seems to be working. For example, after rescheduling the hours of window clerks at the main post office in Providence, Rhode Island, to make service available from 7 A.M. until midnight seven days a week, the division general manager there found that the switch yielded both greater convenience and service to customers and increased revenue. Following the change, managers found more than 20 percent of that office's business occurring after 6 P.M., and revenues from express mail increased 22 percent, largely because customers were able to deposit express items up to 11 P.M. for next-day delivery anywhere in Rhode Island, Connecticut, New Hampshire, or Massachusetts.[10] (Congressionally imposed service cutbacks, discussed at the end of the next chapter, have wreaked some havoc with the "adjusted hours" program, but division managers still have discretion in such matters.)

At USPS headquarters in Washington, D.C., the Postal Service's functional specialists develop, write, and issue the procedural manuals and guidelines that govern or shape almost every phase of operations. The areas covered range from personnel management and organizational unit design, to mail processing and delivery service operations, to financial planning and reporting.

Management by manual and directive has a long history in the U.S. postal system. This seems to have been rooted in two distinct aspects of the organization's situation. First, because the many geographically dispersed operating units are highly interdependent, standardization has been necessary to achieve operational coordination and efficiencies of scale. Second, the appointment of middle- and lower-level managers was traditionally on a patronage basis, with managerial ability only secondarily considered. Consequently, there was a tendency to centralize all important decision-making and ask local managers merely to carry out instructions. The result, which evolved over a century and a half of postal operations, was the *Postal Manual*—the agency's nine-pound administrative bible containing postal regulations, details on rates, and prescriptions for conduct in the face of almost every imaginable contingency.

While a tremendous amount has been done since 1971 to improve the managerial competence of middle- and lower-level managers, the high degree of interdependence among dispersed operating units remains a hallmark of the system. As a result, both custom ("there have always been procedural manuals") and interdependence push the system toward continued reliance on this method of coordination and standardization. This enhances the influence of the technical specialists in headquarters.

But even before the recent reorganization, there have been increasing opportunities for local management to experiment with local solutions to managerial and organizational problems and to recommend systemwide changes to functional specialists at headquarters. This type of communication is achieved through functional staff meetings at the national and regional levels, through training sessions, through temporary work assignments of field managers to headquarters units and vice-versa, and through ongoing day-to-day communications. So, in practice, functional specialists at headquarters have lots of interaction with field units in the development and revision of new programs or written procedures and guidelines. It is customary for new ideas both for technology and management practice to be tested extensively in the field before they are applied on a systemwide basis.

For example, although local managers now have discretion with respect to the extension of retail service hours, the delegation of that authority actually occurred because of a nationwide test that the USPS conducted over a four- or five-month period in 1984 to determine the impact of extended evening and Saturday hours on staffing, revenue, and customer attitudes. The test's objective was to identify ways to make visits to the post office more convenient for customers who hold 9-to-5 jobs and find it hard to pick up parcels or handle other postal business during traditional post office hours. Specialists in the headquarters Office of Delivery and Retail Operations directed the test at three post offices or stations in suburban areas in each of the five regions of the country. Realizing that extended hours may not be right for every office (since customer needs can vary from office to office and from station to station within a large city) and realizing also that it would be difficult to develop a plan or program that would fit each individual station, the goal of functional specialists at headquarters was to develop standard guidelines to help local officials identify changes that would meet customers' needs.

In short, more is being done at headquarters and in the regional offices to help identify ways for local officials to manage more capably. And more areas of discretion are available to local managers now than was the case even ten years ago (and vastly more than twenty years ago). Suggested changes in procedures or programs are incorporated more often and more quickly now than was the case in the past. Still, control over the manuals and other written directives remains at headquarters. There is an elaborate process for interfunctional clearance of changes in, and additions to, existing procedures. And final approval of major issues frequently is exercised at very high levels in the organization.

Despite the continuance of centripetal forces, there is no doubt that the Postal Service has done much to eliminate managerial handicaps that had debilitated the system. Under previous arrangements, managerial creativity and initiative at the local level went unrewarded and was even punished. For field managers, the only safe course was to follow the book. The result, nor surprisingly, was a very rigid, authoritarian system well suited to coordination and to the maintenance of standard operating procedures, but resistant to change, local managerial initiative, and effective cost control. But local officials now are less bound by the rigid dictates of the organization's rules and regulations. They are encouraged to experiment and introduce new methods—in short, to *manage*, finding ways to hold down costs and improve service.

Local Managers and the Pressures of Meeting Performance Objectives

The managerial task at local levels is extremely difficult. As indicated above, the postal system consists of operations that vary widely in their complexity. The pressures are greatest in the large mail processing and customer service facilities, where constant emphasis on meeting cost control and service standards, coupled with dramatic fluctuations in volume and in the mix of mail to be handled, makes for substantial tension and pressure in the work experience of postal managers. Each task being performed under their supervision is relatively simple, but the coordinating, timing, and scheduling requirements are very complex.

The management problem at the operating level in the Postal Service is to use the system's resources—labor, capital, and the mail itself—in the best productive mixture, optimally matching the available work force on each shift or "tour" with the volume of mail to be handled. Achieving this match is particularly important in the large mail processing facilities where thousands of people move the mail and where the great bulk of clerk and mailhandler hours is used. Since labor costs represent 85 percent of total Postal Service expenses, the daily staffing level decisions, especially at these huge facilities, are critical to good system performance.

One great difficulty for postal managers is that they have no control over mail volume. Senders of mail post it primarily at their own convenience, not in consideration of the Postal Service's work load. Moreover, there is little of it that managers can stockpile for later handling. In years past, postal managers relied on third-class mail (bulk business mail, much of it advertising and other so-called junk mail). Since post offices are not committed to moving this mail as quickly as first-class items, it used to be possible to hold off third-class mail for processing during "slow" hours. However, the Postal Service's various efforts over the years to achieve greater efficiency and work-sharing in the processing of mail have reduced the utility of third-class mail as a device for maintaining a more uniform total work load. For example, the Postal Service's encouragement of third-class presort (in which mailers are offered discounted postage rates if they presort their items by ZIP Code) has decreased the amount of processing that bulk-rate third-class mail needs, thus reducing its effectiveness as a flywheel.

Since the productivity and financial well-being of the Postal Service depend in no small measure on the extent to which local managers are effective in making manpower scheduling decisions, postal headquarters has tried at various times to institute management control and information systems to aid local managers in the decision-making process. But the organization's experience with such systems suggests that when also used as performance measuring devices, they invite manipulation by pressured employees.

Reporting the Work Load

In the 1970s, the Postal Service, relying on the advice of McKinsey and Company, management consultants, instituted a computerized data system, the Work Load Reporting System (WLRS), to calculate mail volume, work hours, and cost relations for 70 different mail processing operations. For each post office tied into the system (generally limited to the nation's largest post offices), the WLRS computer produced detailed output reports by shift, day, week, and accounting period. Originally, these data were intended to help local managers in scheduling manpower to meet expected mail volumes, and to help management at all levels in evaluating the effects of technological improvements and changes in methods of processing mail.

But to top management, the WLRS seemed to provide an irresistible additional opportunity—the chance to apply the data on a national basis to evaluate performance of line supervisors, individual post offices, and entire regions, and to compare or rank post offices and regions according to productivity performance. Accordingly, with data furnished by WLRS, headquarters officials instituted the *Eighty Office Productivity Index Report*, which ranked, from best to worst, the performance of the eighty largest post offices. In short, officials at headquarters were trying to use the new WLRS data not only to draw comparisons but to stimulate internal competition in the postal system and to provide local managers with an incentive to use labor as efficiently as possible in meeting their work loads.

Within two years it became clear that this application of the

WLRS data had undermined the original purpose of the system, which was to help local managers in making immediate decisions about staffing to meet the fluctuations in work load more efficiently. Pressures on the managers and employees of the largest post offices to excel in the intensifying interoffice competition led to widespread falsification of WLRS data. Since it was extraordinarily difficult for an office to achieve real productivity increases, and since cutting personnel would affect an office's showings on other performance ratings (such as delivery performance standards), a local manager who wanted to show a strong improvement in the productivity rankings could do so more easily by *appearing* to process more mail with the same (or even a smaller) number of people.

Thus, by early 1973, headquarters officials were finding that falsification of WLRS data was widespread in the field. One common method of adulteration involved the treatment of presorted or "riffle" mail (items presorted by the customer in ZIP-Code sequence). A simple riffling procedure (that is, quickly sliding the thumb along the edge of the envelopes) is enough for a clerk to sort this mail quickly. Some local managers inflated their office productivity measures (some by as much as twenty-five times) by improperly crediting this presorted mail to manual sorting procedures, thereby indicating greater productivity gains than what really existed.[11]

Another, more serious and more widespread falsification was made possible by the shift under WLRS from linear measurement of mail volume to weight measurement on automated electronic scales that transmitted volume data directly to Postal Service computers. Internal audits throughout the postal system in 1974 revealed repeated cases of deliberate inflation of volume figures; managers would have employees run the same mail over the mechanized weight-recording system up to eight times before sending it on to the next processing step. Postal inspectors discovered serious volume inflations by this practice in San Francisco, Washington, D.C., Philadelphia, Houston, and many other cities.[12]

The Washington, D.C., post office, for example, experienced a remarkable rise in the reported productivity of its mail processing operations. In just a couple of years, Washington moved from a relatively low standing among the eighty largest offices to near the number one position on the *Eighty Office Productivity Index Report*. The improved relative standing was the result of reported (though false) increases in mail volume handled without a corresponding increase in man-hours used. A 1974 investigation of the Washington office revealed that total piece handlings there may

have been inflated by more than 110 percent. The officials responsible for these distortions of WLRS data generally attributed their
conduct to excessive pressure from higher management to achieve
unrealistic productivity goals and to the belief that failure to do so
would hurt their careers.[13]

In short, this effort by top officials to extend the use of the
WLRS data hampered the information system's effectiveness as an
everyday managerial tool for efficient manpower scheduling. As
one top postal official said, in trying to explain the problem to a
congressional investigation committee in 1976: "In brief, the system tended to nurture the managing of numbers or 'productivity
statistics' rather than of people and of actual work volumes."[14] This
is a form of "goal displacement," familiar to students of bureaucratic organizations. An instrument such as the statistical index,
intended to further the accomplishment of organizational objectives, becomes an end in itself. Employees begin to think of
maximizing the indexes as their main goal, sometimes at the
expense of the original objective.[15]

As a result of the distortions in the data produced by WLRS,
postal officials were forced to abandon the system. They replaced
it in 1975 with a simplified system of recording work loads (the
Management Operating Data System), the sole purpose of which
was to help local managers in evaluating changes in work loads and
man-hours so they could plan budgets and operations. In the early
1980s, the Postal Service installed yet another new system—the
National Workhour Reporting System—to produce still more refined data for planning, budgeting, and reporting work hours.

The continual development of new information systems reflects
an increased emphasis inside the Postal Service on producing
useful data for managerial purposes; and it can also be seen as part
of a continuing process of "organizational learning," whereby the
organization adapts its processes in light of its experience with
them.[16] These are salutary trends, likely to produce better management systems over time.

Unfortunately, information from these systems is still of little
immediate use or relevance to managers at the operating level,
since they feel that they are being judged more importantly by
meeting service standards than by meeting work-hour budgets and
since the feedback from work-hour reporting systems does not
match the timing requirements for staffing decisions for any given
tour. Moreover, local managers see their budgets of work hours for
each accounting period as being arbitrarily based on previous
years' patterns rather than on careful estimates about the current
year. And in their view, the work-hour tracking process throughout

the year does not allow enough flexibility for changing circumstances such as deviations from planned volume, changes in the timing of certain activities, or unexpected events (such as the need to close a facility temporarily for asbestos removal). Furthermore, the constant comparisons with expenses planned for the period or with data on expenses for the same period of the previous year provide them little helpful insight on their performance given the actual mail volume and mix which the facility has just experienced.

The work pressures on managers at the operating level also have not changed. They still have little or no control over the work load; they have to husband the work hours they have been budgeted and then apply them against the mail as it comes in. This is not at all easy. Managers have to make sure they have enough workers on hand to process the peak loads without having more than are necessary. If they underestimate their requirements on any tour, they cannot meet their service performance standards. If they overestimate them, they exceed their work-hour budget and watch their productivity indicators drop. When asked whether it is more important to meet service standards or budget ceilings, local managers are most likely to respond that both are important, but that in a crunch service standards are more important. This is in part because superiors at higher levels focus attention on the achievement of performance standards, especially the timely delivery of first-class mail as measured by the Origin-Destination Information System (ODIS). Not surprisingly, the use of ODIS statistics to evaluate performance has led to employees' manipulation of this system as well.

Measuring Delivery Performance

The Postal Service is a delivery organization whose customers value not only speed of delivery but also consistency (that is, being able to predict accurately how long delivery will take between two points). Yet for years the old Post Office Department had no formal goals for delivery performance. It simply delivered the mail as quickly as it could, and that was that. The department did have a relatively primitive system, however, for gathering data for internal use on the actual transmission times for first-class mail. From 1954 to 1967, the Post Office's principal test of delivery time involved periodic test mailings to measure the elapsed time between deposit of test letters in a collection box and actual delivery to a home or an office. The Post Office Department conducted nationwide test mailings several times each year, using about 350,000 pieces of airmail and first-class and special delivery letters, and involving the 175 largest post offices in the country. The tests mainly consisted of the interchange of letters between individuals living in 150 test cities. When postal headquarters finished compiling the results of the periodic test, it rated the regions and post offices according to performance. Headquarters analysts based these ratings on a comparison of the test results with the time it should have taken each piece of mail to move through the system, according to the actual pickup, processing, transportation, and delivery schedules and schemes.[17]

The performance ratings were not taken seriously, however, and the test results were not used earnestly for managerial purposes, partly because fundamental weaknesses in the testing method made the results less than satisfactory indicators of actual performance. For example, the system used special test envelopes, easily identifiable by postal employees, who could give them expedited treatment. The studies also used postal employees, not outsiders, as the recipients of test letters, further increasing the possibility of manipulating data. Finally, the tests compared actual transmission times with somewhat unrealistic "scheduled" times.[18]

In 1971 the Postal Service established formal delivery standards: one-day (overnight) delivery within local areas, two-day delivery within a 600-mile radius, and three-day delivery to all other areas. These standards apply only to first-class mail that has proper address and ZIP Code and is posted by the designated collection time, generally 5:00 P.M. The Postal Service goal is to meet these standards 95 percent of the time.

With the establishment of these formal delivery standards, the Postal Service needed a more sophisticated information system that could collect, analyze, and present mail delivery data. Thus, postal managers created a new information system called the Origin-Destination Information System (ODIS), which uses sampling techniques to measure how well the Postal Service is doing in meeting its delivery standards. ODIS samples over 100,000 pieces of mail daily in 1,000 locations nationally—over 34 million pieces in 12,000 post offices during the 303 delivery days of the normal year.

Although ODIS is a far more advanced testing system than its predecessors, it has some conspicuous deficiencies. Unlike the old nationwide test, ODIS measures the interval not from the time of posting to time of delivery but from the time a letter is *postmarked* to the time it is received in the last postal facility before being delivered to the addressee. Thus, actual transmission time for a letter may be as much as a couple of days longer than the figures suggest, depending on how long it sits in a collection box before being picked up, how long it sits in a post office before being postmarked, and how long it takes the carrier to deliver it. [19]

A more important deficiency of the ODIS measure system stems partly from the double use to which the system's data are put. When headquarters managers developed the new measuring system, they wanted to generate data that would be used both in controlling the quality of delivery service *and* in judging performance throughout the system. Thus, raw ODIS data are gathered from around the country, and the results are distributed to the regions, divisions, and individual post offices. Postal officials at each level use the results to judge the performance of managers at the next lower level; headquarters judges the regions, the regions judge division performance, and so on, down to the individual facilities. This use of ODIS data as a performance measure leads to manipulation of the system by anxious local postal officials who have an opportunity to shade the results since they know a day in advance which routes, if any, in their areas will be sampled. The temptation and pressure to adjust figures to reflect better performance undoubtedly were heightened by a field bonus program set up under Postmaster General Albert Casey in 1986. Under it, a division manager could get quarterly and annual lump sums, up to $12,000, if he or she met the standards of overall performance, which are weighted by individual regions. The ODIS service figures are one of the most important factors in that weighted measure.

Manipulation of the ODIS system and its scores is not a new problem. Investigation by General Accounting Office (GAO) auditors and postal inspectors in the mid-1970s found that in Detroit late mail was deliberately being removed from delivery units before ODIS tests in order to improve overnight delivery statistics. Three Detroit mail-processing foremen told the investigators that they had been instructed to examine mail scheduled for ODIS testing and to remove letters that already were late according to Postal Service delivery standards. They then reinserted these letters in the mail processing operation at a point when the letters could not reach the delivery unit in time to be included in the ODIS test. [20]

Other, less overt methods of manipulating ODIS data also appear to have been fairly common practice at times. Since notice of ODIS test dates and of units to be tested were given to mail processing officials at most sectional center facilities (SCFs) well in advance, these managers had an opportunity to expedite mail destined to delivery units scheduled for testing. At the Houston SCF, for example, mail processing and quality control officials in the mid-

1970s admitted to increasing their staff power at units to be tested in order to avoid possible repercussions from higher management about low test scores.[21]

Postal management has tried in recent years to eliminate some of these defects from the ODIS system by restricting the number of persons having access to scheduled test times and sites. But evidence persists that field personnel manipulate their ODIS statistics. In 1987 eleven supervisors in the Atlanta Post Office were demoted or suspended for tampering with ODIS tests. Through one-way mirrors, postal inspectors had filmed supervisors removing mail that might hurt ODIS results. In another investigation focusing on five mail processing facilities around the country, the Postal Inspection Service found that postal clerks recording data "were under pressure to maximize scores." At Newark and Chicago's South Suburban facility, data collection clerks were badgered by supervisors when the results put their post offices in a bad light. Clerks in Cleveland reportedly also told inspectors of "subtle forms of intimidation." Inspectors in Cleveland found that when they monitored the data collection process, the percentage of letters in the "overnight delivery" zone arriving on time dropped from 95 percent to 88 percent. In Oakland and Newark, the declines were 6 percent and 5 percent, respectively. Two postmasters, interviewed by a reporter for the influential *Business Mailers Review*, speculated that if the ODIS tests were conducted by private contractors (as many critics have suggested), the percentage of letters reported to be delivered on time would drop by as much as 20 points.[22]

From time to time private organizations in fact conduct their own tests of delivery speed and usually obtain results sharply at odds with Postal Service data. For example, *Reader's Digest* has found that mail that should get to its destination by the first or second day tends to take one-half day to one day more to do so.[23] In April of 1987 a newspaper in Eureka, California, mailed a total of 190 first-class letters to check both local and long-distance delivery times; 54 of them arrived late. In local delivery, where the Postal Service promises overnight delivery, only 65 percent of 14 test letters mailed in the Washington metropolitan area met that goal (as compared to the 95 percent the Postal Service was claiming for that category at the time). Of 100 letters sent to points less than 500 miles away, which are supposed to arrive in two days, only 68 percent arrived on time. (Aggregate Postal Service statistics suggested an 82 percent delivery rate for this intermediate-range mail.) The Postal Service did best on long-distance mail traveling more than 500 miles. It pledges three-day delivery to distant points, and 78 percent of the 76 test letters met that goal (as opposed to the 85 percent rate reflected by ODIS statistics).[24]

The Larger Managerial Task: Achieving Financial Self-Sufficiency

A broader measure of the Postal Service's performance, as for most businesses, is the net result shown on its annual operating statement. When Congress created the Postal Service as an "independent establishment" of the federal government, one of the primary goals was that the organization achieve financial stability and self-sufficiency. This was a highly elusive goal in the 1970s, primarily for two reasons: (1) the long-standing, serious operating problems the system faced, and (2) severe national economic difficulties in the 1970s such as the oil embargo, high inflation, and recessions.

As the previous chapter demonstrated, executives of the new Postal Service in the early 1970s were charged with righting a huge organization that had already been operating for nearly two centuries. They inherited an organizational legacy that included outmoded physical plants, an inflated work force, rigid standard operating procedures, and a set of established expectations (both inside and outside the organization) about what the Postal Service should do and how it should be done. In short, the new Postal Service, suddenly expected in 1971 to support itself financially, inherited operating problems and deficit-producing services and obligations not of their own making.

Another important factor complicating the Postal Service's fiscal recovery in the 1970s was an unusually high inflation rate, which had particularly devastating effects on this and other labor-intensive industries. For most of the 1970s, for example, the obligations the Postal Service incurred under the cost-of-living adjustment provisions of its labor union contracts amounted to more than the negotiated "up-front" wage increases. Moreover, inflation pushed the Postal Service's aggregate costs for its employees' coverage under the Civil Service Retirement program from $445 million in fiscal 1972 to $1.72 billion in 1982. The soaring cost of fuel was another pressure on the postal budget, increasing the cost of heating the system's 30,500 post offices and dramatically hiking the costs of operating its hundreds of thousands of vehicles; each penny-a-gallon increase in gasoline prices was costing the Postal Service another $3.5 million annually by the late 1970s.

But despite these serious obstacles in the 1970s, the Postal Service has managed to meet its goal of breaking even financially.

Indeed, by the end of fiscal 1987, the Postal Service had achieved surpluses in three of the previous five years and in five of the preceding ten. (In those ten years revenues exceeded expenses by about $500 million.)

While the system as a whole thus seems to have been operating in recent years much in line with the vision of postal reformers, at the operating level it has been difficult to translate the concern with breaking even into meaningful management control measures. The highly interdependent nature of the tasks of different postal facilities and functional units makes it difficult to assign to middle-level managers responsibility for operating surpluses or deficits. Furthermore, the simultaneous need to maintain universal service, meet delivery objectives, and pay competitive wages leads to a number of contradictory signals to middle management. While the USPS remains formally committed to the attainment of self-sufficiency, it is clear from the system's behavior that compromises are frequently made on this dimension to accommodate the attainment of other objectives.

Moreover, as the next chapter shows, many of the Postal Service's efforts over the years to control costs and improve the efficiency of postal operations have run aground whenever they have violated the interests of politically powerful groups, inside or outside the Postal Service.

Endnotes

1. Chester Barnard, *The Functions of the Executive* (Cambridge: Harvard University Press, 1938), p. 217.
2. James G. March, "How We Talk and How We Act: Administrative Theory and Administrative Life," in *Leadership and Organizational Culture*, ed. T. J. Serviovanni and J. E. Corbally (Urbana: University of Illinois Press, 1981), p. 29 (emphasis in the original).
3. Winton M. Blount to postmasters, June 1, 1971. Memorandum in the files of the Postmaster General, U.S. Postal Service, Washington.
4. Quoted in *Union Postal Clerk*, April 1, 1973, p. 3.
5. U.S., Congress, House, Committee on Post Office and Civil Service, *Oversight on Operation of United States Postal Service, Joint Hearings before the Subcommittee on Postal Operations and Services and the Subcommittee on Postal Personnel and Modernization of the Committee on Post Office and Civil Service*, 99th Cong., 1st Sess., 1985, p. 56.
6. *Postal Leader*, February 18, 1986, p. 3.
7. U.S., Congress, House, Committee on Post Office and Civil Service, *Oversight on Reorganization of United States Postal Service, Joint Hearings before the Subcommittee on Postal Operations and Services and the Subcommittee on Postal Personnel and Modernization*, 99th Cong., 2d Sess., 1986, pp. 6–7.

8. Ibid., p. 19.

9. Barnard, *The Functions of the Executive*, pp. 232–33.

10. *Postal Leader*, May 13, 1986, p. 4.

11. U.S., Congress, House, Committee on Post Office and Civil Service, *Operation of the Washington, D.C., Post Office, Hearings before a Subcommittee of the Committee on Post Office and Civil Service*, 94th Cong., 2d Sess., 1976, p. 4.

12. Ibid., pp. 4–6.

13. Ibid.

14. Ibid., p. 7.

15. On the concept of goal displacement, see Robert K. Merton, *Social Theory and Social Structure*, rev. ed. (Glencoe, Ill.: Free Press, 1957), pp. 199, 200. Examples abound in the literature; see, for example, Peter M. Blau, *The Dynamics of Bureaucracy*, rev. ed. (Chicago: University of Chicago Press, 1963), pp. 45–46, 232–33, and 239–41; and James Q. Wilson, *The Investigators: Managing FBI and Narcotics Agents* (New York: Basic Books, 1978), chap. 5.

16. On "organizational learning," see Richard Cyert and James March, *A Behavioral Theory of the Firm* (Englewood Cliffs, N.J.: Prentice-Hall, 1963), pp. 123–25.

17. President's Commission on Postal Organization, Report of the Commission, *Towards Postal Excellence*, Annex, vol. 3, part 4, pp. 83–84.

18. Ibid., part 2, pp. 43–47.

19. Comptroller General of the United States, *System for Measuring Mail Delivery Performance—Its Accuracy and Limits*, report to the Congress (Washington: General Accounting Office, October 17, 1975), p. 2.

20. Ibid., pp. 8–17.

21. Ibid., p. 11.

22. Most of the information in this paragraph is based on reports in a newsletter put out by Van Seagraves. See *Business Mailers Review*, July 13, 1987, and October 12, 1987.

23. *The Friday Report*, August 14, 1987.

24. See [Eureka] *Times-Standard*, May 2, 1987.

Chapter 3

THE MANAGERIAL CHALLENGE: CONTROLLING COSTS WITHOUT COMPROMISING SERVICE

When Congress in 1971 dramatically altered the institutional arrangements governing postal policy, its intention, at least in part, was to make postal management more "businesslike." What that meant was that in the conduct of its business, the Postal Service would apply modern technological and managerial know-how to the system's varied operations, and carry out its tasks and provide its services in the most cost-effective manner. In fact, Congress was quite explicit about the mandate it was giving the Postal Service in this regard. But Congress was equally clear that it continued to expect the Postal Service to pay attention to the needs and preferences of its customers, the American public, and to serve those needs.

Although the Postal Service in the 1980s is managed by people with as much business acumen as one finds in the private sector, its managers are not free to operate in a completely businesslike fashion. The Postal Service is not a business; it is not at liberty to design its services and policies with its eye on the bottom line. It is a governmental organization serving the American public. And that is the way Americans (and their representatives in Congress) continue to think of it—as primarily a public service organization. The "corporate" transformation of the postal system in 1971 did not change that. Citizens (and, by extension, even business mailers) continue to see mail delivery services as a political birthright, the features of which are not to be tampered with—even those, like the ZIP Code, that originated not with Benjamin Franklin but are themselves quite new.

Thus, the Postal Service is saddled with a problem common to many services provided in a governmental context, not just mail delivery. If a particular governmental service (such as mail delivery to the door) has always been the norm, the beneficiaries come to assume that they are somehow entitled to it—that it is inviolable, the natural and correct way of doing things.[1] These fixed expectations are what postal executives confront in trying to fashion a leaner, more cost-effective, and more economically rational postal system. Congress requires the Postal Service to continue supplying certain services (such as Saturday delivery or small rural post offices), not because there are economic demands for them but because they are traditions—established expectations that get reinforced, not so much even by widespread public demands as by the pressures of organized interests.

Consequently, the Postal Service is left trying to serve a wide variety of economically irreconcilable social and political objectives: frequent, speedy, and consistent delivery; universally available letter-mail services at reasonable and uniform rates; support of a large and well-paid work force; continuation of an expensive rural network; maintenance of numerous collection and distribution points; and also the mandate to accomplish all this without a deficit. Clearly, not all of these goals can be achieved simultaneously, but the Postal Service, as a governmental organization, has no choice but to attend to them anyway. This complicates the conduct of "businesslike" management, since there is no way, because of the political pressures and the absence of a market for reconciling impersonally conflicting wants, that these competing goals can be reconciled or reasonable trade-offs among them negotiated.

This chapter examines one aspect of this fundamental problem: the difficulty of negotiating the trade-off between the need for cost controls, on the one hand, and service maintenance, on the other. Contrary to what most Americans would suspect—so culturally conditioned are we to sneer at our postal system—the Postal Service actually has worked hard in recent years to control costs without compromising service and to improve service at reasonable cost. For example, the Postal Service has pursued (or tried to pursue) a variety of strategies for controlling its costs: reducing the total number of employees, increasing the efficiency of mail processing operations through mechanization and automation, reducing the costs of mail delivery operations through greater reliance on centralized delivery methods, and trimming its vast and unwieldy network of post offices.

Some of the Postal Service's efforts to manage the system in a cost-effective fashion have run aground when they have led to alterations in traditional practices with which the public feels comfortable or when those efforts have violated the interests of powerful groups inside or outside the Postal Service that have then successfully importuned on Congress to intervene. And paradoxically, some of the efforts of the Postal Service in recent years to improve service also have been compromised in the late 1980s by elected officials acting in the interest of political expediency and using the postal system to achieve other social, political, and economic objectives.

Controlling the Number of Employees

In the labor-intensive Postal Service, controlling costs is synonymous with controlling *labor* costs, since employee wages and benefits account for 85 percent of the system's total costs. Thus, one obvious cost-control method would involve holding back the rate of increase in employee wages and benefits. But successful pursuit of that strategy has proven difficult at best, as the next chapter explains. ,

Apart from controlling wages, perhaps the most direct method of controlling costs (at least in the short term) is to control the size of the employee work force. This strategy has been pursued with varying degrees of success over the years, the success seeming to depend on how draconian the cuts are and how sharply they affect customer service. A rigorous hiring freeze implemented in the early 1970s proved disastrous, but a more moderate, long-term effort later in the decade to control the size of the work force avoided both untoward effects on service and the political repercussions that usually accompany them.

Perhaps the most direct action taken by postal executives to control costs occurred quite some time ago—in March 1972. Although existing labor contracts did not allow him to lay off any workers, Postmaster General E. T. Klassen was intent on trimming labor costs and announced a ninety-day freeze on all hiring in the Postal Service. Klassen hoped that the organization's normally high attrition rate would shorten the payroll enough to avert a possible $450 million rate increase.[2]

And only five months after the hiring freeze had been imposed, the Postal Service's financial picture actually seemed to be brightening. Along with the usual attrition of staff and an intensive campaign to encourage early retirements, the hiring freeze had succeeded in reducing the postal work force by 33,000 persons. A happy Klassen announced that the staff cuts and other austerity moves (for example, reductions in the frequency of collections from street-corner deposit boxes and curtailment of Saturday window service in post offices) should enable the Postal Service to avoid the rate increase. [3]

Soon, however, some negative effects of the staff cuts became apparent. Not only were post offices operating with fewer workers, but the generous provisions of the early retirement plan had enticed thousands of the more experienced front-line supervisors and postal clerks to leave their jobs. Unfortunately, these departures came during a year when mail volume was increasing at fourteen times the previous year's rate of increase. By the end of the year, the Postal Service quite simply did not have enough skilled employees to handle the massive Christmas rush.

In December 1972 and January 1973, the ensuing public outrage over poor postal service spilled onto the editorial pages of newspapers across the country. By February 1973, Postmaster General Klassen was forced to concede publicly that the cost-control efforts had resulted in a "serious deterioration" of service throughout the country, with service in some areas (such as the New York metropolitan area) particularly hard hit by the staff reductions. [4]

So much mail condemning the poor quality of postal service flowed into congressional offices that committees in both houses of Congress launched full investigative hearings. Citizens complained of extraordinary delays in receiving mail. Postal Service statistics showed that piles of unprocessed mail sat in post offices across the country. Postal union leaders charged that the organization's poor performance resulted from "gross mismanagement" and "blind budget worship."[5] Top postal officials, for their part, admitted that the personnel reductions "may have gone too far."[6] Postmaster General Klassen told a Senate committee: "We may have been so hell-bent on reducing costs that we perhaps lost track of services."[7]

In other words, although the freeze helped reduce the net financial loss for the Postal Service in fiscal 1973 to only $13 million (the lowest it had been since 1945), the reaction of the public and of elected officials to deterioration in service forced postal executives to retreat to a much more moderate form of this cost-cutting strategy.

As the 1970s progressed, Postmasters General Benjamin Bailar and William Bolger continued to emphasize the need to check the expansion of the postal work force. Over the four-year period of

Bailar's administration (1974–1978), the total number of employees dropped from just over 710,000 to just over 655,000. This was a period when the growth in mail volume was very slight. But from 1978 to 1984, when the Postal Service was under the leadership of William Bolger, mail volume expanded by almost a third, reaching 35 billion pieces annually in the last year of Bolger's tenure as postmaster general. During that six years, the total number of employees changed little at first, but rose dramatically in 1984, from almost 679,000 to 702,000. The number of employees has continued to rise rapidly ever since. In 1987, the total number of employees reached 790,000.

Increasing Efficiency and Productivity in Mail Sorting by Automation and the ZIP + 4 Code

The total employment levels of the Postal Service would be even higher than they are had the organization not made clear progress at automating and mechanizing many of its operations in order to improve productivity and efficiency. The inauguration of new mail-processing technologies has made an especially important contribution to the ability of the Postal Service to handle dramatic increases in its work load. But much more needs to be done in this regard.

In the past quarter century, few postal programs have had a more fundamental impact on postal operations than the advent in 1963 of the ZIP (Zone Improvement Plan) Code. Before its initiation, each of the post offices in the United States, in effect, exchanged mail with each of the others. But the ZIP Code system divided the United States into ten large geographic areas, assigning to each a number from zero to nine—to become the first digit in a five-digit ZIP-Code number. Key post offices in each area are designated sectional centers, and each of these is assigned two numbers, which make up the second and third digits in the code. Finally, local post offices within a sectional center's area are designated by the last two digits. (The same system applies to big cities and delivery units within such cities.)

With the advent of the ZIP Code and the institution of sectional centers came improvements in the efficiency of processing mail. First, with simple, five-digit codes designating specific destinations around the country, clerks could sort by numbers, thereby eliminating much of the memorization of sorting schemes and the like that were previously requisite. Moreover, a central postal facility—the sectional center—could be designated to process most of the outgoing mail for all post offices in a given area. Finally, it provided a basis on which to develop machines to expedite the time-consuming and expensive mail-sorting process. By the early 1970s such machines were available.

The most significant step into mechanization was the letter-sorting machine (LSM). An LSM is run by an operator who sits at a keyboard console where, sixty times a minute, a rotating metal arm reaches into a nearby tray of letters and pushes one onto an automatic conveyor and into the view of the operator, who has six-tenths of a second to read the ZIP Code before hearing a click. Then, within the next four-tenths of a second, the operator must press the three keys corresponding to the first three numbers in the ZIP Code, causing the letter to be conveyed by electromechanical signal to one of 277 specific destination bins. Simultaneously, the metal arm deposits another letter before the operator.

Put in place throughout the country in the 1970s, this sorting machinery contributed substantially to increases in operating efficiency and to improvements in the Postal Service's gross productivity figures (the number of pieces of mail processed per postal man-year). The twelve operators of a multiposition letter-sorting machine (MPLSM), for example, can sort up to 43,200 letters an hour and can sort letters to about five times the number of cities that manual sorting allows; the number of letters that need several sortings is thereby reduced. A fully operational MPLSM can thus handle more mail than forty clerks manually sorting letters. Largely because of the implementation of this technology throughout the system in the 1970s, the Postal Service's gross productivity increased 23.4 percent between fiscal 1971 and fiscal 1979. However, by 1980 the Postal Service acknowledged that it was "approaching the saturation point" in its use of the new sorting equipment and that no further significant improvements in productivity were expected as a consequence of that technology.[8]

In anticipating the point where productivity could no longer increase, the Postal Service had been planning a more revolutionary step toward automated mail processing—a step that held promises of a quantum leap in mail-processing productivity, a reduction in postal costs, and for the postal customer, more consistent delivery service. The key to the new generation of automation was an expanded, nine-digit ZIP Code (the traditional ZIP Code followed by a hyphen and four additional digits, thus giving rise to its name, "ZIP + 4"). The Postal Service reasonably believed that with the widespread voluntary use of this expanded code, and with the implementation of the latest optical character reader and bar code sorter equipment, the speed of processing mail would be significantly increased, missorting rates lowered, and substantial work-years saved. The plan was this: when a piece of mail first entered the automated system, an optical character reader would scan the last line of the address containing the ZIP + 4 Code, translate it into a bar code, and then apply the bar code (with an ink jet printer) to the lower right-hand corner of the envelope. From then on, the letter could be sorted automatically by bar code sorters, all the way down to the level of the individual carrier route serving the addressee. All intermediate manual sorting would be eliminated. This automated system would enable the Postal Service to reduce or save processing costs by sorting mail even more efficiently. And while the automation could even be used cost-effectively to process mail bearing only the traditional five-digit ZIP Code, its full savings potential would depend on widespread voluntary adoption of the nine-digit codes by the business community.

Unfortunately, the Postal Service's efforts to implement this new automation program were scrambled repeatedly in the early 1980s. At least four factors contributed to the bumpy transition to automation: (1) the Postal Service's public relations failure in informing Congress and the public of its plans for the nine-digit ZIP Code; (2) congressional intervention that undermined the Postal Service's campaign to win voluntary use of the nine-digit code by the business community; (3) rapid developments in optical character reading technology that suggested the need for a mid-course "correction" in the plan; and (4) a major scandal involving a member of the Postal Service's Board of Governors who joined in a fraudulent scheme to steer a contract for multi-line optical character readers to a particular company.

Public and Congressional Reactions

Although planning for the new automated mail processing system and for ZIP Code changes began much earlier, it was in 1978 that Postmaster General William F. Bolger first publicly announced, to a stunned audience of large mail users at a National Postal Forum, that the Postal Service intended to expand ZIP Codes during 1981. Formal notice of the proposal appeared in the *Federal Register* of June 3, 1980.

The immediate public response was predictably negative (just as it had been in the early 1960s when plans for the original five-digit ZIP Code were unveiled). Editors and cartoonists made great sport of the idea that people would be expected to remember and use nine-digit numbers on their mail. Much of the criticism focused on the plan's contribution to the processes of depersonalization in American society; a commonplace jeer was that Americans might as well just give up their names and henceforth be known by numbers. In this vein, at a hearing held by a Senate Governmental Affairs subcommittee in late November of 1980, Senator Roger Jepsen, Republican of Iowa, mocked the Postal Service's plans for making the nine-digit codes available. The plans included a toll-free telephone number to obtain codes. Jepsen said: "What this boils down to is a system that will require an individual to call a ten-digit number to get the correct nine-digit number that must be placed on the letter. Now, if people can't remember the ten-digit number that must be called, they can always dial a three-digit number to find it."[9]

These criticisms were based on the misconception that the Postal Service was going to expect householders to use nine digits on their personal mail and greeting cards. But the nine-digit code was developed not for personal letters but for business mail. However, the idea fared no better among that constituency. Business firms contacted Congress to complain of the great expense they would incur in converting their mailing lists. And secretaries complained that they would not be able to remember nine digits at a glance while typing. In addition, the postal labor unions naturally complained that the plan was not intended to "zip" the mail but to save money by "zapping" workers from the Postal Service's payroll. And, of course, they were right; that was one of the hoped-for effects, if not the "purpose."

Congress Responds

The vociferous public response to the *Federal Register* notice prompted the House Subcommittee on Government Information and Individual Rights to examine the Postal Service's plan. It became apparent in the course of that subcommittee's hearings that the Postal Service had not adequately addressed many important issues and was not adequately informing the public of its plans. There were many points that needed clarification: whether the program would be voluntary or (eventually) mandatory, whether incentives like those offered mailers for presorting would be available, whether the nine-digit program would replace presort programs that volume mailers were already using, whether the Postal Service had considered the complexities and costs for the private sector to expand the ZIP Code on computerized and manual mailing lists, how much the Postal Service would pay for new equipment and how it would finance the purchases, whether the new equipment would perform up to standard, and what savings the Postal Service expected.

The Postal Service was prepared to respond to most of these points but it provided little information in support of its claims, and what information it did provide was deemed by the subcommittee to be speculative or contradictory. For example, at one point in 1980 Postmaster General Bolger had claimed in a letter to the chairman of the House Post Office and Civil Service Committee that through automation the Postal Service planned to reduce its labor by up to 60,000 work-years by the end of fiscal 1986. A month later, postal officials told the Postal Service Board of Governors that the labor reduction from 1982 to 1986 would be only about 15,600 work-years. The subcommittee also found fault with the Postal Service's failure to inform the public about incentives to encourage mailers to use 9-digit ZIP Codes, noting that as a result the Postal Service found itself in a "Catch-22": it could not make its case to the Postal Rate Commission for discount incentives until it had some idea of how many mailers would use the 9-digit coding, but mailers were reluctant to expand their systems to accommodate the nine digits until they knew what the discounts would be. And finally, not least among its many other criticisms, the subcommittee judged that the Postal Service's expectation that half of all first-class business letters would bear the expanded ZIP Code by 1982 and 90 percent by 1986 was "overly optimistic and unrealistic as a basis for planning." This uncertainty surrounding eventual volumes also undermined the subcommittee's confidence in the Postal Service's claim that it should save $600 million per year in labor costs, since those savings were premised on the "unrealistic" volume estimates. In its report to the House, the whole committee made its view clear: "The committee is concerned that as currently constituted, the Postal Service's planned expansion of the ZIP Code to nine digits could become a colossal failure. It is an idea in search of a plan."[10]

Six months later, in May of 1981, a subcommittee of the House Post Office and Civil Service Committee heard still more pointed criticisms from representatives of the postal labor unions and large mail users such as utilities. Again, a prominent complaint was that the Postal Service seemed to have prepared its plan inadequately and performed poorly in informing its customers of the costs and benefits of the initiative.[11]

In view of the concerns expressed by the business community and the labor unions—and in view of continuing controversies over the likely effects of the program on the public, its probable costs, and its projected return on investment[12]—Congress decided to include a provision in the Omnibus Budget Reconciliation Act of 1981, delaying the implementation of the ZIP + 4 Code until October 1, 1983, but permitting the Postal Service to take certain steps to prepare for implementation. In addition, Congress asked that the General Accounting Office (GAO) study the accuracy and reliability of the automated equipment, the cost-effectiveness of the ZIP + 4 system as a whole, and the impact of the program on postal customers.

In January 1983, the GAO produced its report on the Postal Service's automation system and the ZIP + 4 Code, indicating that the Postal Service should go ahead with its planned equipment purchases once the equipment's ability to perform in accordance with specifications had been demonstrated. The GAO also concluded that the gains to be expected from processing nine-digit rather than five-digit mail on the new automated equipment were so great in comparison with the costs involved that, given a rate incentive sufficient to attract the necessary volumes of ZIP + 4 Coded mail, the move to ZIP + 4 would be fully justified.[13] Such a rate incentive was implemented later in 1983 when the Postal Service established two categories of reduced rates for those voluntarily using the ZIP + 4 Code.

On October 1, 1983, the congressionally imposed moratorium on the 9-digit ZIP Code was lifted, and the Postal Service became legally able to process first-class mail bearing the ZIP + 4 Code on the automated equipment deployed to that date. Unfortunately, largely as a consequence of the moratorium, the Postal Service suffered a crippling loss of momentum in its efforts to involve the American business community in making the voluntary transition to an expanded ZIP Code. In fiscal year 1984, of 68 billion pieces of first-class mail, 1.9 billion pieces carried ZIP + 4 Codes—a far cry from the roughly 15 billion pieces originally projected for 1982. Despite this disappointing rate of adoption, the Postal Service was still gamely projecting that it would meet the overall goal of achieving a 90 percent usage rate of ZIP + 4 Codes on machinable first-class mail by the end of fiscal 1989.[14]

The automation process, however, went ahead as originally planned. And during fiscal year 1984, the first phase of the procurement of the Optical Character Readers (OCRs) and Bar Code Sorters (BCSs) was virtually completed, bringing to 252 the total number of OCRs at 118 sites. The Postal Service also had taken delivery of the 248 BCSs used in conjunction with the OCRs to process the mail. The total equipment cost was $219 million. The Service's experience with OCRs in actual operation indicated that with outgoing business mail, the OCRs were achieving an acceptance rate of approximately 64 percent and a throughput of about 24,000 pieces per hour. The net productivity rate of 6,200 distributed pieces per work-hour represented a substantial increase over the normal productivity of the multiposition letter sorting machines (1,700 pieces per work-hour). And the BCSs demonstrated the capability of equaling or exceeding the contract specifications of 28,000 pieces per hour and a 95 percent acceptance rate on bar-coded mail.[15]

On the basis of its generally favorable experience with the new equipment, the Postal Service decided in 1984 to proceed with the second phase of its automated mail processing system—the purchase, at a total of $278.7 million, of 406 additional single-line OCRs and 452 BCSs. This equipment was to be deployed both at sites already automated and at an additional 91 sites. The Service estimated that the new total of 209 sites would then process 90 percent of the total originating letter mail volume in the United States.[16]

The Shift to Multi-Line Readers

The Postal Service's decision in July 1984 to move ahead with the acquisition of more single-line OCRs followed by one month the release of a critical report by the Office of Technology Assessment (OTA), a congressional staff agency. The OTA argued that such a strategy only made sense if the usage of the nine-digit ZIP Code by large business mailers were in fact to grow as fast as the Postal Service hoped—an eventuality OTA deemed highly unlikely. According to the OTA, an alternative strategy offering a better return on investment involved extensive use of a competing technology— the multi-line optical character reader. Whereas the single-line OCR can read only the "last line" of an address (defined as city, state, and 5- or 9-digit ZIP Code), the multi-line OCR can read an entire address, search an internal computerized directory to determine the ZIP + 4 Code for that address, and print the appropriate bar code on the envelope. Thus, the multi-line readers can process a large amount of 5-digit ZIP mail to the 9-digit level. In other words, the multi-line OCR is not as dependent on the use of ZIP + 4 to realize savings from automation. Moreover, the OTA concluded that, while the multi-line OCR may not have been a technically viable alternative in 1980 when the Postal Service made its initial decision to go with single-line OCRs, by 1984 the multi-line OCR was fully competitive. OTA analysts had found that the multi-line OCR performed as well as the single-line OCR in processing 9-digit ZIP mail, and significantly better than the single-line OCR in processing 5-digit ZIP mail to the 9-digit level. OTA also contended that the purchase and/or conversion and maintenance costs of the multi-line OCR would be only marginally higher than the single-line, and the difference would be negligible when compared to the additional savings expected over the life of the investment. The OTA study's conclusion was that the strategy offering the greatest return to the Postal Service would be for it to proceed with the Phase II single-line OCR procurement, but simultaneously initiate tests on single- to multi-line conversion, and then convert all single-line OCRs to multi-line as quickly as possible, regardless of the level of ZIP + 4 use.[17]

The OTA recommendations did not alter the Postal Service's intentions with respect to Phase II acquisition of single-line OCRs, but the report did have an effect: the Postal Service immediately initiated a research and development effort with the manufacturers of its single-line OCRs (both Phases I and II) to develop multi-line conversion kits.

In 1985, use of the ZIP + 4 by business mailers continued to prove disappointing to the Postal Service. At the same time, however, developments in OCR technology were advancing rapidly. Consequently, Postmaster General William Bolger announced in August that the Postal Service planned to acquire hundreds of multi-line optical character readers for installation in major mail processing facilities. The single-line equipment already at those sites would be redeployed to smaller cities. Bolger said the Service also planned to acquire a kit so that the Phase II single-line OCRs could be expanded to multi-line capacity. This decision reportedly followed extensive study of every aspect of the automation and ZIP + 4 program by a committee of the Board of Governors chaired by Governor Ruth Peters. However, by mid-1986 it had become clear that one of the governors had engaged in a conspiracy to defraud the Postal Service of a fair and unbiased procurement of multi-line OCRs. In addition to derailing temporarily the Postal Service's automation program, the procurement scandal put an end to a five-year period in which the Board of Governors inappropriately tried to "micro-manage" the Postal Service.

The Procurement Scandal

Although the details of the conspiracy are incredibly complicated and fascinating, only the bare bones of it can be revealed here.[18] The essence of it was that early in 1984, Peter Voss, a Reagan-appointed member of the Postal Service Board of Governors, entered into a conspiracy to defraud the U.S. Postal Service, along with John Gnau, a Michigan businessman who had directed Ronald Reagan's campaign in that state during the 1980 presidential election and who was working as a private consultant on public relations and governmental affairs. The agreement was that Voss would furnish Gnau inside Postal Service information and leads to companies seeking to do business with the Postal Service. Voss and Gnau further agreed that Gnau would pay Voss 30 percent of all revenues Gnau realized as a result of Voss's referrals and official influence. Voss also guaranteed Gnau, who had set himself up as Gnau and Associates, Inc. (GAI), access to high-level postal officials.

In 1984 Voss identified a potential client for Gnau—Recognition Equipment, Inc. (REI), a firm headquartered in Texas and engaged in the design, manufacture, and distribution of optical character reading equipment. REI sought a contract to sell the Postal Service multi-line optical character readers. In August 1984, shortly after the Postal Service had awarded the Phase II contract to ElectroCom Automation Incorporated (ECA) for additional single-line optical character readers and additional bar code sorters and had announced that it would consider conversion to multi-line readers, Voss met privately in Texas with an officer of REI and recommended to him that REI retain Gnau in its efforts to convince the Postal Service to deploy multi-line OCRs and to buy them from REI.

After considerable negotiation, REI entered an agreement with GAI wherein GAI, for an initial consulting fee of $30,000 paid in $10,000 installments over three months, would assist REI in pursuing a contract with the Postal Service for the purchase of multi-line OCRs. REI further agreed that upon the award of such a contract to REI by the Postal Service, REI would pay GAI an additional fee of 1 percent of the contract price, minus the initial $30,000 fee.

Then, using his position as a member of the board's Technology and Development Committee and having duped an apparently unwitting colleague on the board to assist his cause, Voss pushed from the inside to secure the contract for REI by putting direct pressure on top management (including the deputy postmaster general) and by consistently trying to steer the decision-making process in REI's favor. For example, in April 1985, as part of a regular pattern of sharing information, Voss furnished GAI with an internal memorandum prepared by the deputy postmaster general that expressed management's views on automation. GAI prepared for Voss a rebuttal to management's views, along with recommendations to management that included a call for the immediate acquisition of multi-line OCRs from REI. Then Voss managed to get the GAI-prepared recommendations attached to a May 5, 1985 memorandum for the Board of Governors, which was signed by all three members of the board's Technology and Development Committee. The effect was to misrepresent to the remaining members of the board and to Postal Service management that the content of the report was the independent work and ideas of the board committee.

As the spring turned to summer, it became increasingly clear to Voss and his associates outside the Postal Service that postal management was not going to award a sole source contract to REI despite the relentless pressure Voss had been applying. Voss apparently grew increasingly convinced that the stumbling block to attaining a contract for REI was Paul Carlin, the postmaster general. With his associates, Voss plotted to get Carlin fired. Inside the Postal Service, Voss tried to foster the impression that Carlin had lost the confidence of top field managers and was incapable of managing the Postal Service. And the message for public (and congressional) consumption was no different. For example, in testimony before a subcommittee of the House Government Operations Committee in the fall of 1985, Voss repeatedly questioned the competence and integrity of top management while simultaneously misrepresenting his own interests.[19]

Voss finally persuaded John McKean, the chairman of the Board of Governors, to initiate a search for Carlin's replacement. Moreover, Voss managed to get McKean to retain an executive placement firm headed by William A. Spartin, who also was president of Gnau and Associates. Paul Carlin was in fact fired and was replaced in early January 1986 by Albert Casey. A few other high postal officials whose integrity had proven nettlesome to Voss—most conspicuously, William R. Cummings, then senior assistant postmaster general in charge of the finance group—lost their positions as a consequence of Voss's maneuvering.

But Voss never got to find out whether personnel changes at the top would make it easier for him to have his way. Since early 1985, the Postal Inspection Service—the Postal Service's own highly regarded internal investigative arm—had been aware and concerned that members of the Technology and Development Committee of the Board of Governors were expressing an intense interest in postal automation and were applying heavy pressure on postal executives to accelerate the procurement of multi-line OCRs. As the Inspection Service later put it in a report on its investigation:[20]

We observed that once Peter Voss was appointed to the Technology and Development Committee, the actions of the committee on this issue were raised to a level inconsistent with normal business interests. The repeated invitations to REI for sales presentations and the quantity of committee memorandums to management suggested there was much more to the actions than merely an interest in assuring the USPS was pursuing the correct policy on the automation of its mail processing system. The combination of the Technology and Development Committee's efforts with those of REI and their congressional supporters amounted to a "flood tide" of facts and opinions designed to sweep away any objection to a noncompetitive award to REI.

The Inspection Service began to monitor with great care the overall automation procurement effort and gradually uncovered the whole conspiracy. The incredible means by which the Inspection Service revealed the scope and details of Voss's maneuvers would make for an interesting Hollywood who-dunnit. Suffice it to say that as the exhaustive investigation progressed over many months, postal inspectors not only documented his concerted efforts surrounding the OCR purchase, but also found details of embezzlement by Voss and of the illegal payments to him from Gnau and Spartin. They discovered, for example, that beginning with the second travel voucher he submitted after his appointment to the postal board, Voss had submitted vouchers containing false claims for travel and administrative expenses. Eighty-one instances were identified where he falsified the amount claimed for air travel. He received $70,023 when his actual expenditures totaled $26,205. He also claimed reimbursement for lodging in Washington, D.C., at the rate of $60 per night, when he actually stayed in a private residence instead of a hotel. Moreover, from October 1985 through February 1986, Voss had received airline tickets valued at approximately $4,300 from William Spartin. The tickets represented Spartin's kickback to Voss for the executive search work that Voss had steered to Spartin. Also during January and February 1986, Voss had received approximately $5,000 in the form of two equal cash payments from John Gnau as compensation for his official actions to assist REI in obtaining a contract from the Postal Service.

When faced with all the compelling evidence against him, Voss resigned from the Board of Governors and on May 30, 1986, pleaded guilty in federal district court to a three count information of agreeing to accept a gratuity, accepting a gratuity, and embezzlement of Postal Service property. He was sentenced to a four-year period of incarceration and an $11,000 fine. John R. Gnau, Jr., eventually pleaded guilty to paying Voss a gratuity and to conspiracy charges for his role in defrauding the United States Postal Service of a fair and unbiased procurement. Gnau was sentenced to three years incarceration and a $10,000 fine.

Automated Mail Processing: Back on Track

In the wake of the procurement conspiracy scandal, the Postal Service suspended its multi-line procurement program. But in early 1988, after almost two years of delay and regrouping, the Postal Service's automation program was back on track as the Service began converting its single-line OCRs to multi-line technology. The renewed commitment to the automation program reflected not only an interest in taking advantage of the potential savings from the multi-line technology but also a coming to terms with the fact that widespread adoption by the business community of the ZIP + 4 Code simply was not in the cards but that with developments in multi-line OCR technology, the Postal Service finally was in a position to take full advantage of bar coding—ZIP + 4 or not.

The stakes for the Postal Service are high. Postal officials estimated in early 1988 that when the converted machines or new units are deployed by May 1989, the multi-line technology will save the Postal Service almost $950,000 a day, or $250 million a year. Much of this saving was expected to come from reductions in the work-hours involved in handling incoming secondary sortation (the sorting step prior to casing for delivery). At that time, most letter mail that was sorted to the carrier was worked by a 16 to 18-person crew on a multi-position letter sorting machine at the rate of between 26,000 to 32,000 pieces an hour, or by hand at the rate of between 650 to 900 pieces an hour. The prototype of the retrofitted multi-line OCR (used at the Denver Post Office since 1986) put a nine-digit bar code on letters at the rate of about 10 letters per second, or roughly 32,000 to 38,000 pieces an hour. The automated system needed only two people to operate it and another two people to operate the bar code sorter which, at about the same rate as the OCR, read the code and automatically sorted mail down to the carrier route. The Postal Service's stated objective in early 1988 was to have approximately 700 multi-line OCRs in operation by August 1991, capable of bar coding 85 percent of letter mail directly to the carrier.[21]

The ultimate goal of the Postal Service, enunciated by Postmaster General Tisch early in 1988, is to put a bar code on every piece of mail. The point is to have every piece of mail take advantage of the ZIP + 4 Code, which is the heart of the whole automation strategy. But because the new multi-line OCR technology makes it unnecessary for the mailer to put the nine-digit code on an envelope, the Postal Service quietly ceased its largely unsuccessful effort to get businesses to adopt the nine-digit ZIP Code. While the use of the nine-digit ZIP certainly is not discouraged, the goal now is to get large mailers to do their own bar coding so that the mail can be sent directly to bar code sorters for processing. As the deputy postmaster general put it: "Our strategy is based on offering customers a number of options—options to pre-bar code their mail, put ZIP + 4 Codes on their mail, presort their mail, or do nothing at all. How they respond depends on what makes the most economic sense for them. But regardless of what they do, our objective is to have a nine-digit bar code on every piece of mail. If they don't put it on, we will."[22] Plans call for half the volume of letter mail to contain a bar code by 1990. But postal officials have learned that progress toward that goal is bound to be slower than they hope, especially since only a small percentage of first- and third-class letter mail now contains a bar code—either applied by the Postal Service or by mailers.

Other Advances in Technology and Automation

Although the ZIP + 4 program and the developments in auto-mated mail sorting have been attracting most of the attention in the past decade, the Postal Service has been making many other, heretofore less conspicuous advances in technology and automa-tion that also seem likely over time not only to help contain costs but to improve service. These efforts are too numerous to take account of in their entirety here. But noteworthy developments are occurring in two particular areas—the adoption of improved facer-cancelling equipment, and assorted improvements in the speed and efficiency of post office window services.

The Postal Service has been working on ways to make even more efficient use of its new automated sorting equipment by improving the mechanization of the facing and cancelling of mail. The Mark II and M36 facer-cancelers generally in use around the country in the 1980s orient and cancel approximately 90 million pieces per day of originating letter mail collected from local mail boxes and other deposit points. These machines scan the upper-right and lower-left corners of every envelope, imprinting the cancellation mark on the stamp. But these facer-cancelers cannot distinguish the mail's processing characteristics. As a result the majority of the mail is directed to multi-position letter sorting machines. Any mail that is nonmachinable is processed at manual sorting stations. But about 60 percent of this mail could be processed more efficiently on optical character readers. The ability to separate this mail at the facer-canceler operation would allow more efficient use of the new automation.

Consequently,. the Postal Service has been testing a new facer-canceler (the FC200) that can separate originating letter mail according to its processing characteristics. This new machine contains electronic sensors that enable it to identify and separate letter mail into three basic groups: OCR readable, FIM mail (facing identification mark), and OCR nonreadable mail. OCR readable mail contains typewritten or machine printed addresses that can be recognized by optical character readers. After being separated by the FC200, this mail will go to optical character readers for processing. FIM mail, which bears orientation marks and a bar code applied by the mailer, will bypass the OCR and go directly to bar code sorters—economical automated equipment that reads the mailer-applied bar code and translates it into sorting information. The remaining mail, that which is not readable by OCRs, is comprised primarily of hand-addressed pieces and will be processed on regular letter sorting machines. In short, the Postal Service will be able to steer various types of letters more efficiently to processing operations that are best suited for each type of mail.

The behind-the-scenes processing of mail is not alone in receiving the attention of the Postal Service. In an era when customers place ever-increasing value on convenience and time, the Postal Service also has been trying to improve its over-the-counter services to customers at post offices, working especially on providing quicker and more accurate retail transactions, clearer information for retail customers, and more efficient ways for employees to apply complex rate data and mailing rules. The rapid growth of computerized point-of-sale systems and automated transaction machine systems has presented opportunities for significant improvement. Most conspicuously, the Postal Service began in 1982 to install at post office counters a new piece of equipment called the Integrated Retail Terminal (IRT). These terminals combine the functions of an electronic scale and a microcomputer in a single unit. Each IRT is equipped with floppy disks that contain all data needed to conduct business, such as rates and fees (both domestic and international), special services, money-order, and meter information. When any of the data become obsolete—because of changes in rates or mailing requirements, for example—the Postal Service immediately supplies replacement disks containing up-to-the-minute programmed information. By mid-1990 there will be roughly 53,000 IRTs deployed around the country. These terminals provide a substantial increase in the efficiency of window operations through faster service and the automatic recording of retail transactions.

In addition to adopting automated means of assisting window clerks, the Postal Service has been developing state-of-the-art self-service machines to dispense postal products and services. Postal management has estimated that such self-service machines are capable of handling transactions that now account for nearly 68 percent of all window time—from stamp and commodity sales to weighing parcels and providing postal information. In 1987 the Postal Service unveiled the computerized mailing and information stations that are expected to speed up services and save money. Patterned after the automatic teller machines used by many banks, the mailing stations feature video screens that, at the touch of a button, provide text and video answers to the customer's questions about products, rates, mailing procedures, regulations, and other postal matters. The machines will accept most currency, from coins to $20 bills, and will even accept automatic bank teller cards for customers who want to charge their transaction to their bank account. Using these stations, a customer will be able to weigh a letter, flat, or parcel; select the desired class of mail; and receive a postage strip and a receipt upon payment. The machine will also dispense labels for insured, priority, and certified mail. These automated postal tellers will be hooked to a central computer that will keep track of sales, revenues, and the kinds of questions answered and will use remote diagnostics to detect problems and dispatch rapid service or maintenance.

Increasing the Efficiency of Delivery

Over the past two decades, the Postal Service has had an opportunity to introduce mechanization and automation in the mail processing sector of its operations. Similar opportunities are less readily available in the area of delivery services. But the delivery function nevertheless commands special attention from postal management because of the very significant proportion of total postal costs it represents. Delivery is the most expensive of all the Postal Service's functions, accounting for nearly 37 percent of total postal costs and about 39 percent of the system's total work-hour distribution (compared with 29 percent for mail processing and 16 percent for retail customer service operations). Another reason the delivery function is of special concern to postal management is that the number of delivery points, or addresses, continues to grow by more than 1.5 million each year—a growth rate with serious impacts on delivery service costs.

Since there is now very little mechanization in the delivery area, it is particularly challenging to find ways to reduce delivery costs through technology. Nearly all of the operations in this area are performed manually. But there are opportunities for significant gains from investing in new technology for this functional area. Experts in the Postal Service's Technology Resource Department have been placing their heaviest emphasis on finding ways to reduce the amount of time carriers spend in the office (approximately three hours each day) manually preparing the day's mail for delivery; this time currently accounts for 43 percent of city delivery route work-hours. The objective of the principal development program (known as the "carrier in-office project") is to reduce this preparation time through mechanization and automation and ultimately eliminate it altogether, freeing carriers for street delivery, and resulting in more mail being delivered per carrier. But the specifics by which this wonder might occur have yet to be revealed—or, for that matter, worked out.

But most of the cost of delivery is an institutional cost—that is, a cost incurred simply by putting the letter carriers on the street, regardless of how much mail they are carrying. The most effective ways of controlling costs in the delivery function thus involve changes in either the frequency of delivery (now six days a week) or in the mode of delivery (whether to the door, to a curbside box, and so on). But changes in either the frequency or mode of delivery incite great controversy, invite organized opposition, and induce primal screams from people who feel that God-given rights are being violated.

Eliminating Saturday Delivery: An Option Foreclosed

With respect to the frequency of delivery, market research conducted by the Postal Service has shown that the demands of over 90 percent of its customers could be met with only three-day-a-week delivery. But when the Postal Service has tried to take even modest steps in this direction, strong opposition has arisen to block its efforts. For example, in May 1977, the Postal Service declared its intention of eliminating Saturday deliveries—a move that reportedly would have saved $400 million a year. The Postal Service decided to go ahead with the plan after an A. C. Nielsen Co. poll, conducted for a postal study commission, found that 79 percent of the public would be willing to forgo the sixth delivery day if such a move would help hold down the rate of increase in postal rates (as its proponents claimed it would).[23]

But the postal employee unions (particularly the letter carriers' organization) feared that eliminating Saturday delivery would lead to eventual reductions in the postal work force and a corresponding decline in union membership. Officers of the National Association of Letter Carriers, announcing that their union would "do everything in our power—use every means available—to make sure that five-day delivery never becomes a reality," persuaded Congressman Charles Wilson (Democrat from California and chairman at the time of a House postal subcommittee) to introduce in the House of Representatives a concurrent resolution that six-day delivery be retained.[24] The political vigor with which the union demonstrated its feelings on the matter showed through in the final outcome; the House overwhelmingly passed the Wilson resolution in late September 1977 by a vote of 377 to 9. Though the resolution had no force of law, it was enough to dissuade the Postal Service from pressing ahead with its plan.

The Clusterbox Controversy

The Postal Service's effort over time to move toward more efficient modes of residential delivery also have stimulated controversy and the opposition both of organized interests and of members of Congress. For years it has been evident to postal management that the nationwide proliferation of sprawling new suburban communities would quickly stretch system capacities and costs beyond limits if letter carriers continued to deliver mail to the door. Thus, in the mid-1960s the old Post Office Department directed local offices to provide curbside delivery to all new service areas. But citizens and housing developers across the country disliked the new policy and made their views known to Congress. Elderly and handicapped residents worried about getting out to the curb to retrieve their mail. And Larry Blackmon, the president of the National Association of Home Builders, described the postal department's move as a "step backward," calling it inconsistent with the efforts of the Johnson administration to beautify and improve city and suburban environments. Blackmon said: "Rows of curbline mailboxes detract from the beauty of these areas, whether the mailboxes are of uniform or mixed design."[25] Pressed by the public and by groups such as the home builders, several congressmen introduced legislation to require the Post Office Department to provide delivery to the door in residential communities. The postmaster general finally backed down in the face of gathering opposition to this cost-saving measure and opened the way for door service to more than 4 million homes that would have been affected by the ban.

After the reconstitution of the postal system in 1971, Postal Service executives once again explored alternatives to door delivery in residential areas, especially suburbs. Postal officials determined that the Service could save $210 million annually by replacing door delivery whenever possible with either curbside or clusterbox delivery. A clusterbox, sometimes known as an NDCBU (Neighborhood Delivery and Collection Box Unit), is a centralized unit, with anywhere from 18 to 100 lockboxes, to which all the mail for a given neighborhood is delivered. Whereas the average annual cost of door delivery in the early 1970s was $49 a household, curbside delivery cost the Postal Service only $39 annually, and delivery to a clusterbox cut the cost still more—to $24.[26]

With this potential saving in view, the Postal Service in 1972 established a policy that made almost all new housing developments ineligible for delivery to the door. For new residential housing areas, the policy limited the delivery options to curbside service or lockbox service at a clusterbox located within 300 feet of the residence. Centralized delivery to clusterboxes is especially attractive to the Postal Service because of the economic savings: there is greater fuel efficiency in delivery vehicles and greater productivity on the part of letter carriers when they make one stop instead of 14 or 16 individual stops.

Once again, Congress was flooded with complaints. Community associations and irate owners of new homes expressed their unhappiness to members of Congress. The National Association of Home Builders, claiming to be worried about "discrimination against persons who buy homes in a new area," also objected to the Postal Service's policy.[27] However, it seems more likely that the home builders' opposition stemmed primarily from the fact that they had to bear the costs and responsibility for purchasing, installing, and maintaining neighborhood clusterboxes.

In any case, Congress quickly acted to block the policy's application. Through amendments in 1976 to the Postal Reorganization Act, Congress directed that until April of 1977 (when a special study commission established to examine the Postal Service would be issuing its report) the Postal Service had to provide (depending on the average dimensions of the lots in a new development) either door delivery or curbside delivery to all new residential addresses. But the commission report essentially was silent on the subject, and the Postal Service no longer was bound by the congressional direction.

Thus unshackled, the Postal Service in 1978 published new regulations in the *Federal Register* stipulating that thenceforth in new residential areas, door delivery would no longer be an option. The options for service in such areas would be delivery to curbside mailboxes, to sidewalk mailboxes, or to clusterboxes. Postal Service policy provides that door delivery be considered for an individual customer where service through any delivery option other than door delivery would place an extreme hardship on the customer. In general, such exceptions are granted where an infirm elderly or handicapped person living alone would experience extreme dificulty receiving mail at a receptacle located away from the home. Exceptions are made on a case-by-case basis after an examination of the relevant facts. Individual customers may request a change in the mode of delivery based on disabilities that may prevent their access to centralized mail receptacles. They submit these requests to their local postmasters for approval. And if the request is denied at the local level, it is subject to further review within the management structure, with a final decision made at the regional level.

The Postal Service tried in 1981 to defuse some of the likely opposition to its policy by assuming responsibility for purchasing, installing, and maintaining neighborhood delivery and collection boxes, thus lifting that cost and responsibility from the shoulders of home builders. This change in policy also had the advantage, from the Postal Service's perspective, of permitting it greater control over the quality and condition of clusterboxes.

But the clusterbox issue continued to emerge from time to time in the early 1980s as Representative Glenn English (D., Okla.), chairman of a government operations subcommittee in the House, assumed an aggressive oversight role vis-à-vis the Postal Service and organized a series of hearings on a variety of postal issues that he and his staffers found vexing—clusterboxes not least among them. The subcommittee's hearings proved a hospitable forum for the cost-saving program's critics, most of whom criticized the Postal Service's policies on clusterbox procurement or disputed the claimed economic savings from the centralized delivery policy.[28] Other complaints also came to the attention of legislators. In testimony before a different House subcommittee, some witnesses insisted that the centralized delivery policy constitutes a change in postal services on a nationwide basis and should thus be subjected to review by the Postal Rate Commission and by Congress. Other witnesses claimed that as homeowners in new residential areas, they had not in fact been offered an option among delivery services but had had clusterbox delivery imposed on them by the Postal Service.[29]

Having been asked by members of Congress to review the implementation of the clusterbox program, the General Accounting Office in 1987 investigated the situation in fifteen communities around the country. The ensuing GAO report revealed that although postal managers are supposed to make developers of new housing areas aware that they have a choice among three modes of delivery service, five of the twenty-four developers interviewed in those communities said that they had not been offered a choice by local postal officials. The GAO's investigation also indicated that local postal officials are under pressure from higher levels to promote delivery to clusterboxes and thus have an incentive to conceal the options.[30]

Still, the centralized delivery program remains on-track. In 1985, of the approximately 70 million possible delivery points in the United States, roughly 23 percent were centralized.[31] During fiscal year 1987, approximately 50 percent of all new possible deliveries were centralized in some fashion, with half of those new centralized deliveries provided through clusterboxes. By the end of 1987, there were approximately 4.7 million clusterbox deliveries, comprising about 5 percent of all possible deliveries. (At the time, the annual cost per delivery point was estimated at $118 for door delivery, $83 for curb, and $71 for centralized modes such as clusterboxes.)[32]

Trimming the Network of Post Offices

Besides trying to cut costs in mail processing and delivery, the Postal Service has also focused attention on trying to trim its vast network of post offices. The Postal Service in 1987 maintained almost 30,000 post offices and another 10,000 stations, branches, and community post offices—a network that has been gradually diminishing in size ever since 1901, when the number peaked at 76,945. Though thousands of small, uneconomical post offices have been closed over the years, thousands still remain. Yet, the Postal Service faces sharp constraints on its ability to prune the system of these uneconomical facilities.

One important limitation was imposed by Congress when it passed the Postal Reorganization Act in 1970. Some legislators were worried that a business-minded postal corporation might be overzealous in its efforts at economy, so the act contains language that clarifies the congressional intent on post office closings:[33]

> *The Postal Service shall provide a maximum degree of effective and*
> *regular postal services to rural areas, communities, and small towns*
> *where post offices are not self-sustaining. No small post office shall*
> *be closed solely for operating at a deficit, it being the specific intent*
> *of the Congress that effective postal services be insured to residents*
> *of both urban and rural communities.*

Thus, when the Postal Service has closed rural offices, it has argued that the closings are not inconsistent with this statutory direction, since the Service ensures "effective postal services" to the affected communities through well-equipped rural carriers who are "traveling post offices," selling stamps, accepting packages, registering mail, and so forth.

Even so, the Postal Service has found its efforts in this regard vigorously opposed by its own managers (postmasters concerned about their jobs), by members of Congress, and by persons in the affected communities who argue that small rural post offices are the social heartbeat of isolated communities, gathering places for the exchange of news, and centers for the nourishment of local identities. This array of opposition has guaranteed predictably lively controversies over post office closings.

In the early 1970s post office closings created relatively little stir since the newly reconstituted Postal Service was closing post offices at no higher rate than the old Post Office Department had—roughly 300 offices a year. But a controversy arose in 1975 when the General Accounting Office issued a report contending that if the Postal Service closed down 12,000 small rural post offices, $100 million could be saved annually without diminishing the quality of postal services in the affected areas. The GAO based its report on a review of previous closings where alternative means of providing service had proved adequate. The review also showed, however, that users of the affected facilities had not felt in many cases that they were adequately consulted about the changes or informed of the way things would be handled after the change. Thus, the GAO recommended that the Postal Service alter its practices to achieve more savings from closings and also to give more attention to community reactions and especially to social effects on the community unrelated to mail services.[34]

Postal management saw the GAO report as an indication that Congress would soon be pressing for more effective efforts to generate savings through more efficient deployment of its small facilities. Thus, the Postal Service began to move more vigorously to consolidate its network. In late 1975 it revised its procedural guidelines for closing post offices, allowing closings even in cases where the postmastership was not vacant (previously, closings had occurred only where there was a vacancy). The change increased substantially the number of offices that might be subject to closing. Moreover, the Postal Service took advantage of the widespread publicity generated by the GAO report and began releasing data to the press, indicating how uneconomical many small rural post offices are.

But postal management's effort to build public support for cutting costs backfired. Rural postmasters' rising concern over their job prospects, combined with the Postal Service's news releases that seemed to cast all rural post offices in a bad light, prompted the National League of Postmasters to fight back. Arguing that an annual savings of $100 million, though substantial, would be relatively inconsequential in view of the Postal Service's enormous budget (then about $13.5 billion), and that the rural post offices were important to community identity at America's crossroads, the league filed a civil action to stop any policy of increased office closings, and, more important, initiated a massive lobbying effort on Capitol Hill to persuade Congress to intervene.

The political storm grew more fierce as the postmasters' formidable lobbying campaign began to show results. Individual members of Congress were hard-pressed to see how the closing of one or more post offices in their districts was essential to the fiscal stability of the vast postal system. The congressional attitude, understandably, was that surely the Postal Service could find other ways of economizing. Many congressional critics charged that the Postal Service was moving too far toward a business-minded approach to its operations and forgetting its "service" responsibilities. Others argued that economy and efficiency alone were not good enough reasons to close rural post offices and that the Postal Service had to pay more attention to the important role rural post offices play as informal town halls and community centers.[35]

In 1976 members of Congress responded to the postmasters' pleas and to their own electoral concerns by amending the Postal Reorganization Act to include a stipulation that, in deciding whether to close an office, the Postal Service must carefully and formally consider the effects on the community. The amendment also directed that the Postal Service may close or consolidate an office only after the citizens of the community have been formally advised of the plans and have had an opportunity to present their views. It further established the right of any customer using such a facility to appeal the decision to the Postal Rate Commission (PRC) which would provide an impartial opinion as to whether the decision to close met the conditions set forth in the law. The PRC could either endorse the Postal Service decision or remand it to the Postal Service for further consideration.

Finding itself under fire, the Postal Service temporarily suspended its efforts to close post offices; in 1977 none was closed. But by the next year postal management, responding to congressional mandates, had developed a more thorough and systematic policy for handling closings. Regional and district managers once again were encouraged to suggest to sectional center managers that they look for situations where it might be appropriate to close an office. In addition, they were to make sure that local managers developed a careful case detailing not only the cost savings and service maintenance rationale, but also potential effects on the community as required by the revised statute.

For several years, the Postal Service moved rather tentatively in its efforts to close post offices. Not only was top management sensitive to the political ramifications of a headlong rush toward office closings, but there was a new uncertainty introduced into the decision-making process as a result of the inclusion by Congress of an appellate role for the Postal Rate Commission. That is, in judging appeals on closings or consolidations of offices, the PRC was given a function analogous to that of a U.S. Court of Appeals entertaining a petition for review of an administrative agency's action. Like those courts, the PRC is restricted in these cases to reviewing the administrative record made by the agency; it is not free to conduct its own fact-finding hearings. And when presented in 1979 with its first cases to review, the PRC showed that it intended to exercise its powers deliberately. The Postal Service had decided to close or consolidate 69 small post offices that year and replace them with alternative forms of service. Twenty-three cases were appealed to the PRC. The commission affirmed only one decision and remanded 22 to the Postal Service, insisting that postal management had not paid enough attention to the congressional instruction that it consider an office closing's "effect on the community." The PRC believed in particular that the Postal Service was not considering effects unrelated to mail service, even though the legislative history of the 1976 amendment clearly showed that its sponsors were at least as concerned with preserving the economic and social benefits of local post offices as with ensuring satisfactory mail service. The rate commission criticized the Postal Service for acting too much as the prudent manager of its own operations and not enough as the guardian of the public interest.[36]

In response to these criticisms, the Postal Service continued its efforts to improve the care with which local managers prepared their cases, encouraging them to develop more detailed records, to address community concerns more fully, and to explain more completely their reasons for proposing a post office closing or consolidation. The track record of the Postal Service began to improve. In 1980, the Postal Service decided that 128 of its offices should be closed or consolidated. Many of these involved small offices operated in the homes of retiring postmasters. Ten cases were appealed by customers to the Postal Rate Commission. Four of these appeals failed or were dropped. Two cases were remanded for further consideration of nonpostal effects on the communities, and four were withdrawn by the Postal Service. In 1981 only 86 offices were slated to be closed, and only three were appealed to the PRC, which upheld the Postal Service in two cases.

In September 1982, the General Accounting Office again entered the fray, issuing a report estimating that the Postal Service could save between $125 million and $150 million annually by 1990 if it replaced about 7,000 post offices with contract units or rural delivery. More specifically, the GAO recommended:[37]

- A further reduction of the emphasis placed on postmaster vacancies as a trigger for considering possible closings.
- A quicker time frame for considering closing of offices suspended for loss of quarters or other temporary problems.
- A joint attempt with the PRC to streamline closing procedures.
- Periodic determination of the costs involved in the overall effort to close or consolidate post offices (the administrative resources committed to processing a case should not exceed the costs of retaining an unneeded office).

The Postal Service took steps to implement some of the GAO's recommendations. In particular, it reviewed its investigative procedures and analytic standards to determine ways in which they could be simplified and expedited within the existing legal requirements without adversely affecting customers. But the Postal Service took exception to the GAO's recommendation that 7,000 small offices be closed (and did so again a couple of years later in response to similar suggestions made by the President's Private Sector Survey on Cost Control, also known as the Grace Commission). The Postal Service expressed its firm commitment to the preservation of its unique characteristic as a communications system—its universal delivery network.

Even so, the rate of post office closings began to increase in 1983. There were 165 offices slated for closing that year, 200 in 1984, 230 in 1985, 219 in 1986, and 74 in 1987. In short, in the nine years from 1979 through 1987, the Postal Service closed down over 1,200 post offices. Moreover, appeals to the PRC of such closings typically amounted to less than 10 percent of the total, and the PRC affirmed the Postal Service's decision in a majority of these appealed cases.

The increased rate of closings in the mid-1980s reflected improved procedures on the part of the Postal Service both for gathering input from the communities likely to be affected by such actions and for explaining the reasons for (and advantages and disadvantages of) the proposed action. Still, the Postal Service has learned from past experience that Congress will find a large-scale campaign of office closings politically unpalatable. The Postal Service thus tries consistently in its reports to Congress to demonstrate its responsiveness and responsibility. This passage from the 1984 *Comprehensive Statement on Postal Operations* is typical:[38]

> *The Postal Service is committed to the preservation of the universal mail delivery system, and believes that it would be a false economy to sacrifice that universal system in the name of cost reduction. Accordingly, the Postal Service does not intend to take any action for the immediate closing of large numbers of small post offices. Similarly, the Postal Service does not intend to implement any actions which would impair the quality of delivery or retail services provided to rural America. In the Fiscal Year 1985 postal appropriations measure, Congress provided that rural service should be maintained at the previous year's level and registered its disapproval of wholesale post office closings. The Postal Service recognizes its responsibilities in each of these areas.*

In its report to Congress the next year, the Postal Service, mindful both of its own restraint in this area and of continued congressional hand-wringing, was a bit more saucy in its treatment of this subject: "Inasmuch as the Postal Service is not contemplating wholesale closings of post offices, the language on this subject which continually finds its way into the annual Treasury-Postal Service-General Government appropriations measure would appear superfluous."[39]

The Ultimate Irony: Congress Forces Service Cutbacks

The mid-1980s was a period when the Postal Service demonstrated not only a renewed commitment to maintaining its distinctive network of small rural facilities, but a new commitment to service across the board. During William Bolger's last year as Postmaster

General in 1984, he launched the Postal Service on what came to be known for a while as the "All Services" campaign, which was an effort to encourage courtesy and helpfulness on the part of postal employees, to instill in them a sense of pride in providing good service, and to increase customers' knowledge of postal products and services (this last, largely through an ambitious advertising series). The campaign enjoyed the support also of Bolger's immediate successors as Postmaster General, Paul Carlin and Albert Casey.

But under the leadership of Postmaster General Preston Tisch, who assumed office in August 1986, the campaign to improve service acquired new vigor, and new pressure from the top. Tisch worked to improve service to major business mailers; he personally visited mail order companies, publishing houses, and other heavy users of the mails to talk about how the Postal Service could help them solve their mailing problems. Tisch wanted to make sure that a new organizational commitment to improve service was not merely symbolic. To institutionalize efforts to improve understanding between the Postal Service and its customers, and to encourage one-on-one meetings between postal executives and decision-makers in industry, Tisch established a Senior Management Account Focus Program. Patterned after the Xerox Corporation's highly acclaimed national acounts marketing effort, this program focuses on having Postal Service officers and other senior managers spend time with major customers, listening to what they have to say, getting inside their businesses, learning what they do and how they do it, and determining how to serve them better. This corporate marketing effort involves major customers at every level of the Postal Service, with corporate officers working closely with national accounts, regional and divisional managers working with key accounts, and account representatives at the division level working with major local accounts.

And for business and household mailers alike, the Postal Service had been trying to improve both the geniality and the convenience of its services. Throughout the organization intensified efforts were made to get employees to be more courteous and friendly to customers. Officials in local post offices were being encouraged to tailor their retail hours to customer needs by, for example, opening window services earlier in the morning and keeping them open later into the evening and on Saturdays. By the end of 1987 over 3,800 postal facilities around the country had implemented adjusted window hours in an effort to make it more convenient for customers to do business with the Postal Service, and at the same time helping to eliminate long lobby lines and reduce traffic congestion around post offices. And in 1987 the Postal Service took another step to accommodate customers' needs by establishing a new program enabling customers to order stamps by phone or by mail, billing the purchase to their credit cards.

The increased emphasis on service and customer convenience could also be seen in individual mail services. For its Express Mail (overnight delivery) service, for example, the Postal Service had initiated improved proof of delivery using a computerized system for entering complete delivery receipt data; deployed an additional 10,000 new Express Mail outdoor collection boxes in strategic locations near office buildings, in industrial parks, and other convenient locations (and another 3,600 indoor collection boxes in high-rise office buildings); increased the number of mobile Express Mail acceptance vans; and inaugurated the Express Mail Corporate Account, a centralized, nationwide advance deposit account that permits customers to mail at any acceptance location by simply using an account number.

But this rather remarkable momentum in the direction of improved sensitivity to customer service was stopped cold in late 1987 as a consequence of an effort by Congress to deal with the federal budget deficit in a typically short-sighted way.

When Congress passed the fiscal 1988 budget-reconciliation bill in the early morning hours of December 22, 1987, its intention was to cut the anticipated overall federal deficit by an estimated $17.6 billion in fiscal 1988 and $22 billion in fiscal 1989. Normally, these budget-reconciliation bills are meant to bring existing laws into line with instructions in congressional budget resolutions, passed earlier, to reduce federal spending and increase revenues. But in 1987 the deficit-reduction targets set in the budget resolution had been changed twice by December—first by new targets set in a revised budget-balancing measure signed into law in September and, second, by an agreement reached in late November by negotiators at budget "summit" talks between Congress and the White House. The budget summit had been prompted by congressional failure to meet the deficit-reduction targets set in the budget resolution had been changed twice by December—first by new targets set in a revised budget-balancing measure signed into law in September and, second, by an agreement reached in late November by negotiators at budget "summit" talks between Congress and the White House. The budget summit had been prompted by congressional failure to meet the deficit-reduction targets and by concern over the stock market crash of October 19, 1987, which many analysts linked to the budget deficit. The summit agreement set a two-year deficit-reduction target of $76 billion—$30.2 billion in fiscal 1988 and $45.8 billion in 1989—and called for $9 billion and $14 billion, respectively, in new taxes for the two years. A pre-summit version of the reconciliation bill had passed the House in late October. Following the summit, Senate committees reworked major sections of a Senate version that had not yet reached the floor. The changes were made to conform to targets set at the summit. Then, in eight days of conference negotiations, House-Senate differences in the bill were settled.

The Postal Service's troubles began in early December when it became clear that the Senate's version included a plan to shift to the Postal Service about $1.7 billion in costs associated with cost-of-living, retirement, and health care benefits for thousands of postal workers who retired before the Service became an independent establishment in 1971. The federal government had been continuing to provide the pension benefits for those workers, as former federal employees, whereas the Postal Service had responsibility for paying the benefits of those workers who became annuitants after the reconstitution of the postal organization. This had not typically posed a problem for legislators concerned about the federal budget deficit because those costs for a long time had not been included in federal budget totals, the Postal Service having been taken "off-budget" shortly after the postal system's reorganization in 1971. Only the small annual appropriation payment to the Postal Service was normally included in the budget totals. But in 1985 the Postal Service was brought back "on-budget," so the long-standing annuity obligations became part of the fiscal headache for Congress and the White House.

Postal officials were willing to accept the extra cost of the annuities and were prepared to find ways to cope with it. But the difficulty was that the Senate's proposed legislation tied the Postal Service's hands in terms of how it could cover the new costs. The measure short-sightedly prohibited the Postal Service from borrowing funds or adjusting postage rates in order to compensate for the unanticipated expenses. Instead, the measure's language required the Postal Service to offset the additional costs by cutting spending for its capital construction projects and by reducing its operating expenses.

In the face of the Senate's proposal, Postmaster General Preston Tisch convened a news conference on December 14 to outline the Postal Service's possible responses to the legislative proposal: cutbacks in the number of weekday hours that retail window services would be available at local post offices, discontinuance of Saturday retail services, elimination of Saturday deliveries, delays in mail processing and delivery, cancellations of major construction

and renovation projects around the country, halts to the acquisition
of automated mail-sorting equipment, hiring freezes, and possibly
the closing of 10,000 to 12,000 small post offices, primarily those
in rural areas.[40] Tisch told reporters gathered in Washington:[41]

> *In my many years in the private sector, I have never encountered a
> corporation that could shoulder an unexpected $2 billion obligation
> without compromising its financial position and the service it pro-
> vides its customers. . . . I find this development particularly disturb-
> ing, especially since I made the commitment to the American people
> when I became Postmaster General that I would improve service,
> not reduce it.*

Some Washington officials, including James C. Miller, director
of the White House Office of Management and Budget, contended
that the postmaster general was "bluffing." They viewed his pro-
nouncement as a classic Washington strategy of fighting budget
cuts by threatening steps that would surely prompt an angry public
response—a "Washington Monument" strategy, named for the
Interior Department's legendary tradition of fighting spending
cuts by threatening to close popular tourist attractions in Washington.

But the Postal Service's public warnings as to the measure's
likely effects touched a few nerves in Congress, which finally
passed a bill that required the Postal Service to reduce spending
by $1.25 billion over fiscal years 1988 and 1989—$700 million less
than the cuts originally proposed by the Senate. However, the
legislation specifically required the Postal Service to meet this new
cost by cutting $430 million from the postal operating budget and
taking the remaining $800 million away from planned capital
expenditures.

This move by Congress forced the Postal Service to cancel 50
percent of the postal facility construction projects scheduled for
fiscal years 1988 and 1989, overall, and 75 percent of those that
would have gone forward in 1988. The acquisition of equipment
intended to improve productivity and customer services also was
sharply curtailed in the wake of Congress's action. The net effect
was to wipe out plans to build or modernize badly needed postal
facilities throughout the country.

On the operations side, the impact of the congressional decision
was less severe than it would have been had the original Senate
proposal been enacted. Still, the Postal Service was forced to make
adjustments in postal operations—adjustments that unfortunately
would be felt by customers. In mid-January 1988, the Postal
Service decided that post offices around the country would have to

shorten their lobby hours by an average of half a day a week to absorb the budget cuts. The managers of the 74 postal divisions around the country were given authority to determine how to time the shutdowns, so that not all of the post offices in any given area would be closed at the same hours. Moreover, local managers were given flexibility in reducing hours of service at low-use times (such as Wednesday afternoons), rather than retreating from the new program aimed at expanding window service for earlier and later hours in a day to serve people who cannot do postal business from 8 A.M. to 5 P.M. Postal Service headquarters directed field managers to make sure that offices in affluent and in poor areas were affected equally.

In addition, the Postal Service eliminated the 3 P.M. to midnight shift on Sundays, the work shift that sorted most of the roughly 20 million first-class letters collected from mail boxes around the country on an average Sunday. This cost-saving step meant that mail collected on Sundays would not be sorted until the shift ending at 8 A.M. Mondays, thus delaying by one day the delivery of the mail put in mail boxes on Sundays. Letters destined for local delivery started arriving on Tuesday rather than Monday; delivery of mail to more distant locations also was delayed a day.

Although all the effects of this particular cutback were not yet apparent when this book went to press, the speculation among observers in the postal policy community—postal executives, labor leaders, business mailers, and others—was that they would go beyond mere delays in the delivery of first-class letters mailed on Sundays. Users of business bulk mail (third-class advertising material) worried that the delays would be cumulative, affecting mail processing on subsequent days of the week. This would make it harder for businesses with time-sensitive mailings to predict when mail would arrive. Union officials also predicted trouble, noting that the elimination of the Sunday sorting shift would increase work loads. This, combined with steady increases in mail volume each year (estimated at 5.5 percent for 1987–1988), might cause severe service disruptions in some metropolitan areas—especially key cities with outmoded facilities (the improvement of which also was forestalled by the congressional action).[42]

Thus, the full impact of the congressional action in late 1987 was likely to be more sharply felt in the long run than in the short, since the effects of cancelled construction projects and equipment acquisitions would be apparent in the system for years to come, as the Postal Service's mail handling facilities struggle to cope with ever-higher mail volumes.

What Congress did to the Postal Service in late 1987 was short-sighted in the extreme and served little productive purpose since the imposition of spending restraints was merely an accounting measure—"smoke and mirrors" as one observer put it—aimed at helping politicians make the federal budget deficit appear smaller than it really is.[43] In barring the Postal Service from spending its revenue, Congress was merely engaging in the kind of sleight of hand that citizens would find so repugnant if they knew of it.

In view of the progress the Postal Service was making by 1986 and 1987 to improve service to its customers, and also in view of the regularity and near religiosity with which Congress has intervened in postal operations and policies over the years on behalf of powerful and organized interests (but in the name of the larger "public" interest), it may at first appear anomalous and surprising that Congress would force the Postal Service to make such conspicuous reductions in service delivery. But the congressional action is easier to understand when it is considered as part of the long-standing tendency of most members of Congress to treat the Postal Service as a political expedient, something to be tinkered with or disregarded, depending on what suits their political needs of the moment.

Endnotes

1. For a good example of this "entitlement ethic" at work, see Robert D. Behn and Kim Sperduto, "Medical Schools and the 'Entitlement Ethic,' " *Public Interest*, no. 57 (Fall 1979), p. 55.
2. U.S. Postal Service, General Release No. 28, March 29, 1972.
3. *New York Times*, August 29, 1972, p. 1.
4. *New York Times*, February 18, 1973, p. 1.
5. From statement of Morris Biller, president of the Manhattan-Bronx Postal Union, in U.S., Congress, House, Committee on Post Office and Civil Service, *Oversight Hearings on the Postal Service, Hearings before a Subcommittee of the Committee on Post Office and Civil Service*, 93rd Cong., 1st Sess., 1973, p. 243.
6. E. V. Dorsey, senior assistant postmaster general for operations, testimony in ibid., p. 272.
7. U.S., Congress, Senate, Committee on Post Office and Civil Service, *Postal Oversight, Hearings before the Committee on Post Office and Civil Service*, 93rd Cong., 1st Sess., 1973, p. 68.
8. U.S. Postal Service, *Comprehensive Statement on Postal Operations*, January 1980, p. 28.
9. Quoted in *New York Times*, November 26, 1980, p. B4.
10. U.S., Congress, House, Committee on Government Operations, *U.S. Postal Service Plan for the Nine-Digit ZIP Code, Thirtieth Report by the Committee*

on *Government Operations*, House Report No. 96-1531, 96th Cong., 2d Sess., 1980, pp. 6, 7.

11. U.S., Congress, House, Committee on Post Office and Civil Service, *Nine-Digit ZIP Code System, Hearings before the Subcommittee on Postal Operations and Services of the Committee on Post Office and Civil Service*, 97th Cong., 1st Sess., 1981.

12. U.S., Congress, House, Committee on Government Operations, *The Nine-Digit ZIP Code Investment: More Digits, Less Savings, Nineteenth Report by the Committee on Government Operations*, House Report No. 97-397, 97th Cong., 1st Sess., 1981.

13. Comptroller General of the United States, *Conversion to Automated Mail Processing Should Continue; Nine-Digit ZIP Code Should Be Adopted If Conditions Are Met*, report to the Congress (Washington: General Accounting Office, January 6, 1983), No. GGD-83-24, pp. ii–iii. Also see Comptroller General of the United States, *Conversion to Automated Mail Processing and Nine-Digit ZIP Code—A Status Report*, report to the Congress (Washington: General Accounting Office, January 6, 1983), No. GGD-83-84.

14. U.S. Postal Service, *Comprehensive Statement on Postal Operations*, 1984, pp. 37–38.

15. Ibid., p. 37.

16. Ibid.

17. *Review of Postal Automation Strategy: A Technical and Decision Analysis—A Technical Memorandum* (Washington: U.S. Congress, Office of Technology Assessment, OTA-TM-CIT-22, June 1984), pp. 2–3.

18. All of the information in this section on the procurement scandal is drawn from a report by the Postal Inspection Service on its investigation of the conspiracy: U.S. Postal Inspection Service, "ZIP + 4/Automation Investigative Report," January 1987, pp. 290–323. This section of the confidential Inspection Service Report has been released to the public and is reproduced in U.S., Congress, House, Committee on Post Office and Civil Service, *Oversight on Operation of the United States Postal Service, Joint Hearings before the Subcommittee on Postal Operations and Services and the Subcommittee on Postal Personnel and Modernization of the Committee on Post Office and Civil Service*, 100th Cong., 1st Sess., 1987, pp. 31–64.

19. See U.S., Congress, House, Committee on Government Operations, *ZIP + 4 After 5 Years: Postal Service Oversight, Hearings before a Subcommittee of the Committee on Government Operations*, 99th Cong., 2d Sess., 1985, esp. pp. 116–61.

20. Postal Inspection Service, "ZIP + 4/Automation Investigative Report," p. 296.

21. *Postal Leader*, January 19, 1988, pp. 1, 4.

22. Ibid., p. 5.

23. Commission on Postal Service, *Report of the Commission on Postal Service* (Washington: U.S. Government Printing Office, 1977), vol. 1, p. 50.

24. *Postal Record*, May 1977, p. 4.

25. Quoted in *Washington Post*, May 21, 1966, p. F3.

26. Comptroller General of the United States, letter report to Senator Alan Cranston (No. GGD-75-92), June 7, 1975, p. 3.

27. U.S., Congress, Senate, Committee on Post Office and Civil Service, *Postal Reorganization, Hearings before the Committee on Post Office and Civil Service*, 94th Cong., 2d Sess., 1976, pp. 304–06.

28. See U.S., Congress, House, Committee on Government Operations, *Postal Service Move Toward Centralized Mail Delivery, Hearing before a Subcommittee of the Committee on Government Operations*, 98th Cong., 1st Sess., 1983; U.S., Congress, House, Committee on Government Operations, *Continued Examination of the Postal Service Move Toward Centralized Mail Delivery*, 98th Cong., 2d Sess., 1984.

29. See U.S., Congress, House, Committee on Post Office and Civil Service, *Prohibit Use of Clusterboxes for Certain Residential Mail Delivery, Hearing before the Subcommittee on Postal Operations and Services of the Committee on Post Office and Civil Service*, 99th Cong., 1st Sess., 1985.

30. Comptroller General of the United States, *Mail Delivery to New Residential Addresses: Adherence to Policy Can Be Improved*, report to the Congress (Washington: General Accounting Office, June 1987), No. GGD-87-66.

31. U.S., Congress, *Postal Service Move Toward Centralized Mail Delivery*, p. 154.

32. U.S. Postal Service, *Comprehensive Statement on Postal Operations*, 1987, pp. 30–31.

33. *United States Code*, Title 39, sec. 101(b).

34. Comptroller General of the United States, *$100 Million Could Be Saved Annually in Postal Operations in Rural America without Affecting the Quality of Service*, report to the Congress (Washington: General Accounting Office, June 4, 1975), No. GGD-75-87.

35. See U.S., Congress, House, Committee on Post Office and Civil Service, *Cutbacks in Postal Service, Hearings before the Subcommittee on Postal Service of the Committee on Post Office and Civil Service*, 94th Cong., 2d Sess., 1976, p. 15; and U.S., Congress, Committee on Post Office and Civil Service, *GAO's Recommendations That 12,000 Small Post Offices Be Closed, Joint Hearings before the Subcommittee on Postal Service and Postal Facilities, Mail, and Labor Management of the Committee on Post Office and Civil Service*, 94th Cong., 1st Sess., 1975, pp. 4–5, 20.

36. U.S., Postal Rate Commission, *Commission Opinion Remanding Determinations for Further Consideration*, Docket Nos. A79-1 through A79-9 (Washington: Postal Rate Commission, May 7, 1979), pp. 1, 3, 4, 16; Docket Nos. A79-10 through A79-21 (Washington: Postal Rate Commission, July 20, 1979), p. 1.

37. Comptroller General of the United States, *Replacing Post Offices with Alternative Services: A Debated But Unresolved Issue*, report to the Congress (Washington: General Accounting Office, September 2, 1982), No. GGD-82-89.

38. U.S. Postal Service, *Comprehensive Statement on Postal Operations*, 1984, p. 4.

39. U.S. Postal Service, *Comprehensive Statement on Postal Operations*, 1985, p. 6.

40. *New York Times*, December 15, 1987, p. A18.

41. *Postal Leader*, December 22, 1987, p. 1.
42. *New York Times*, January 30, 1988, p. 6.
43. Leonard Weiss, staff director of the United States Senate Committee on Governmental Affairs, which oversees the Postal Service, quoted in ibid.

Chapter 4

COLLECTIVE BARGAINING, FAIR WAGES, AND QUALITY OF WORK LIFE

After a brief examination of the composition of the postal work force and the structure of union representation of postal workers, this chapter focuses on three principal topics: (1) the nature of the collective bargaining process, (2) the question of whether postal workers are paid excessive wages, and (3) the difficulties the Postal Service has in motivating its changing workforce and more general issues relating to quality of work life in the postal system. The collective bargaining process receives principal attention here for a reason that is perhaps best indicated by the juxtaposition of two facts about the postal system. First, with roughly 800,000 employees, the U.S. Postal Service has a work force that is larger than that of General Motors, the nation's largest company. Second, compensating this work force accounts for 85 percent of the total cost of operating the system. Thus, if we are to understand the sources of rising costs in the postal system, our analysis must include a close examination of the collective bargaining process.

Composition of the Postal Work Force

More than three-quarters of a million individuals—a shade over 1 percent of the total U.S. labor force—work for the U.S. Postal Service. These persons work in facilities with work contingents ranging in size from a single person to over 40,000 workers. Some of the tasks they perform, such as moving mail within large

112

processing facilities, require physical strength and dexterity but virtually no skill. Other tasks, such as the maintenance and operation of sophisticated electronic equipment and computers, demand considerable technical skill and knowledge. Some postal jobs (window clerk, for example) bring workers into constant contact with the public, while other jobs (such as sorting-machine operators) entail no such contact. Some postal work involves close monitoring by supervisory personnel (mail sorting, for example), while other work (such as delivery) involves very little supervision.

One could draw multiple contrasts of this sort across many different dimensions of postal work. Despite the great variety in occupation and working conditions that one finds within the Postal Service, it is nevertheless possible to identify the most common postal jobs or, at least, those that account for the largest percentages of the postal work force.

Easily the largest category of postal employees consists of clerks and mailhandlers who process the mail. Together they constitute 44 percent of the work force or about 350,000 individuals. Most mail processing personnel work in large sectional center processing facilities that serve a surrounding geographical area. These facilities are large buildings full of conveyors and noisy machines that expedite the sorting and routing of mail. For the clerks and mailhandlers who staff these facilities, the work experience is much like that of a factory or production line worker. But for other clerks—such as those who staff the window services of post offices—the work experience is more like that of a bank teller or retail clerk.

The next largest category of postal workers—237,000 or 30 percent of the total—consists of delivery carriers and vehicle drivers. Some of these carriers have the familiar task of delivering mail to homes, apartment buildings, and office buildings. Others are responsible for moving the mail from collection points at corner boxes or other collection receptacles to central processing facilities and taking mail from these facilities to carrier stations for distribution. All of these jobs involve knowledge of a particular route that is repeated day after day for months at a time. Moreover, most of those who perform these jobs spend the great part of their workday alone, out on the route.

The system's 65,000 full- and part-time rural delivery carriers (8 percent of the total) share many of the same work experiences of their city counterparts, but must also perform many of the tasks of the window clerk—selling postage stamps, accepting registered mail, answering questions about postal regulations, listening to complaints, and the like. These carriers tend to stay with their routes for many years and to become familiar figures in the communities they serve.

Over 50,000 people serve in supervisory and managerial positions, and over 29,000 perform building and vehicle maintenance services. There are 28,000 postmasters in facilities of remarkably varying size. And the remaining 31,000 people fill dozens of specialized jobs ranging from security officer to the postmaster general.

The vast majority of the Postal Service's employees are craft workers who are members of national labor unions that are affiliated with the American Federation of Labor–Congress of Industrial Organization (AFL-CIO) and that represent them in collective bargaining with management over pay and conditions of employment. Even some management personnel—most supervisors and postmasters—have associations representing their members' interests to the Postal Service. Unlike the craft unions, the postmasters' and supervisors' national associations cannot bargain with postal management, but like the craft employee unions, they have a long history of representing their members' interests in congressional deliberations on postal policy and of seeking a voice in management decisions that affect their members.

Union Representation of Postal Workers

The history of American postal unionism is unusually rich. Postal employees were the first federal employees to join unions in significant numbers. Although skilled craftsmen working in the shipyards of the U.S. Navy and in the U.S. Government Printing Office had organized earlier in the nineteenth century, it was in the nation's post offices that federal employee unionism caught hold and grew.[1] The city letter carriers were the first postal employees to unite for concerted action, forming the National Association of Letter Carriers (NALC) in 1889. A year later, the postal clerks also established a national association. And by 1908, the rural letter carriers, the postmasters, and the postal supervisors had created associations too. Today, four major organizations are recognized to represent postal employees in collective bargaining with management over pay and other terms and conditions of employment: the NALC; the American Postal Workers Union (APWU); the National Rural Letter Carriers' Association (NRLCA); and the National Post Office Mail Handlers, Watchmen, Messengers, and Group Leaders Division of Laborers' International Union of North America (Mail Handlers).

The two largest of these recognized unions—the APWU and the NALC, representing clerks and carriers, respectively—are quite different from one another in their organizational genesis and their internal stability and harmony.

The principal organization representing the interests of clerks is the APWU, formed in July 1971 as a result of a merger of several postal workers' associations. The two largest of these groups were the United Federation of Postal Clerks (175,000 members) and the National Postal Union (70,000 members), the latter of which had split off from the former in 1958 and included among its members the nation's largest and most militant local, the 27,000-member Manhattan-Bronx Postal Union. Other parties to the merger were the National Association of Post Office and General Services Maintenance Employees, the National Federation of Post Office Motor Vehicle Operators, and the National Association of Special Delivery Messengers. The resulting organization is somewhat of a federation inasmuch as each of the four founding crafts—the clerks, maintenance workers, motor vehicle workers, and special delivery messengers—constitutes a separate division with its own president and staff.

The creation of the APWU seemed to signal at least a temporary end to long-standing organizational divisions and internal dissension that had torn the ranks of the postal clerks ever since 1890, when the first organization of postal clerks, the National Association of Post Office Clerks, was formed. But, in fact, two factors that contributed to the long series of bitter splits and cautious alliances among warring factions of clerks remain today and continue to unsettle the ranks of the APWU. First, the great variety in clerical duties—ranging from keeping records to selling stamps or operating high-speed letter-sorting machines—makes it difficult for these workers to feel a common bond and perceive shared stakes. Second, promotions to the supervisory ranks have traditionally been made from the clerical ranks—a situation further exacerbating the jealousies, rivalries, and factionalism among post office clerks.

By contrast, the organizational experience of the letter carriers has been relatively free of internal strife. Perhaps one key to this organizational tranquility is the fact that unlike the clerks, most city carriers share roughly the same kind of work experiences and most of them remain carriers throughout their postal careers, often on the same route. Thus, it is easier for carriers to perceive shared economic and political stakes. Whatever is responsible for this relative cohesion, the National Association of Letter Carriers, which in 1989 celebrates the 100th anniversary of its founding, certainly has benefited from having a united membership rather than a factious membership beset by quarrels and squabbles. Its cohesive membership has freed it from having to devote time and other resources to the resolution of internal disputes. Moreover, having a cohesive membership generally has placed it in a strengthened position in the eyes of government policymakers.

Although one can identify important differences among the postal unions, those differences fade when one considers how much better organized and more strategically positioned postal unions are for advancing their interests than are other associations of federal employees. Two factors combine to give postal workers a measure of political and economic power unmatched by any other group of federal workers. First, they have long had effective organizations in place to represent the interests of postal workers in national political arenas. And second, the postal unions since 1970 have enjoyed the right to bargain collectively with postal management on wages and working conditions.

The Postal Reform Movement and the Onset of Collective Bargaining

The sweeping postal reorganization proposal floated by the Nixon administration in 1969, containing a provision for collective bargaining, elicited its strongest opposition from the postal employee unions. These groups vigorously opposed any serious changes in postal policy, fearing a sharp reduction in their influence if the role of Congress in making postal policy were curtailed. The unions had great influence on Capitol Hill and had been very successful in achieving their goals through legislation. They feared that the plan's proposed change to direct collective bargaining would work to the political and economic disadvantage of postal workers, especially since the reorganization proposal retained the prohibition on strikes by postal workers. Moreover, the unions believed that the whole political discussion in Washington about postal reorganization was obscuring an issue they felt merited more immediate attention—a pay raise for postal workers.

Early in 1969, at the same time the Post Office Department was preparing initial drafts of postal reorganization legislation, the postal labor unions were starting to push for a wage increase. On February 12, 1969, the Nixon administration revealed its intention of increasing postal pay by just under 3 percent. The postal unions argued for a more substantial increase, and after some prodding the administration offered to raise the increase to just over 4 percent. The unions still were dissatisfied, so they turned to Congress for help.

On Capitol Hill, the subject of postal pay quickly overshadowed the postal reorganization legislation and continued to do so throughout 1969. In October the House overwhelmingly approved a postal pay bill that provided for an 11 percent pay increase. But by Thanksgiving neither house of Congress yet had taken substantial action on the reorganization measure. The Post Office Department, fearing that the chances for passage of the reorganization might fade if action on it were delayed too long, sought to use the pay issue as leverage to gain support from the unions for the reorganization package. The President became involved in the process, and the parties began in earnest to negotiate a settlement on a combination pay package and reorganization plan. Despite apparent breakthroughs in December, the year ended with no progress on either measure.[2]

The new year began with still no break in the impasse. The Nixon administration was willing and able to withhold action on the pay raise until it won some measure of support from the unions for the reorganization proposal. The unions, on the other hand, had virtual veto power over any reorganization legislation, and they could be counted on to exercise it until their pay demands were met. When this stalemate persisted into February 1970, rank-and-file postal workers began to talk of a postal strike.

The department acted quickly to try to stem the growing discontent of postal workers and to save the reorganization proposal. David Nelson, the general counsel of the Post Office Department, along with John Gabusi, a staff member of a House postal subcommittee, drafted a substitute reorganization proposal providing for an 11 percent pay increase retroactive to January 1, 1970. The House Post Office and Civil Service Committee approved and reported the bill on March 12, 1970. The bill also drew the support of the National Association of Letter Carriers. But all the accompanying rhetoric about the new measure being "an important first step," and "a workable bill," did not convince militant postal workers. On March 18, 1970, postal workers in New York City went on a strike that spread throughout the nation and lasted for eight days—crippling business activities and severely disrupting commerce.[3]

With workers still out on strike on March 24, the leaders of the main postal unions seemed to worsen the prospects of settlement when they announced that they would no longer even consider a pay raise tied to a postal reorganization proposal. When Labor Secretary George Schultz, who had been called in to help solve the dispute, argued that "to link the justifiable demands of postal employees with reform, and to leave the thing pending seems to be a colossal error," Postmaster General Winton Blount announced that the administration was willing to discuss all issues involved in the strike, and that postal reorganization would not necessarily be a prerequisite to pay legislation.[4]

The next afternoon, March 25, 1970, negotiations began in Washington between postal labor and management. The talks went on for almost a week without progress. Finally, on April 1, a compromise plan emerged. The proposal offered the unions a two-step pay increase: the first, an immediate 6 percent increase, retroactive to December 29, 1969; the second, an 8 percent increase contingent on union support for postal reorganization. The proposal also included an offer to have the unions participate in formulating the details of the reform plan. Both sides agreed to the compromise resolution on April 2, 1970.

Further negotiations continued for two weeks in an attempt to develop a reorganization package that would have the support of the Post Office and the unions alike. On April 16 the parties finally reached an agreement on the terms of a postal reorganization proposal. The agreement included most of the same features the Post Office had been pushing all along, but there was one important change intended to secure beyond doubt the support of the unions: the proposal called for third-party binding arbitration—a provision the unions had sought as compensation for the reduction in Congress's role in making postal policy and the consequent severing of the unions' principal line of influence over postal labor policies. In short, the unions finally gave their support to the postal reorganization proposal only after exacting a 14 percent pay increase and a provision for binding arbitration.

The Postal Reorganization Act that was passed by Congress in the summer of 1970 revolutionized postal labor-management relations. The act provided that the Postal Service be governed by the National Labor Relations Act. It further provided that the Postal Service negotiate agreements on wages, benefits, and working conditions through collective bargaining with the labor organizations that held exclusive recognition rights nationwide as of August 12, 1970, the date of the reorganization plan's enactment. These unions represented the maintenance employees, special delivery messengers, motor-vehicle employees, postal clerks, letter carriers, mailhandlers, and rural letter carriers.

The collective bargaining process established in 1970 radically altered the institutional arrangements and procedures for setting postal wages, benefits, and working conditions. These changes had some important consequences for the tenor of the relationship between postal workers and management and also led to substantial increases in employee wages. It is possible to identify three relatively distinct periods in postal labor-management relations since 1970. The first period—including the negotiations of 1971, 1973, and 1975—was characterized chiefly by management concessions to unions that were just learning how to flex their muscles in the new bargaining arena. The hallmark of the second period—including the negotiations of 1978, 1981, and 1984—was the development of an openly bitter and acrimonious relationship between unions and management. Though it is too soon to judge, the negotiations of 1987 seemed to signal the onset of another new phase, marked by a more conciliatory tone.

The Period of Management Concessions: 1971–1975

Ending congressional and presidential responsibility for establishing postal wages was supposed to accomplish two objectives: (1) to give postal management a more direct part in determining the compensation levels of postal workers; and (2) to enable postal management to control labor costs and reduce the percentage of the system's total costs accounted for by employee wages and benefits. This second objective was the more problematical, for its implicit assumption was that management would be better able than elected officials to stand firm before union wage demands. But in the first half decade of experience with collective bargaining, from 1970 to 1975, that assumption proved false as the Postal Service repeatedly backed down in the face of the unions' demands.

Having given in to the inclusion of a no-layoff clause in the contentious first round of collective bargaining in 1971, the Postal Service entered the 1973 talks with what seemed to be a firm, nononsense bargaining position: it adamantly insisted that substantial increases in wages and fringe benefits were out of the question since management needed to hold the line on the system's rapidly rising costs. Moreover, the Postal Service began issuing press releases to the effect that postal workers had never had it so good. The reports called attention to the attractiveness of postal salaries by citing the long waiting lists around the country for postal jobs. The unions, angered by management's tactic, countered by announcing plans to mobilize massive demonstrations against postal management in Washington and around the country. More important, the unions contacted business organizations heavily reliant on the postal system and told them there was a distinct possibility of a strike on July 21 unless a new contract was signed and ratified by then. The large mailers, in turn, put pressure on postal management, saying that if there was a strike, they would seek out permanent alternative methods of getting their material to the public.[5]

Management's position then changed dramatically. Senior Assistant Postmaster General Darrel F. Brown, management's principal representative at the negotiations, yielded on a number of important points, and his public statements stood in sharp contrast to management's earlier posture:[6]

> I am impressed with the need and urgency for improvement in labor relations. . . . We shall not abdicate our authority to manage, but we do have an obligation to share many things with the unions. . . . We want our negotiations and the subsequent agreement to be a model for all.

In what many observers have since come to regard as an extraordinary capitulation by postal management, the Postal Service reached an early and generous agreement with the unions. Postal workers won retention of the controversial no-layoff clause and a money package providing for a 14 percent wage increase over two years. The contract also provided for four cost-of-living adjustments over the life of the contract, increasing base salary schedules one cent an hour for each 0.4 percent increase in the consumer price index. This last provision actually ended up giving postal workers more of an increase than the guaranteed "up-front" wage boost of $1,100; the four cost-of-living adjustments during the 1973–1975 contract totaled $1,310. The 1973 agreement also included significant improvements in fringe benefits. Whereas the Postal Service's share of the cost of employee life insurance previously had been about one-third, the Service began paying 100 percent of the cost on July 20, 1974. Moreover, whereas the employer's share of health insurance premiums previously had been 40 percent, the 1973 contract increased them to 55 percent in July 1973, and to 65 percent in July 1974.

Union leaders could not hide their pleasure over the favorable contract. The president of the powerful letter carriers' union told the members that he thought the contract was "in the dreamboat category," and a leader of the APWU proudly claimed: "The fact is that we have gained substantially larger raises across the board in negotiations with postal management than we ever did politicking on Capitol Hill."[7]

Two years later, in the 1975 contract, postal workers won a $1,500 wage hike and an increase to 75 percent in the employer's share of health insurance premiums, and managed also to hold onto the no-layoff clause and the lucrative cost-of-living adjustments.

As this account suggests, the early years of postal collective bargaining were characterized chiefly by a reluctance on the part of the Postal Service to stand too firmly in the face of union strike threats. With the 1970 strike still fresh in their memories, postal executives feared that a massive strike would be a blow from which the Postal Service might never fully recover. Users of second-, third-, and fourth-class mail might be driven to find alternative delivery systems from which the Postal Service might be unable to recapture them. Moreover, the Postal Service was under pressure from those same mailers, and also from the general public and political elites, to avoid a strike because of the potential crippling effect on the economy and because of the general inconvenience it would cause those who depend on the mail system.

The early 1970s also were years of growing animosity between postal management and the unions representing most postal workers. Prior to the reorganization of the postal system and the onset of the collective bargaining process, the presence of third-party decision makers (Congress, the President, and the Bureau of the Budget) had tempered relations between the Post Office Department and its rank-and-file employees. But after 1970, the unions and management faced each other across a bargaining table without the luxury of intermediaries on whom responsibility devolved. Whereas before the reorganization both parties saw themselves as constituent parts of the same service agency, after it they came to see themselves as independent adversaries. This development made it more and more difficult to achieve consensus throughout the Postal Service about the organization's prevailing practices or future policies. It is not uncommon for government agencies to adopt an "us versus them" outlook toward Congress and the White House or toward various external clientele groups; in the Postal Service, however, this adversary relationship came to be institutionalized inside the organization by the advent of collective bargaining.

The difference in attitude was most pronounced on the side of the unions, whose members' principal attachments had changed: being Postal Service employees had become secondary to being union members. This change had followed as the postal unions matured with the privilege of bargaining directly with management. The unions gradually adopted a more aggressive posture throughout the 1970s. Some of this stemmed from the generally increasing militancy of public employees throughout the late 1960s and 1970s. Strikes by municipal workers had become common-place. This development had encouraged the postal unions to use demonstrations and strike threats to back their demands for improved wages and benefits. Strikes by other public employees increased the potency and credibility of the postal unions' strike threats by showing that it was not the legal right to strike that counted, but the will and the ability to do so.

Acrimonious Bargaining: 1978–1984

By the time negotiations were ready to begin for a new contract in 1978, the atmosphere of postal labor-management relations had become still more highly charged. The Postal Service had just come under the leadership of a new postmaster general, William F. Bolger, who succeeded Benjamin F. Bailar. Bolger had committed himself to a strenuous cost-cutting campaign. In addition, the Postal Service was under pressure to hold down costs. The White House, as part of President Carter's inflation-control campaign, was publicly pressing postal management to stand firm and exercise restraint in the coming wage negotiations.[8]

On the union side of the fence, matters were similarly charged. The two largest postal unions—the APWU and the NALC—faced closely contested presidential elections before the end of the year, and their leaders were under tremendous pressure from members (and from the challengers for their jobs) to improve on the 1975 contract. The president of the NALC, J. Joseph Vacca, was in his first term, and he lacked the substantial base of support given his predecessor, James H. Rademacher, who had led the union during the previous bargaining talks. In addition, Emmett Andrews had just succeeded the late Francis S. Filbey as president of the APWU, and had not yet faced an election of his own. The Postal Service worried about the effect these election races would have on the coming negotiations. As one Postal Service manager warned: "Those guys will be bargaining and running for election at the same time."[9]

The 1978 Negotiations

In light of these pressures on both sides, it is no surprise that the 1978 negotiations were particularly bitter and protracted. Once again, all the important issues (no-layoff clause, cost-of-living ad-

geles, and Chicago—union members prepared to follow the lead of the Jersey City and San Francisco workers.[16]

The dissatisfaction with the proposed contract was fanned by Vincent Sombrotto, president of the huge Manhattan-Bronx branch of the NALC. Sombrotto, who was preparing to challenge NALC national president J. Joseph Vacca in the upcoming union election, announced: "I am absolutely dissatisfied with the way our leaders negotiated in Washington. It was a meaningless charade that they entered into with the Postmaster General and the White House."[17]

The next few weeks were filled with similar attacks against the national unions' leadership from Sombrotto and from Moe Biller, the president of the APWU's New York Metropolitan Area Chapter, which then represented 23,000 workers, including many of the 4,500 at the Jersey City facility. Like Sombrotto, Biller had plans at some point to seek the presidency of the national union. (Both would win—Sombrotto in 1978, Biller in 1980—partly as a result of their militant posture, which appeals to many union members in the large cities.)

A wider strike was forestalled for the time being when Postmaster General Bolger, signaling his intention to deal firmly with those who might walk off the job, fired eighty strikers in Jersey City and forty-two in San Francisco and announced his intention to "do the same thing wherever this happens."[18]

But by the last week in August, the prospects of a nationwide postal strike again appeared strong as the results of the union membership ratification votes were tabulated. The NALC members rejected the tentative contract by a 72,288 to 58,832 vote. The letter carriers' union was the first to vote, and it was bound by its constitution to strike if bargaining did not resume within five days, even though postal strikes are illegal under federal law. Vacca, caught between the conflicting requirements of the law and of his union's constitution, called on Postmaster General William Bolger to reopen contract talks. Bolger had earlier insisted that the Postal Service absolutely would not resume negotiations, since the law provided a clearly defined procedure for such situations— fact-finding and binding arbitration.

The likelihood of a postal strike seemed to increase still further when, two days later, the rank-and-file members of two more unions joined the letter carriers in rejecting the proposed contract. The APWU voted 94,400 to 78,487 against the contract—roughly the same margin by which the letter carriers had earlier turned down the pact. The mail handlers also rejected the settlement. The APWU vote elicited a statement from Postmaster General

Bolger, who described the situation as serious but gave no indication that the Postal Service would meet union demands for a new round of bargaining, even though the Federal Mediation and Conciliation Service was urging the Postal Service to abandon its no-bargaining stance.[19]

As the strike deadline approached, the leaders of the NALC and the APWU faced a no-win predicament: defy the law and risk jail and fines for the unions, or defy official directives of their own unions and risk internal political reprisals.

The nation was once again girding for a postal strike, when with fewer than eight hours to go before another midnight strike deadline, the Postal Service and union leaders agreed to a compromise procedure (permitted under the terms of the reorganization act) for resolving their contract dispute. The agreement, drawn by the chief federal mediator, Wayne Horvitz, combined the unions' demand for more negotiations and management's call for arbitration. The agreement provided for a resumption of bargaining followed by binding arbitration if the two sides failed to reach a settlement within fifteen days.

The Federal Mediation and Conciliation Service selected James J. Healy, a professor of industrial relations at Harvard Business School, to mediate the talks between the Postal Service and the unions. But during the fifteen-day discussions, Healy was unable to secure a resolution of the disputes between the two parties, so on September 15, 1978, he imposed a binding settlement. The arbitrator gave postal workers a salary increase slightly larger than the one contained in the rejected contract (21.3 percent rather than 19.5 percent). More important, Healy removed the cap that had been put on the cost-of-living raises. Whereas the rejected pact would have limited the total cost-of-living increase over the three-year life of the contract to 73 cents an hour (roughly $1,300), the arbitrated settlement permitted six semiannual increases based on a 1-cent raise for each full 0.4-point increase in the consumer price index. (The effect of this decision was substantial, providing postal workers once again with a larger pay increase under the cost-of-living provision than under the up-front wage boost.)

But in spite of these increases in the proposed contract's wage provisions, Healy granted postal management little in exchange. The Postal Service had been hoping to eliminate the no-layoff provision. Instead of eliminating or watering down the job-protection language, Healy strengthened it for workers already employed by the Postal Service as of September 15, 1978, ordering that they should be guarded from layoffs for their "work lifetime" rather than just for the lifetime of each contract.

The 1981 Negotiations

By 1981 the positions of the postal unions and management were worlds apart. The unions had new leaders eager to prove their mettle, and the Postal Service faced serious economic pressures fueled by high labor costs.

Well before the start of the 1981 contract talks, union leaders were promising an aggressive challenge to what they described as "the antilabor policies" of postal management.[20] The unions' posture was not surprising since militant hard-liners headed both of the big unions. Vincent Sombrotto had been reelected president of the NALC, swamping three opponents in the union's national election and picking up 85 percent of the votes. And Moe Biller, the militant leader of the New York Metro Area Postal Union, had defeated the incumbent to win the national presidency of the APWU. Biller was openly hostile to the administration of Postmaster General William Bolger because of Bolger's dismissal in 1978 of workers who went on strike illegally in New Jersey and San Francisco. Upon taking office Biller staked out a familiar position: he held out the possibility of a strike if the union's wage demands were not met, and he denounced Postal Service plans to increase productivity and improve efficiency.[21]

For its part, the Postal Service was ready to adopt an equally hard line in the negotiations. Its financial position allowed little flexibility. The Postal Service had been running chronically in the red during the 1970s (a $306.4 million deficit in 1980) and was facing congressional mandates to make this deficit-prone operation financially self-sufficient by 1985. To get back in the black, postal management would have to trim its labor costs and increase efficiency in order to make the Postal Service more competitive with the growing numbers of highly automated private providers of mail and other information services. Studies commissioned by the Postal Service—and supported by other research—indicated that postal workers earned more than comparable workers in every sector of the private economy except mining. And to show how well postal workers had done since being extended collective bargaining privileges in 1970, the Postal Service released studies showing that postal workers' wages had increased faster than those of federal general service workers in the preceding decade. For example, the pay for a federal worker at GS5, Step 4, increased by 87.4 percent between 1970 and 1981, as compared to a 173.5 percent increase for a postal employee in the same grade.[22]

The Postal Service fired the first round in the 1981 labor bargaining, delaying the onset of talks by a surprise petition to the

National Labor Relations Board, asking it to determine which of the four unions representing nearly 600,000 postal employees should negotiate a new contract with the Postal Service. From 1971 to 1975, all four unions enjoying recognition rights bargained as a single unit with the Postal Service and signed a common contract. But in the 1978 talks, the rural letter carriers' union had split off from the others and had bargained separately. By 1981, the two smaller unions—representing the rural letter carriers and the mail handlers—were fighting with the APWU and the NALC and were thus seeking independent contracts with the Postal Service. (The NALC had been trying to organize the rural letter carriers, and the APWU had been wooing clerks who belonged to the mail handlers' unions.) In a letter to the postal system's 667,000 employees explaining the reasons for his petition to the NLRB, Postmaster General Bolger said:[23]

> *The problem of reaching goals we all want is further complicated by the increasing rivalry and dissension between the two sets of unions. Jurisdictional disputes between these unions have led to harsh words, frayed feelings, and active raiding campaigns by two of the unions to win over members of the other two unions. Such animosity also reduces the possibility of reaching sound agreements.*

Although the NLRB dismissed the petition, the only real consequences for the Postal Service were that contract talks commenced nearly two months later than they normally would have started and that the two big postal unions were emboldened by the rebuff to postal management. The unions' pay pitch, laid on the table only two weeks before the expiration of the 1978 contract, called for annual pay raises of 5 percent over each of the three years of the contract. The unions also asked for a special $577 "catch-up" raise at the outset to compensate for purchasing power lost since the 1978 agreement and for an improved cost-of-living formula.

The Postal Service immediately attacked the unions' demands as inflationary, saying that the pay proposals would raise the price of mailing a first-class letter to at least 40 cents in 1983. Management's analysis of this pay proposal also showed that if the Postal Service complied with the unions' wishes, the total cost to ratepayers over the three-year contract would amount to $25 billion and would result in employee compensation and benefits rising 44.3 percent a year.[24]

When the Postal Service still had not countered with its own wage proposals a week before the old contract's expiration, the unions accused the postmaster general of trying to provoke a nationwide mail strike. But to make it clear that he would not tolerate a strike, Bolger sent union leaders copies of a letter from the assistant attorney general in charge of the Justice Department's criminal division, advising that any striking postal worker could be arrested and prosecuted on criminal felony charges without having to first exhaust civil or administrative remedies.[25]

Less than four days before the contract's expiration, negotiators for the Postal Service issued their first economic proposal, calling for a three-year wage freeze, reduction in health benefits, and a cost-of-living adjustment not to exceed about $3,000 in three years. Naturally, unions reacted with programmed outrage. Sombrotto of the NALC called the offer a "devastating insult," and Biller of the APWU said: "This offer is a recessive bunch of garbage that could take us back 20 years. The Postmaster General, who still refuses to bargain in good faith, is bringing this nation to the brink of disaster as he tries to bring the unions to their knees."[26]

The Postal Service's rationale for its proposed wage freeze was that the Postal Reorganization Act provides that the wages of postal workers must be based on comparability with workers in private industry and that comparability had been achieved.

Although the day of the contract expiration brought reports from the negotiating table of "no progress," the talks continued past the midnight deadline as both sides attempted to head off a nationwide mail strike. After a frantic thirty-hour bargaining session, the Postal Service and the two unions finally agreed on a three-year contract that included a $900 basic wage increase over three years; productivity bonuses of $350 in each year of the contract; an uncapped cost-of-living allowance identical to that in the old contract; inclusion of $3,600 in previous cost-of-living increases in the base pay for purposes of calculating pensions, shift differentials, and other benefits; health benefits similar to those in the expired pact; and a $150 "sweetener" bonus for each employee if the contract won approval within forty-five days.

The 1984 Negotiations

The character of the 1984 contract talks was evident before they even began. They promised to be primarily a struggle over the Postal Service's contention that pay and benefits had soared out of line with earnings in comparable private sector jobs. The Postal Service's negotiating team went to the bargaining table with a directive from the Board of Governors, issued at an April 3, 1984, board meeting, that said postal pay and benefits exceeded the rewards of comparable private sector jobs and called on the system's management to "seek correction of this situation."[27] The board's instruction was somewhat unusual inasmuch as the board in the past had typically watched labor negotiations quietly from the sidelines, approving contracts after the fact. But President Reagan's five appointees to the board had given it a more conservative cast since the 1981 negotiations, and this transformed board was not reluctant to try to guide management's hand.

As the talks proceeded, one of the major issues was a Postal Service proposal to create lower wage schedules and fringe benefit packages for new employees. These proposals were designed, management insisted, to close the gap it said existed between average postal wage levels and those paid in the private sector for comparable levels of work—and to do so without adversely affecting the existing basic wage rates of current employees. This concept is commonly referred to as a "two-tier" pay structure in the private sector, and hundreds of thousands of employees are covered by this form of wage and salary plan. (Several private employers such as the Boeing Company and American Airlines had won such packages in the preceding period.)

After extensive negotiations, labor and management were still at an impasse when the existing labor agreements expired on July 20, 1984. On July 24, the director of the Federal Mediation and Conciliation Service initiated the fact-finding procedures of the Postal Reorganization Act, which also provides that if the fact-finding process does not assist the parties to reach agreement, the matters in dispute will be referred to binding third-party arbitration.

But on July 25 the Postal Service announced that it would take advantage of the expiration of its labor contracts to hire new workers at pay levels about 20 percent below the wages of its current employees. Union leaders understandably denounced this move as a "provocative, union-busting tactic."[28] Unions typically dislike two-tier wage schedules on the grounds that they pit old workers against newcomers: younger workers come to resent older ones who earn more money; the older workers, in turn, fear that management will find an excuse to edge them out so less expensive newcomers can take their places. Of course, the unions are worried that their organizational power will be undermined if their members are split into two warring camps. Interestingly, however, the strong opposition of union leaders to two-tier pay systems is often overruled by the rank and file, who prefer to pass economy measures on to the next generation of workers.

In any case, postal management's plans to begin hiring new employees at lower wages were blocked on August 10 when Congress voted

to prohibit the action. The vote came on an amendment to a supplemental appropriation bill for 1984. The amendment, sponsored by
Representative Silvio Conte, was passed 378 to 1 in the House and
was accepted by the Senate as part of the spending bill. Supporters of
the amendment argued that the Postal Service should abide by the
terms of its lapsed contracts until new labor agreements had been
signed. They further argued that because postal employees were
legally prohibited from striking it was only fair that postal management
be barred from unilaterally changing its rules.[29]

Even with the help of federal mediators, postal management and
labor failed to reach an agreement. An interest arbitration panel,
chaired by Clark Kerr, was convened to resolve the bargaining
impasse. The Kerr panel's award, rendered in December of 1984,
applied to nearly 550,000 postal employees and was the largest
interest arbitration ever conducted in the United States. Among
other things, the award adopted the Postal Service's argument
that, during the period since the passage of the Postal Reorganization Act, wage rates in the Postal Service had gone up substantially
faster than those in the private sector. Kerr concluded that the
principle of "moderate restraint" should govern future postal wage
determinations. Under this principle, the rate of postal wage
increases should be less than the overall rate of increases occurring
in the private sector of the economy. And the arbitration award
also approved the introduction of lower starting wages for new
postal employees as one of several means of bringing postal wages
into equilibrium with those prevailing in the private sector.[30]

1987 and Beyond

The 1987 contract talks were characterized by relatively little overt
conflict and produced a contract far more favorable to labor's
interests than to management's. The pay package contained an
immediate increase of 2 percent of each worker's base pay, further
wage increases averaging $525 a year, plus cost-of-living increases
ranging from $779 to $849 (assuming a 4.5 percent rate of inflation)
in the third year of the contract. Under this contract the typical
clerk or carrier's pay (not including benefits) was to rise from
$25,829 to $29,886.

Moreover, management ended up capitulating completely on
the one matter it claimed to care most about in these talks: winning
more freedom to hire casual and other part-time workers. The
Postal Service's hope was to double the percentage of casuals
(supplemental employees subject to specific limited periods of

employment in each calendar year, such as the Christmas season) to 10 percent from the 5 percent ceiling under the 1984 contract. Also, postal management wanted to keep the casuals for nearly a year in contrast to the existing 180-day limit. Finally, management wanted to increase the percentage of part-time workers getting regular wages from 10 to 16 percent of the work force. But when the negotiating was over and the new contract was initialed, the Postal Service prevailed on none of these points.

In defending the settlement, Postmaster General Preston Tisch said: "We entered these negotiations with a new attitude. We learned from past mistakes and realized that we would accomplish little over the life of a new contract if we left the bargaining table in an atmosphere of contention and acrimony."[31]

Wage Comparability with the Private Sector

A common criticism of the Postal Service is that postal employees are paid too much. People hear of postal clerks and letter carriers earning close to $30,000 and may believe such a wage to be excessive. Surely, it is true that postal workers have done well financially since 1970 through the collective bargaining process. Of course, "doing well financially" is a highly subjective notion, and in a free society it is very difficult to devise a formula to determine unambiguously what is a fair wage, a reasonable salary, just and equitable compensation. There is no rigid standard by which the adequacy or excessiveness of compensation can be measured. These matters seem especially difficult in public sector employment.

Federal law directs the Postal Service to "maintain compensation for its officers and employees comparable to the rates and types of compensation paid in the private sector of the economy of the United States."[32] The difficulty, of course, comes from trying to identify comparable levels of work in the private sector.

A number of studies have been conducted over the past fifteen years examining wage differentials between the Postal Service and other industries. These studies aimed to determine whether postal workers are paid more than their counterparts in other sectors and, if they are, to estimate the size of the pay differential.

Joseph Quinn investigated the difference in wages between the Postal Service and private industry prior to the postal reorganization in 1970. His analysis focused on what the average postal wage rate would have been in 1969 if postal workers retained their own productivity-related characteristics such as educational attainment and years of work experience, but worked in the private sector. After controlling for individual differences in worker, job, and locational characteristics, Quinn found that older white male postal workers were overpaid prior to postal reorganization.[33]

Douglas Adie investigated the wage differential for 1972 and concluded that postal employees generally were overpaid relative to workers in other industries. To calculate this wage differential, Adie postulated a relationship between an industry's quit rate and its wages relative to other industries. The idea is that a firm wishing to minimize the cost of its personnel operations can increase its wage relative to other firms and decrease the number of workers who leave. While this decreases the cost of personnel operations, it increases the firm's wage bill. Adie determined the optimum trade-off between quit rates and wage rates to produce an estimate of the optimal wage and turnover level to minimize total labor and personnel costs. His conclusion was that the Postal Service paid 35 percent more in 1972 than its computed optimal wage and that this differential was higher than for every other industry studied.[34]

A study by Sharon Smith compared the wages of both male and female postal employees with those of similar workers in the private sector and in the rest of the federal government. She found that in 1973 and 1975, postal workers received wages that were at least equal to those received by comparable workers in other sectors. However, there were differences by gender and union status. Female postal employees earned considerably more than comparable female workers in the private sector and moderately more than those in the rest of the federal government. Smith's comparison of postal workers with nonunionized private sector workers also showed postal workers enjoying a relatively high wage premium.[35]

Although their methodologies thus vary, these and other studies by independent researchers suggest that postal workers do enjoy a wage advantage by virtue of their employment with the Postal Service. But the differential appears to vary by gender and race: female and nonwhite workers earn substantially more in the Postal Service than they do in other industries. This is because the Postal Service is the only industry in which nonwhites and females earn as much as comparable white males. In other words, comparable postal employees receive equal wages regardless of their race or gender. Thus, it may not even be that the Postal Service overpays its workers, but merely that it does not permit the wage-depressing and discriminatory race and sex differentials commonly found in private sector industries.

The wage differential between the Postal Service and the private sector also seems to depend on union status. When postal workers are compared with similar workers in the nonunionized private sector, there is a substantial wage advantage or premium for postal workers. But when these same workers are compared to similar workers in the unionized private sector, the premium disappears. Thus, it may be that the Postal Service is paying a substantial premium because it is employing union labor.

The wage comparability issue also has been examined by researchers hired by the Postal Service to study the problem. One such study, released in 1984 at the start of that year's contract negotiations, was by Michael Wachter, an economics professor at the University of Pennsylvania. Wachter found that the Postal Service pays a wage premium of approximately 23 percent compared to workers in the private sector. Indeed, according to Wachter, the Postal Service pays a wage that is higher than the wage paid in every major industrial sector of the American economy. This wage premium varies across industries—from a high of 33.4 percent with respect to the retail and wholesale trade sector to a low of 2.9 percent in relation to the high-wage durable manufacturing and mining sectors. Wachter argued also that even when compared only with unionized workers in the private sector, postal workers still earn approximately 15 percent more, except in the construction and mining sectors, where the positive private sector differentials may be explained by the health and safety risks in mining and the job security risks in both construction and mining.[36]

As this last point suggests, one explanation for high wages is that they are offered to attract workers to jobs with few available takers. In other words, in a competitive labor market, a firm raises its wages when it cannot easily retain current employees and attract new employees. But, as Wachter noted, attracting applicants is not a problem for the Postal Service, which hires off long registers whenever it seeks to fill a job. Retaining workers is not a serious problem either. Wachter presented quit-rate data, expressed as monthly quits per 100 workers, showing that the Postal Service has a very low quit rate when compared to private sector firms and that the quit rate differential had expanded in the early 1980s. Nor can high postal wages be explained, as high wages often are, as a compensating differential for the higher risks of layoffs. After all, the Postal Service has a history of not laying off workers, and postal employees often point to job security as one of the more attractive features of their work.[37]

The Wachter study also argued that the positive relative wage differential paid by the Postal Service had increased substantially between 1969 and 1983. In that period, postal worker wages increased 21.9 percent faster than average private sector wages. He attributed these increases in part to sizable gains by heavily unionized industries generally—that is, across all sectors of the economy, union wages pulled away from nonunion wages. This increase in union wage differentials is, in turn, related to the spreading prevalence of union contracts with cost-of-living-allowance (COLA) clauses that use the consumer price index to value wages against inflation.[38]

A problem with all these studies is that there is no consensus as to which workers in the private sector in fact have comparable skills or perform comparable work and should thus form the basis for comparison with postal workers. It may be, for example, that the more meaningful data would compare postal workers to employees in competing private delivery services. Systematic and reliable data for such an analysis are difficult to obtain. But the *New York Times* reported in 1984 that drivers for Federal Express in the Washington area were earning base pay of $25,000 a year to start, compared with $21,511 for beginning Postal Service letter carriers. At United Parcel Service, where workers are represented by the International Brotherhood of Teamsters, drivers and package handlers were earning $28,000, and a package of fringe benefits even more generous than the Postal Service offered.[39]

The emphasis on cross-industry wage comparisons also is problematic inasmuch as it tends to divert attention from two different pay inequity problems inside the Postal Service. First, there is a wholly inadequate differential between the wages in the top carrier and clerk grades and those of supervisors and postmasters. This stems in part from the serious pay compression that is caused by the cap on the postmaster general's salary, which is the top level of pay in the postal system. The pay of supervisors and postmasters gets squeezed from both ends. Above them are many layers in the postal hierarchy, where differentials also are maintained. Beneath them are the craft employees whose pay keeps getting pushed up against theirs because the craft employees benefit from collective bargaining privileges the supervisors and postmasters lack. The national associations representing postmasters and supervisors (the National Association of Postmasters of the United States, the National League of Postmasters, and the National Association of Postal Supervisors) cannot bargain with postal management because the Postal Reorganization Act bars the National Labor Relations Board from recognizing a bargaining unit that includes "any management official or supervisor."

The second internal pay inequity in need of resolution stems from the Postal Service's practice of using the same wage structure across the entire country. The national uniformity of wages provides postal workers in small towns and rural areas with wages that are often far greater than those received by privately employed workers with similar skills and, in some cases, even greater than highly trained professionals in those areas. This practice also inadequately compensates postal workers in some of the large cities where the cost of living is high and the job pressures are great.

Quality of Work Life Issues

Although wage rates are the central focus of the collective bargaining process, labor-management relations today involve issues that stretch far beyond wage negotiations. The increasingly complicated contours of labor-management relations stem largely from the changing nature of work and the changing expectations of workers. Workers no longer sell their time and labor to employers simply for financial compensation. Rather, workers have expectations and aspirations that employers must respond to if they are to maintain and strengthen the commitment of their employees. To put it more simply, employees do not work as hard when they think their needs are not being met.

This has become a serious problem for the U.S. Postal Service, whose workers—according to a study commissioned by the Postal Service in 1983—have, at best, a "muted" commitment to the organization and are not performing their jobs as effectively as they could, if given the right conditions. The study, conducted by the firm of Yankelovich, Skelly and White, Inc. (YSW), concluded that the Postal Service is only marginally utilizing its most expensive asset—its employees. The study contended that a principal reason for this is that a shift in work values and expectations has profoundly changed the workplace in the last few decades. A majority of workers have replaced the traditional work ethic goals—money, success, rigid moral standards, company loyalty—with new values. Doing the job as well as possible is no longer the goal and the source of satisfaction. Rather what is important is having work that allows freedom, autonomy, and opportunities to be creative and innovative. Workers holding "new values" are less willing to subordinate their needs to those of their employer.[40]

Many factors have contributed to these changes in work values and are reflected in the postal work system. Increased automation and mechanization of tasks removes workers from control over the process or the results of their work and leaves them feeling like mere "cogs in the machine," easily replaced and easily controlled. At the same time, the gradual increase in the level of formal education attained by workers makes them feel they should have more control over their lives than their parents or grandparents had. In addition, the focus of mass education now is mainly on imparting information and training people for particular occupations—a shift from its traditional emphasis on instilling values such as punctuality, discipline, and the value of work. And once on the job, a worker is less likely to draw his or her principal satisfaction from it, as increased leisure time allows pursuit of activities outside of work that offer satisfactions the job may not provide.[41]

Whatever the reasons for the changing values and expectations of its workers, the Postal Service has not kept pace with those changes. While the majority of postal employees hold these so-called new values, the Postal Service continues to operate within a controlled, authoritarian value structure. Thus, in the words of the YSW study, "there is a mismatch between the current (and likely future) work values of many Postal Service employees, and the organizational realities of the Postal Service." This "mismatch" is most apparent at lower organizational levels, where the commitment on the part of craft workers is particularly weak. The work values and attitudes of these employees indicate that under the right circumstances they are inclined to "contribute substantially to the Postal Service," but generally speaking, these employees are not exerting what the Yankelovich study called "discretionary effort"—any effort beyond what one has to expend in order to avoid being penalized or fired.[42]

The heart of the problem seems to be that these postal workers feel that management does not care about their needs and expectations and does not listen to them or permit them to be involved in their jobs through discussions about work-related issues or concerns. Moreover, the organization still has within its front-line managerial ranks too many supervisors whose authoritarian behavior and know-it-all attitudes dampen the enthusiasm and commitment of workers.

The clear challenge for the Postal Service during the next decade is to find ways to narrow this gap between employees' potential (their untapped commitment) and their actual performance. The Postal Service is pursuing two principal strategies toward this goal.

First, the Postal Service is trying to do a better job of training front-line supervisors and educating them about the benefits of communicating with employees and getting them directly involved in decisions to improve service, labor-management relations, and the work environment. The theory behind this effort is that those supervisors who demonstrably listen to their workers and are responsive to their suggestions elicit better work from them.

Toward this end, the Postal Service in 1985 completely redesigned its training programs for newly appointed first-level supervisors and associate office managers (some 4,000 to 6,000 a year) to try to develop in them strong interpersonal skills and participative management styles. The new program, called the Supervisory Training System (STS), is divided into three major phases. The first part, called "Supervisory Basics," provides training in the human relations, administrative, and functional skills needed immediately for on-the-job success. This phase is an eighty-hour program presented by the local Postal Employee Development Center immediately upon the promotion of an individual to an initial-level supervisory position. Approximately two to four months later, the supervisor attends the Postal Service's Management Academy for eighty more hours of resident training entitled "Skills Building." This segment of STS divides the curriculum evenly between emphasis on human relations skills building and on specific functional skills. The final segment of STS, presented five to six months after the student has completed the "Skills Building" course, consists of a one-week resident course in "Supervisory Leadership." This capstone to the STS teaches advanced interpersonal, analytical, and problem-solving skills. In sum, this program represents a major commitment on the part of the Postal Service to training supervisory personnel to value craft employees, to communicate with them, and to encourage innovative ideas.

A more important step in that same direction—and the second part of the Postal Service's overall strategy to narrow the gap between employees' potential and their actual performance—more directly focuses on employee involvement. The Postal Service has established an extensive process to involve employees in decision-making and to improve the work environment by creating a management environment that is more participatory and less adversarial. The Employee Involvement/Quality of Work Life (EI/ QWL) process is based on the belief that the Postal Service, its employees, and the public will reap benefits when management and employees develop more effective ways of working together. The groundwork for the EI/QWL process was laid in 1982, when Postal Service management signed agreements with three of the four principal postal unions (all but the APWU). Each of the participating unions established steering committees with postal management at the national, regional, and local levels to implement the process at selected sites. By the end of 1987 the process had expanded around the country to include over 4,850 active work teams or "quality circles" operating in virtually every division, management sectional center, bulk mail center and airport mail facility in the country.

The Postal Service's EI/QWL process has not been without its share of problems and disappointments. Some employees lack the patience required to deal with such a large-scale effort to change things, and others fail to recognize that the Postal Service has adopted the process as a business policy. Moreover, although an estimated 60,000 postal employees have received training and are involved in some capacity in one of the structured processes, both union and management officials agree that they have only scratched the surface in making EI/QWL an integral part of the way the Postal Service conducts its daily business. Still, both sides are enthusiastic with the results to date. Hundreds of effective programs and productive ideas for work changes have been developed by employee involvement work teams around the country, leading to improved customer service, enhanced safety in the workplace, more effective operations, and decreases in the use of sick leave and the number of grievances filed at work units. In short, there seems to be sufficient accomplishment to date to indicate that EI/QWL continues to be an appropriate strategy for the Postal Service to pursue.

The Postal Service is taking seriously these issues of work life quality since top management apparently has become committed to the view that only by achieving better teamwork and harmony from within can the Postal Service meet the challenges of the future: keeping the size of the rapidly expanding postal work force in check, compensating workers fairly but not excessively, and eliciting efficient, productive work from postal employees.

Endnotes

1. See Michael L. Brookshire and Michael L. Rogers, *Collective Bargaining in the Public Sector* (Lexington, Mass: Lexington Books, 1977), p. 2.
2. There had been an apparent break in the impasse when James Rademacher, president of the National Association of Letter Carriers, and President Richard Nixon met at the White House and reached an agreement that called for union support of a noncorporate "postal authority" in return for White House support for postal pay raises. But the other postal unions and some members of Congress felt displeased over having been excluded from the meeting at which the decision was reached, and the compromise collapsed.

See Harold E. Dolenga, "An Analytical Case Study of the Policy Formation
Process: Postal Reform and Reorganization" (Ph.D. diss., Northwestern University, 1973), pp. 529–40.
3. *New York Times*, March 18, 1970, p. 1.
4. *New York Times*, March 25, 1970, p. 1.
5. These tactics of the assorted interests are described in *Postal Record* (August 1974), pp. 10, 11.
6. Ibid.
7. Ibid., and *American Postal Worker* (October 1973), p. 10.
8. *New York Times*, April 19, 1978, p. 15.
9. Ibid.
10. *Washington Post*, March 22, 1978, p. E2.
11. *Washington Post*, May 17, 1978, p. D2.
12. *New York Times*, June 19, 1978, p. 16.
13. *Washington Post*, June 14, 1978, p. C2.
14. *New York Times*, June 19, 1978, p. 16.
15. *New York Times*, July 15, 1978, p. 43.
16. *New York Times*, July 22, 1978, p. 8; *New York Times*, July 24, 1978, p. 1.
17. *New York Times*, July 22, 1978, p. 1.
18. *Associated Press*, July 25, 1978.
19. *Washington Post*, August 26, 1978, p. A1.
20. *New York Times*, November 14, 1980, p. A18.
21. Ibid., and *New York Times*, November 2, 1980, p. 51.
22. *Washington Post*, July 20, 1981, p. A11.
23. Quoted in *New York Times*, April 16, 1981, p. B14.
24. *Washington Post*, July 10, 1981, p. E4: and *New York Times*, July 15, 1981, p. A12.
25. *New York Times*, July 17, 1981, p. A10.
26. *New York Times*, July 19, 1981, p. A22.
27. *Postal Leader*, April 17, 1984, p. 5.
28. *New York Times*, July 26, 1984, pp. A1, A18.
29. *New York Times*, August 12, 1984, p. 28.
30. See U.S. Postal Service, *Comprehensive Statement on Postal Operations*, 1985, p. 7.
31. *Postal Leader*, August 4, 1987, p. 2.
32. *United States Code*, Title 39, sec. 101(C).
33. Joseph F. Quinn, "Postal Sector Wages," *Industrial Relations* 18 (Winter 1979): 92–96.
34. Douglas K. Adie, *An Evaluation of Postal Service Wage Rates* (Washington, D.C.: American Enterprise Institute, 1977). See also Douglas K. Adie, "How Have Postal Workers Fared Since the 1970 Act?" in *Perspectives on Postal Service Issues*, ed. Roger Sherman (Washington, D.C.: American Enterprise Institute, 1980), pp. 74–93.
35. Sharon Smith, "Are Postal Workers Over- or Underpaid?" *Industrial Relations* 15 (May 1976): 168–76.
36. Michael L. Wachter, "Wage Comparability in the United States Postal Service" (May 1984), typewritten.
37. Ibid.

38. Ibid.
39. *New York Times,* July 30, 1984, p. A8.
40. Yankelovich, Skelly and White, Inc., "A Study of the Work Values and Commitment of United States Postal Service Employees—Summary Report" (October 1983).
41. These points are drawn from Sharon Greene Patton, "The Changing Work Force," *Postal Life* (September/October, 1986): 3–9.
42. Yankelovich, Skelly and White, Inc., pp. 5, 6.

Chapter 5

POSTAL RATES AND RATE-MAKING

Few things about the Postal Service in recent years are more noticeable to the citizen-client than the sharp increase in the rates charged for mail services. Since the passage of the Postal Reorganization Act in 1970, first-class letter rates have been increased on eight different occasions, raising the price of a first-class stamp fourfold, from 6 cents to 25 cents (see Exhibit 5-1). Sharp increases of this kind for all mail classes (and much higher percentage increases in second-class, for example) are the consequence of two factors. First, the postal system's costs have soared in this period for reasons examined earlier. Second, the Postal Reorganization Act requires that operating revenue equal, "as nearly as practicable," the system's total costs—in other words, the Postal Service is expected to try to break even. Thus, as its costs increase, so do its revenue requirements and, thus, so do its rates.

But while the increases in the price of stamps are quite noticeable to consumers of postal services, the complicated legal and political processes that determine the frequency and size of those increases are little understood. This chapter describes the institutions responsible for postal rate-making and analyzes the procedures they follow. It also explores some of the difficulties associated with this whole process and the controversies surrounding it.

The Institutional Context of Rate-Making

Usually overlooked as a reason for why postal rates have gone up so much since the reorganization of the postal system in 1970 is

May 16, 1971	8 cents
March 2, 1974	10 cents
December 31, 1975	13 cents
May 29, 1978	15 cents
March 22, 1981	18 cents
November 1, 1981	20 cents
February 17, 1985	22 cents
April 3, 1988	25 cents

Exhibit 5-1   First-Class Rate Increases, 1971-1988 (cost of first ounce).

the fact that until that time rates were artificially depressed by legislative rate-making in which political considerations were more highly valued than economic ones. Rates were set by Congress and the President through routine legislative processes that were informal, generally perfunctory, and highly politicized, affording powerful special mailing interests opportunities to shape postal rate structures in their own best interests.

As Chapter 1 showed, the many deficiencies of legislative rate-making were fully apparent to postal reformers, who found a better alternative in the standard model for public utility regulation. At the time, the Post Office was the only public service of national importance for which the legislature had retained the prerogative for setting rates. The rates for natural gas, electricity, telephone, and transportation services all were being regulated by full-time commissions that, with the aid of technically trained staffs, approved rates after reviewing extensive accounting and engineering data and economic evidence. These commissions based rate decisions on the record of evidentiary proceedings in which due process safeguards were carefully observed. Postal reformers wanted postal rates set under similar arrangements.

Although reformers appreciated the differences between postal service and the services rendered by traditional public utilities, the differences, they argued, were primarily in form. And although postal reformers recognized that other factors besides cost and economic efficiency were properly to be considered in establishing rates and fees for postal services, they concluded that "economic science does provide standards for postal rate-making"; and they urged, therefore, that procedures and economic principles observed in the operation and regulation of other economic enterprises should be applied to postal services also.[1]

Thus, when Congress designed the current postal rate-making

process in 1970, it created the Postal Rate Commission (PRC) as an independent establishment of the executive branch of the federal government. The PRC has a staff of about seventy persons (mostly lawyers, economists, and accountants), headed by five commissioners who are appointed by the President and confirmed by the Senate. The President designates one commissioner as chairman, and the chairman's tenure during his or her term of office is at the pleasure of the President. The commission's major responsibility is to submit recommended decisions to the governors of the Postal Service on postage rates and fees and mail classifications. The commission publishes proposals in the *Federal Register*, schedules public hearings on rate and classification changes, conducts those hearings and assembles from witnesses' testimony a factual record for decision, analyzes the record, and renders a recommended decision.

Congress made it quite clear that the Postal Rate Commission was to be an expert body charged with independently evaluating presentations—including evidence intended to prove facts, as well as legal and policy views—by both the Postal Service and interested members of the public. The commission must utilize its expertise to apply technical costing and important policy criteria to reach independent recommendations on postal rate and classification matters. The commission is required to make detailed findings of fact based on the evidence of record; affirmatively evaluate numerous statutory factors; and balance the goal of a healthy postal service with the needs and rights of American individuals and businesses.

The legislative history of the Postal Reorganization Act emphasizes the need for an independent rate commission that would balance these considerations fairly. The due process rights accorded to parties appearing before the PRC are meant to assure that all interested persons will have a fair opportunity to learn how Postal Service proposals will affect them, and offer suggestions or criticisms, *before* those proposals are implemented. The detailed opinions issued by the PRC evaluate both the position of postal management and the comments of attentive interests, and provide the governors with a carefully documented analysis of all factors material to its recommended decision. This process is meant to assure balanced consideration of all relevant issues, and it is a process that, on balance, has worked quite well. (It is worth noting that when the General Accounting Office surveyed representatives of the large mail-users' organizations that appear before the PRC, the respondents generally gave high marks to the current rate-making process. In particular, a majority found the hearing process efficient and effective.)[2]

The commission has distinct responsibilities separate from those of any other body. It provides expert technical analysis of factual matters and applicable theoretical concepts. It also provides the only opportunity for interested persons to present to an independent body their views concerning potential rate and classification changes.

The commission also is required by law to appoint an Officer of the Commission (OOC) "to represent the interests of the general public" in proceedings before the commission.[3] This has proved to be an important provision because the OOC, assisted by attorneys and rate analysts, has normally represented the public interest by reviewing and testing the proposals of other participants and also by proposing its own alternative comprehensive rate proposals.

The Postal Rate-Making Process

The process of making new postal rates is complicated.[4] It begins when the operating management of the Postal Service believes it needs to change rates and asks the Board of Governors to authorize a formal request to the PRC. When the governors have given such authorization, the Postal Service's general counsel files a request with the PRC. This formal request includes the material considered to be the Postal Service's direct testimony and consists of volumes of information and data explaining the nature, scope, significance, and effect of the proposed rate and fee changes. Perhaps the most important parts of the request are the data explaining the attribution and assignment of costs to specific services or classes of mail and the design of rates based on those costing data.

Within five days of receiving the Postal Service's formal request for a rate increase, the PRC provides notice of the proposed rate change in the *Federal Register* and gives interested parties a fixed period of time to file petitions to intervene in the rate proceeding. Persons granted permission to intervene are considered parties to the proceeding and may actively participate in the rate proceeding. (To convey a sense of the array of intervening interests, Exhibit 5-2 lists the intervenors in Docket No. R87-1, the omnibus rate case concluded in March 1988.) Interested persons not requesting intervenor status may file petitions as "limited participants" who are entitled to file briefs and present evidence that is relevant to the issues in which they are interested.

Advo-system, Inc.
Agricultural Publishers Association, Inc.*
Air Courier Conference of America
Alliance of Nonprofit Mailers
American Bankers Association
American Newspaper Publishers Association
American Postal Workers Union (AFL-CIO)
American Retail Federation
The Association of American Publishers, Inc. and The Recording Industry
    Association of America, Inc.
Association of Business Publishers
Association of Paid Circulation Publications*
The Brooklyn Union Gas Company
Elmer Cerin*
Classroom Publishers Association*
Coalition of Non-Postal Media
Coalition of Religious Press Associations
Council of Public Utility Mailers
Direct Marketing Association, Inc.
Direct Marketing Sector, Harte-Hanks Communications, Inc.
Reuben H. Donnelley Corporation
Dow Jones & Company, Inc.
Envelope Manufacturers Association of America
Federal Express Corporation
Financial Stationers Association*
Fingerhut Corporation
The First Class Group
Florida Gift Fruit Shippers Association
The Hearst Corporation*
Industry Council for Tangible Assets
International Circulation Managers Association*
Magazine Publishers Association
Mail Advertising Service Association International*
Mail Order Association of America
Mayhill Publications, Inc.*
McGraw-Hill, Inc.
Meredith Corporation*
National Association of Letter Carriers (AFL-CIO)
National Association of Presort Mailers
National Newspaper Association
Newsweek, Inc.
New York State Consumer Protection Board
Nonprofit Mailers Federation*
Office of the Consumer Advocate (OCA), Postal Rate Commission

Exhibit 5-2   Intervenors in Docket No. R87-1.

Parcel Shippers Association
J. C. Penney Company, Inc.
Pi Electronics Corporation
Pitney Bowes Inc.*
David B. Popkin*
Post Card Distributors & Manufacturers Associations*
The Reader's Digest Association, Inc.
Red Tag News Publications Association, Inc.*
Small Business Legislative Council*
TCOM Systems, Inc.*
Third Class Mail Association
Time Incorporated
Times Mirror Company*
Triangle Publications, Inc.*
United Parcel Service
U.S. News & World Report*
U.S. Telephone Association
Warshawsky & Company
Westvaco Corporation*
United States Postal Service

*Denotes limited participants

Exhibit 5-2 Continued.

Once intervenor petitions are approved and limited participants identified, the PRC schedules the first prehearing conference, which is not required but is useful for expediting the process inasmuch as it provides an opportunity for defining and simplifying the issues and reaching agreement on the various exhibits that will constitute the evidence to be presented at the hearings. Consistent with the arrangements made at the conference, intervenors and the Officer of the Commission begin discovery on the Postal Service's direct testimony. Discovery includes three basic components:

1. *Interrogatories.* Participants prepare written requests for relevant information from other participants in the proceeding that must be answered. Each interrogatory must be answered separately and fully in writing and under oath, unless the party objects to answering the interrogatory (in which case the reasons for objection are stated in lieu of an answer).
2. *Requests for Production of Documents.* Any participant may request any other participant to produce and permit the participant making the request to inspect and copy any

documents or things that are relevant to the rate proceeding
and that are in the custody or control of the participant upon
whom the request is served.
3. *Requests for Admissions*. Any participant may serve upon any
other participant a written request for the admission of any
relevant, unprivileged facts, including the genuineness of any
documents or exhibits to be presented in the hearing.

Parties have ten days in which to object to answering these
requests. Otherwise, answers must be provided within twenty
days to the requesting party, the PRC, and any other party
requesting to receive such information.

If a party fails to comply with another party's request to provide
information, the requesting party may make a motion to the
presiding officer to compel the requested party to provide the
information. The presiding officer rules on motions to compel
answers (no time limit is established). Parties may, within five
days, appeal to the presiding officer to request that all of the
commissioners consider a motion; however, such appeals are appropriate only in extremely limited circumstances. (Motions, rul-
ings, and appeals may occur at any phase of the proceedings.)

Since the Postal Service files direct testimony in support of its
application for a rate change, the OOC and intervenors first direct
discovery to the Postal Service. This process allows parties to (1)
understand fully the Service's case and (2) select questions and
answers they believe should be included in the record and submit
them as their "written cross-examination" of the particular Postal
Service witness.

After this process is complete, the OOC and intervenors submit
their written cross-examination for the record and orally cross-
examine the witnesses to the extent necessary to round out the
written cross-examination. (Under PRC rules, unlike court rules,
permission must be granted to engage in oral cross-examination.)
A second conference may be held prior to this hearing. On the
basis of the OOC's and intervenor's views of the Postal Service's
request for a rate change and other data obtained during discovery,
the OOC and intervenors file their direct written testimony with
the PRC.

Following this filing, the Postal Service has the opportunity for
discovery concerning the presentations of the OOC and intervenors. During this stage, intervenors also begin discovery of the
OOC and other intervenors and vice versa. This phase of discovery
also leads to the filing of written cross-examination.

The Postal Service files its written cross-examination and conducts any necessary oral examination of OOC and intervenor witnesses at further public hearings. Similarly, the OOC and intervenors cross-examine each other's witnesses. Before these hearings, a third prehearing conference may be held.

Any party—intervenors, the OOC or the Postal Service—may offer rebuttal testimony, also subject to cross-examination, at another set of public hearings. The PRC then closes the evidentiary record.

Once the evidentiary record is closed, the briefing period begins in which the commission gives all parties the opportunities to file briefs. A brief is to contain a clear, concise, definitive statement of the party's position regarding the Postal Service proposal; a discussion of the evidence; and proposed findings and conclusions. After the briefs are filed, the commission may allow all parties to present oral argument, when time permits and the nature and complexity of the issues warrant such argument. All these procedures are intended to provide an open forum for all interested parties to attempt to prove relevant facts and express their legal and policy views—either pro or con—on proposed Postal Service changes in postal rates.

When this whole process is over, the commission has before it the monumental task of analyzing the entire record—the various filings, testimony of experts, interrogatories and answers, exhibits, briefs and replies, and oral arguments. The commission, in evaluating all this information (running to tens of thousands of pages in total), is required to take into account the following criteria set down by Congress in section 3622(b) of the Postal Reorganization Act (*United States Code*, Title 39):

1. The establishment and maintenance of a fair and equitable schedule.

2. The value of the mail service actually provided each class or type of mail service to both the sender and the recipient, including but not limited to the collection, mode of transportation, and priority of delivery.

3. The requirement that each class of mail or type of mail service bear the direct and indirect postal costs attributable to that class or type plus that portion of all other costs of the Postal Service reasonably assignable to such class or type.

4. The effect of rate increases upon the general public, business mail users, and enterprises in the private sector of the economy engaged in the delivery of mail matter other than letters.

5. The available alternative means of sending and receiving letters and other mail matter at reasonable costs.

6. The degree of preparation of mail for delivery into the postal

*system performed by the mailer and its effect upon reducing costs
to the Postal Service.*

*7. Simplicity of structure for the entire schedule and simple,
identifiable relationships between the rates or fees charged the
various classes of mail for postal services.*

8. Such other factors as the Commission deems appropriate.

When the commission has finally made its judgment of the rate
proposal, it issues a recommended decision to the Postal Service
Board of Governors. This recommended decision comes as a
detailed and extensive document that explains the legal and policy
principles governing the commission's recommendation and includes supporting evidence and data. The PRC must render its
decision on rate cases within ten months from when the Postal
Service submits its original request. If, however, the commission
determines that the Postal Service has unreasonably delayed the
rate proceedings by failing to respond within a reasonable time to
any lawful order of the commission, the PRC may extend the ten-
month period by one day for each day of such delay. If the PRC
fails to render a decision or extend the proceedings within the ten-
month period, the Postal Service may establish temporary changes
in rates and fees in accordance with the proposed changes under
consideration by the commission. These temporary changes cannot
remain in effect longer than 150 days after the PRC renders its
decision to the governors.

When the Postal Service's Board of Governors receives a recommended decision from the commission, the board may approve
the recommendation and order the rates to be put in effect, or it
may completely reject the proposal and start all over. The governors are also free to reject the PRC's recommended decision and
resubmit the rate request to the commission for its reconsideration. When the PRC then renders a new decision, the governors
can modify the decision by a unanimous vote.

Professionalism, Expertise, and Information in
Postal Rate-Making

Persons long familiar with postal rate-making processes cannot
help but be struck by the sharp contrasts between the current
process and the legislative rate-making method that was ended by
the 1970 reorganization of the postal system. Perhaps the most
obvious difference is in the relations among the Postal Service, the
organized mail users, and the rate reviewers (previously Congress,
now the rate commissioners). Legislative rate-making was handled

in a highly informal, hail-fellow atmosphere in which political maneuvering was the rule. But that process made it too easy for organized mailing interests to exercise untoward influence over postal rates. The current process, with its formal, depoliticized, legalistic, adversary hearings is much more rigorous and professional.

Some of the rules under which the Postal Rate Commission operates are meant to safeguard procedural fairness and to isolate PRC commissioners and staff members from the pressures and blandishments of organized mail users. For example, rules governing *ex parte* communications prohibit employees of the commission, and the commissioners themselves, from engaging in one-sided discussions regarding either a substantive or a procedural matter that is at issue or that may become an issue before the commission.[5] The rule, common among regulatory agencies, requires the commission to solicit rebuttal information from all interested parties if it accepts information from any interested party.

Other rules of conduct tightly restrict commissioners and employees in their financial holdings in any entity that may be significantly affected by rates, fees, or classifications of mail. Soliciting or accepting gifts, favors, entertainment, and the like from parties having or wanting business with the Postal Service is forbidden. The rules even direct each employee to pay personal bills "in a manner which the commission determines does not, under the circumstances, reflect adversely on the commission as his employer."[6] These and other provisions are intended to increase the likelihood of integrity and independence in regulating postal rates.

Much of the rigor (and contentiousness) of the postal rate-making process stems from its trial-like, adversary proceedings, which place a premium on expertise and challenge. Each party to a rate case strives for every possible advantage and tries to expose weaknesses in opponents' arguments; intervenors must therefore try to have good enough data to make credible arguments, and to be successful must have evidence that can withstand all-around close scrutiny. Rate cases center on careful analysis of extensive data about postal revenue requirements, cost attributions, demand elasticities, economic effects on large mailers, and the like. Information and expertise are thus among the most important resources for influence in the postal rate-making process.

Consequently, mailers' associations participating in the rate proceedings hire professional economists and cost analysts to bolster their arguments and to dissect the presentations of other intervenors. For example, the huge Direct Marketing Association (DMA) hires Arthur Eden, a former assistant postmaster general for rates and classifications, to help present its own case and to dissect the Postal Service's cost attributions and assignments.

High-priced Washington lawyers also figure prominently in the process. After all, the legal formalities are almost as tangled and complex as the economic ones. Since evidentiary hearings are very strict on procedure, an intervenor's chances of successful participation rest on the shoulders of counsel who can maneuver through the labyrinth of legal notices, pleadings, interrogatories, examination and cross-examination, and findings. So important is expert legal assistance in this process that the large mailers' associations spare no expense in retaining the best legal help they can find. The DMA, for example, hires partners from the prestigious Washington law firm, Covington and Burling. The Parcel Shippers Association hires the services of Timothy J. May, a former Post Office Department counsel who now works under the shingle of Patton, Boggs, and Blow. And when the Federal Express Corporation was looking for someone to represent it before the PRC in the 1987–88 omnibus rate case, it turned to Jim Finch, who once served as deputy postmaster general and senior assistant postmaster general for finance.

The heavy reliance on economists and lawyers and other professionals in the rate-making process means that the costs of intervening in these lengthy rate proceedings are substantial—ranging from tens of thousands of dollars to over a million. Large organizations or trade associations—such as the DMA, Advo-System, Inc., the American Newspaper Publishers Association, Federal Express, the Magazine Publishers Association, Newsweek, Time Incorporated, and United Parcel Service—have an advantage in that they can afford to participate in the lengthy legal proceedings. They can hire the lawyers to present their case, the consultants to prepare their economic forecasts or their economic analyses of the rate proposals, and the expert witnesses to substantiate their case. They have the resources to prepare the many required copies of each document, and they have the staff resources to devote to monitoring legislative and regulatory hearings that may affect the ongoing proceeding. But all these costs are so great as virtually to preclude the involvement of small organizations of mail users or interested individual mailers anxious to press their case but lacking substantial financial resources. This does not necessarily mean that the interests and concerns of the general public get ignored in this process since, as noted above, the PRC has within it a whole suborganization (the OOC) charged with representing the general public's interests.

One problem with the current process is that although mail users and competing delivery systems invest huge sums of money in acquiring their own information and expertise, they still find themselves at a disadvantage in facing the Postal Service, which is in a superior position as a result of its control over scarce information. The Postal Service chooses what kinds of data it will generate and release. Though the Postal Service is supposed to honor requests from rate-case participants for information, it can effectively refrain from doing so merely by dragging its feet or claiming not to have the data. Even the Postal Rate Commission has to depend on the Postal Service's goodwill and informational beneficence since the PRC lacks explicit statutory authority to prescribe or require the Postal Service to collect or release particular types of data. Postal management sees such matters as its exclusive domain, thus tying the PRC and parties to the proceedings to the data the Postal Service is willing to make available.

In the 1970s the Postal Service was the subject of bitter complaint from the PRC and from intervenors who believed the Service was not sufficiently forthcoming and open with information and data. But the antagonism on this score has diminished in recent years as the Postal Service and the rate commission have established a more cooperative relationship that has led to more accessible and intelligible information. For example, the commission now has access to valuable information about the Postal Service's congressional budget submission—information that makes it easier for the commission to do financial analyses of the Postal Service.

The revolution in computer technology in the late 1970s also has changed both the nature of some of the data and the character of the disputes over information. That is, increasingly the struggles over information have to do with whether one party's data can be mounted on the computers of other parties. This is especially problematic when the Postal Service bases its analyses on computerized cost models of great mathematical complexity and then refuses to release sufficient documentation on the model to permit other parties to judge whether it meets threshold standards of reliability. This happened in the rate case that led to the 1981 rate increases. The Postal Service would not release sufficient documentation of its Mail Processing Cost Model, so the rate commission was forced to strike testimony that relied on that model for its basic numbers, thus foregoing useful evidence and diminishing the case record.

This is no small problem for the rate commission since it has been receiving a growing amount of evidence in recent years based on computer studies. In staking out its position on the issue of the admissibility of computer-based evidence, the Postal Rate Commission has followed the lead of the federal courts, which require that such evidence have a foundation in the form of documentation allowing that kind of analysis. The premise is that findings of fact cannot be based on the output of a "black box"—a computer program or study that is unexplained and cannot be replicated and tested by interested parties.[7]

Controversies over Postal Costing and Pricing Methods

When Congress created the current institutional arrangements for setting postal rates, it intended that rate-making would be in the hands of experts who would set rates reasonably—that is, at levels that would not prove burdensome to the public but that would produce sufficient revenue to cover costs. For the most part, all this has happened. Congress may or may not have anticipated the extent to which the postal rate-making process would remain highly controversial and contentious.

Postal rate-making involves three major elements: the determination of the revenue requirement (that is, the total revenues needed by the Postal Service to cover its projected costs); the assigning of that revenue to various classes of mail; and the definition of a detailed rate structure for each subclass of mail. As the following analysis shows, there is virtually universal agreement with the principle that each class should cover the costs that it causes directly (its avoidable or incremental costs). In postal rate cases, this is defined as those costs that vary directly with the volume of that class. But there are also joint and common costs within the postal system—costs that cannot be assigned to any particular class but which are incurred on behalf of all. Assigning the joint and common costs requires discretion; there is no way around it. Disagreement over the exercise of that discretion by the Postal Service and the Postal Rate Commission has fueled high-stakes controversies over postal rates and rate-making.

At issue in these disputes are two basic questions: (1) whether the Postal Service has accurately determined the costs it incurs in providing each class of mail service; and (2) whether the rates for the various classes are imposing on them more or less than their legally prescribed share of the system's total costs. There is sharp disagreement on these questions in part because the financial stakes are high for mailing interests and in part because it is difficult to produce the data needed to answer them. Moreover, those data that exist are by no means incontestable.

The issue of cross-subsidization seems especially controversial. Virtually every interest argues that it is paying the freight for somebody else. Business mailers contend they are cross-subsidizing occasional users. Presorters say that the discounts they receive for presorting are insufficient in view of the avoided cost that their work-sharing produces, and that they are therefore subsidizing nonpresorted mail. Senders say they cross-subsidize receivers. Newspaper publishers, eager for advertising revenues, complain that direct-mail advertisers have an unfair advantage because their third-class mail rates are, in effect, subsidized by more expensive first-class mail. Although there is no unambiguous answer to the question of whether (or to what extent or in what directions) cross-subsidization is occurring, many observers point to it as a persistent problem. Kathleen Conkey of Ralph Nader's Center for Study of Responsive Law has articulated this view about as clearly as anyone:[8]

> *The reorganized Postal Service has not eliminated cross subsidies—it has simply hidden them in a jungle of economic theory and costing methodologies. Indeed, the inability to establish a firm rate structure based on sound economic and social judgments has been one of the reorganization's most profound failures. Rates remain as confused and unfair as they were when Congress set them according to the whims of strong special interests.*

The source of the problem here is that the Postal Service is an industry that produces more than one output (in this case, different classes or kinds of mail services for letters, parcels, circulars, "overnight mail," and so on) through the use of many of the same primary resources (post offices, delivery vehicles, personnel, and the like). These shared production resources create common costs of production—that is, "institutional costs," which are simply part of making the system itself available and are thus common to all classes of mail. But the presence of these institutional costs greatly complicates determination of the basic cost structure, the correct allocation of costs among the various classes of service, and establishment of an appropriate and generally acceptable set of rates. Hence the continuing controversies.

At the heart of the matter is the question of how the total costs of operating the Postal Service are allocated among the various classes of mail. When a congressional conference committee met in 1970 to thrash out the final version of the reorganization bill, it adopted a Senate provision that contained one of the act's most important standards: "Each class of mail or type of mail service should bear the direct and indirect postal costs attributable to that class plus that portion of other costs of the postal service reasonably assignable to such class or type."[9] In short, Congress directed that each class was thenceforth to pay the costs directly attributable to it plus some share of the system's common, or institutional, costs.

But the act left unspecified (and thus gave the Postal Service discretion in choosing) the methods to be used in calculating the attributable costs and assigning the remaining institutional costs among the various classes of mail. Most of the debate in rate hearings and resulting court challenges is over just how to do this. A series of court cases, known as the "Greeting Card" cases, arose out of challenges to recommended decisions by the Postal Rate Commission. These cases produced a conflict between two federal district courts, which was eventually resolved by the Supreme Court. The nub of the issue involved in these cases concerned the criteria (in section 3622[b]) to be used in assigning costs—that is, the nine criteria (listed earlier) that Congress required be used for judging the fairness of rate increases.

The law does not prescribe specific methods for rate determination, so the Postal Service and the Postal Rate Commission tried over the years to fashion a workable rate-making methodology using the rather ambiguous language and conflicting goals specified by Congress. Private intervenors challenged these methods in court, hoping to influence future rate-making decisions. Eventually, the court decisions became determinative. Although the courts cannot actually set rates, their expressions of dissatisfaction with the rate process have always strongly influenced the actions of the Postal Service and the Postal Rate Commission. For several years, the two agencies followed the D.C. Circuit Court's interpretation of section 3622(b), even though they did not agree with that interpretation.

The Initial Costing and Pricing Methods

In the first three rate cases after the postal system's reorganization (leading to the rate increases of 1972, 1975, and 1976), postal management used a "short-run" costing method that attributed to mail classes only volume-related costs, leaving out long-run capacity costs. That is, to be attributed to a particular class under this costing method, a cost had to be variable, fluctuating from year to year with changes in the volume of mail in that class. Thus, included in the many costs left unattributed by this short-run costing method were:[10]

> . . . *all costs for the purchase and lease of buildings, the purchase of equipment and vehicles, expenses for vehicle drivers, vehicle maintenance, building and equipment maintenance and custodial cost, the cost of a mailman's driving or walking his route to deliver mail, one-third of purchased transportation, most supplies including gasoline and oil, and a considerable portion of clerk's time (including window service).*

Most economists consider expenses such as these to be long-run incremental costs, which under proper costing practices should be assigned to the classes of mail for whose benefit the outlays are made.[11] But in the first three rate cases, the Postal Service argued (and the rate commission agreed) that accurate data simply were not available to permit long-run incremental costing. The rate commission and the intervenors had no way to challenge the assertion.

It is also true, however, that the Postal Service had no incentive to move quickly to produce those data. The short-run costing method was attractive because at the time it left 51 percent of the system's total costs for the Postal Service to "assign" among the various classes of mail according to its discretion. Since assigning these unattributed, "institutional" costs allowed the Postal Service room to juggle the total rate burden among the various mail classes, the methods used in that assignment naturally raised substantial disagreement.

Also controversial was the Postal Service's use of a pricing formula, developed by two Postal Service economists, that included three factors: (1) the estimated elasticity of demand for each class of mail; (2) the "value" of each class of mail; and (3) the competitive stance of the Postal Service in those classes in which it lacked a legal monopoly. The first of these factors was purportedly the most important of the three. That is, postal economists spread the organization's institutional costs primarily by marking up the marginal cost of each product in inverse proportion to the presumed elasticity of its demand.[12]

The Postal Service claimed that this application of the "inverse elasticity rule" (IER) was the best way to find the optimum rate for each class of mail and service. In theory, the optimum rate is the rate that maximizes the volume of mail while recovering all the related attributable costs and making some contribution to the fixed overhead, so that in the end total costs are recovered. If prices for each service were set at marginal cost, the Postal Service would fail to recover its substantial institutional costs. Thus, the Postal Service used the IER as a guide in setting prices above marginal costs to recover the institutional costs, at the same time interfering as little as possible with an economically efficient allocation of resources.[13] Theoretically, that is, in a comparison of two products, if a rate is raised more for the product with a less elastic demand, the change in price will induce proportionately less change in volume than if the rate is raised for a product with a more elastic demand. And the smaller the change from the volumes that would have been in effect if marginal cost prices had prevailed, the smaller the deviation from the economically optimal use that would usually occur at marginal cost prices.[14]

But the application of the IER in postal costing and rate-making caused controversies because economic theory approves the use of the IER only if two prerequisites are met: (1) the enterprise must be at a stage of productive capacity at which it has decreasing costs with scale; and (2) the correct elasticities of demand must be known and applied.[15]

The Postal Service has not, however, been incontestably in accord with either of these criteria. The debate over economies of scale in the postal system is far from being settled one way or another. And as for the second prerequisite, top postal economists have openly acknowledged that "the techniques for measuring demand elasticity are generally inadequate," holding that "conventional techniques for computing demand elasticity can, at best, provide only approximate indicators of price sensitivity."[16]

Because of this unreliability of the data on the elasticity of demand for various postal services, postal economists took what they felt was the "pragmatic course" of ranking the main categories of mail in accordance with *their judgment* of the relative demand elasticity for each class, and then using these rankings as their primary, but not exclusive, basis for assigning unattributed costs among the various classes.

Even if the inverse elasticity rule is appropriate in setting postal rates, its use in conjunction with the short-run costing method was a recipe for controversy. According to critics, the net effect of the postal costing and pricing methods was to permit the Postal Service to place an inappropriate share of the rate burden on first-class mail, which to date has had a less elastic demand than other classes largely because the Postal Service has a legal monopoly over it. The short-run incremental costing method leaves a large share of the postal system's costs in the "fixed" cost category, thus providing the Postal Service with more discretion in assigning all those costs however it likes.

Challenges to the Methods

Naturally, these costing and pricing methods adopted by the Postal Service and sanctioned by the Postal Rate Commission generated considerable controversy. Perhaps most critical was Seymour J. Wenner, who was the hearing examiner in the first two rate cases. In the initial decision he rendered in the first rate case, Wenner criticized the Postal Service's loose approach to cost attribution and its judgmental cost assignments. He reasoned that the Postal Service's decision to allocate only short-run costs to the different classes did not sufficiently reflect the costs caused by each class of mail. Wenner also criticized the method by which demand elasticities were determined and used. But his foremost concern was the degree of discretion exercised by postal managers in setting rates: "The scope for judgment in setting rates should be reduced. Distributing billions of dollars on the basis of thinly supported judgments is not an acceptable method."[17]

But Wenner acknowledged the difficulties the Postal Service faced in developing all new costing data and rate-design techniques for the first case, and he contented himself for the time with urging that the assignment of costs on a judgmental basis be reduced in future rate proposals by a more diligent effort to link long-term and indirect costs to the classes of service that give rise to them.

The rate schedule produced in the first rate case brought the Postal Service another challenge (this time in federal court) by the Association of American Publishers and other organizations that thought the rates had been unfairly increased for special fourth-class mail (books, films, sound recordings, and the like), while parcel post rates were left untouched. The court denied and dismissed the petitioners' request that the rates be set aside but used the opportunity to comment on the Postal Service's cost-accounting and assignment practices. Chief Judge David Bazelon, joined by Circuit Judge Edward A. Tamm and Senior District Court Judge Charles E. Wyzanski, Jr., wrote that the Postal Service had "some distance to go" to reach the objectives of postal reform. The court characterized the Postal Service's response to the rate guidelines established by Congress as "questionable at best." And the judges also criticized the Service's pricing formula on the grounds that it vested "an unstructured and well-nigh unreviewable discretion in two individuals [the two postal econo-

mists who originated the formula] to propose allocation of over half
the Service's budget." The court also held that discretionary or
"reasonable" assignment of costs should apply only when the Postal
Service absolutely could not attribute costs. For the Postal Service
to correct its errors, the court said, it would have to "itemize its
costs in more detail, determine which classes of service caused
them, and attribute those costs solely on that basis. Only very
long-term costs and overhead could be 'reasonably assigned.' "[18]

In spite of Wenner's warnings and those of the court, the Postal
Service initiated the second rate case in 1973 with the same low
level of attributable costs and the same discretionary pricing
formula. Seymour Wenner, now an administrative law judge, held
evidentiary hearings to consider the Postal Service's requests. He
did not like what he found. In advising the Postal Rate Commission
why he thought it should reject the Postal Service's rate request,
Wenner wrote:[19]

> *The Postal Service has become a tax-collecting agency, collecting
> money from first-class mailers to distribute to other favored classes.
> Every time a person pays 10 cents to mail a first-class letter he is
> paying his appropriate attributable share of residual costs, and in
> addition, he is contributing almost 2 cents to pay the costs of other
> services.*

In the same initial decision, issued on May 8, 1975, Wenner
shocked the Postal Service by advocating rejection of both marginal
cost pricing and the inverse elasticity rule. His most significant
recommendation was to redistribute the cost burden among the
various classes of mail, limiting the increase in the cost of a first-
class stamp to 8.5 cents, compared with the 10-cent rate requested
by the Postal Service. This recommendation was based on Wenner's application of a cost allocation method that assigned each
class of mail an "equitable" portion of all unattributable costs.
Applying this method, Wenner had attributed about 71 percent of
postal costs to various mail classes, whereas under Postal Service
cost allocation methods, only about 45 percent of costs had been
attributed to the different classes.

For many weeks after the release of Wenner's initial decision,
the Postal Rate Commission worked through the briefs submitted
by the Postal Service and by the intervenors in exception to the
examiner's proposal. Almost two full years after the original rate
request had been filed, the commission on August 18, 1975, issued
its own recommended decision, which was immediately accepted
by the postal Board of Governors. While the rate commission
produced cost attributions of 52 percent of the total, the PRC

refused to go beyond that, arguing that the record provided inadequate basis for doing more. And although the PRC admonished the Postal Service to present better data in the future or face the possibility of having its rate request rejected, the commission accepted the Postal Service's costing methods once again.[20]

Less than three weeks later, on September 18, 1975, the Postal Service initiated the third postal rate case, projecting revenue requirements of $14.2 billion for fiscal year 1977, a revenue increase of $2.3 billion. Part of this total included revenue needed to offset an estimated revenue deficit of $2.31 billion that could be carried over from 1976. Though the rate request called for higher rates in each class, it proposed an extraordinary hike for first-class rates from 10 cents to 13 cents for the first ounce.

The rate commissioners, who removed Seymour Wenner from the scene and heard this case themselves, responded favorably to all of the rate requests. The only changes they made were to attribute additional costs (above those attributed by the Postal Service) to various mail classes. Costs attributed to the Postal Service were 54 percent of the total; the PRC increased this to 59.5 percent attributable. As a result, the PRC approved the Postal Service's recommended increase in first-class letters to 13 cents for the first ounce, and the postal Board of Governors accepted the rate commission's recommendation.

The D.C. Circuit Court Dictates New Approach

By 1975 the handwriting was on the wall for all parties to see. The Postal Rate Commission appeared to have no intention of rejecting or seriously modifying postal rate requests, thus seeming to leave the Postal Service in control over its own rate structure. Moreover, rates seemed certain to continue to climb rapidly since the Postal Service was demonstrably failing to control costs at the time.

The National Association of Greeting Card Publishers (NAGCP)—an organization with obvious concerns over soaring first-class rates—was alarmed by these trends and stung by the decision in the second rate case, and thus turned to the D.C. Circuit Court for review of the Postal Service's rate-making process. The NAGCP's legal action relied heavily on Seymour Wenner's fully distributed cost allocation approach. The petitioners alleged that, by using the inverse elasticity rule to supplement marginal cost pricing, the Postal Service had invalidly restricted direct cost attribution, and had thereby allocated too much cost to first-class mail.

The court's opinion in this case, finally issued on December 28, 1976, sent another shock wave through the postal community. The court agreed with the petitioners' position, although it did not invalidate the first-class rates at issue. Judge David Bazelon, writing for the majority, held that the Postal Service's methods of costing and setting rates failed to comply with the law, and the court rendered invalid and illegal the methodologies used by the Postal Service and endorsed by the rate commission. Praising the cost-attribution methods used by Seymour Wenner in his controversial proposal, the court said that the costing methods of the Postal Service had failed to attribute enough costs directly to the classes of mail. Judge Bazelon argued that the Postal Service and the rate commission had misread subsection 3622(b)(3) of the law by insisting on applying only a two-tiered cost allocation method. Judge Bazelon's interpretation required a three-tier cost allocation scheme: (1) direct and indirect attributable costs should be assigned to each class of mail; (2) a portion of all other costs should be assigned on a reasonable basis of "cost causality" to each class; and (3) any remaining cost not "reasonably assignable" to any single class should be allocated to the different classes based on the subsection's noncost factors. Judge Bazelon believed this approach would lead to greater accuracy in the rate-making process.[21] He ruled this way in spite of the long history of deference by the courts in allowing regulatory bodies to determine the details of cost allocation procedures[22] and in spite of the Senate report on the Postal Reorganization Act, which stated specifically:[23]

> *[N]o particular cost accounting system is recommended and no particular classification of mail is required to recover a designated portion of its costs beyond its incremental costs. That decision is for the Postal Rate Commission to determine, in accordance with the general criteria enacted by law.*

The decision in this case (which is commonly referred to in the postal community as *NAGCP* I, to distinguish it from later court cases brought by the greeting card publishers) had a significant effect on the Postal Rate Commission and the Postal Service by, in effect, dictating the "proper" approach to use in formulating future cost allocations. The PRC and the Postal Service interpreted the decision as a mandate that they adhere to Judge Bazelon's opinion in formulating all future rate increases.

Because of a continuing rapid rise in its total operating costs, the Postal Service decided early in 1977 to request a general rate increase. The request it filed on July 13, 1977, was the first to be formulated under the restrictions of the court's decision in *NAGCP*

I. It was also the first request to be governed by a new set of amendments to the Postal Reorganization Act, adopted in 1976, one of which imposed a ten-month limit on the PRC for reaching its recommendations. The combined rate increases in the request were expected to generate revenues of $17.64 billion, an increase of $2.4 billion.

Although the Service had little choice but to increase its cost attributions, it took this step with understandable reluctance. The users of second-, third-, and fourth-class mail could be expected to look more earnestly for alternative delivery methods if the Postal Service increased their rates. But knowing that a continuation of their former cost-accounting practices would be rejected in the courts, the Postal Service and the Postal Rate Commission set out to satisfy the new three-tier requirement established by Judge Bazelon in *NAGCP* I. The Postal Service formulated its rate request by applying a new concept known as "service-related costs." These costs are fixed delivery costs attributable to a six-day delivery week versus a three-day delivery week. According to this theory, the six-day week is required only for delivery of so-called "preferential" mail. The Postal Service reasoned that if all the mail it delivers were nonpreferential, it would require only a three-day delivery week, and its fixed costs would then decline substantially. The costs of providing the extra three days of service were assumed by the Postal Service to be "assignable" to those classes of mail receiving preferential service.

The Postal Rate Commission's recommended rate increases were very close to the Postal Service's request, except that it set the projected revenue requirements at a slightly lower figure ($17.58 billion). In its recommended decision, the PRC was careful to indicate that it was attempting to conform to the new three-tier system established by Judge Bazelon. It argued that it was required to do so, but also stated that:[24]

> We would mislead the reader if we left the impression that we regard NAGCP I as unquestionably sound and our previous methods as incompatible with the Act. On the contrary, and with all due respect to the court, we believe that the NAGCP I ruling was not inevitably required by the statute and has caused us difficulties in its application. Whether or not it remains the law, however, it is the law today and we are bound to follow it to the best of our ability. This opinion represents, in our view, a comprehensive and workable application of the principles of NAGCP I, as we understand them, to the record before us.

Using this methodology, the PRC was able to identify 65 percent of total costs as attributable and another 9.6 percent as reasonably assignable. The postal Board of Governors approved the rate commission's recommendations, and the new rates were put into effect on May 29, 1978, slightly over the ten-month deadline.

The results of this rate case were challenged in federal court by the NAGCP and other petitioners who objected to the rate increase on grounds that it applied both the three-tier cost allocation method and the service-related costs concept. The petitioners were not trying to invalidate any particular rate, but were appealing the application of Judge Bazelon's rate methodology and his interpretation of section 3622(b) of the Postal Reorganization Act (PRA). The D.C. Circuit Court held that the Postal Service and the Postal Rate Commission had acted properly and affirmed the Postal Service's rate increase.[25]

This case also gave the D.C. Circuit Court an opportunity to reaffirm Judge Bazelon's interpretation of the PRA. In doing so, a large portion of the court's opinion was devoted to a comparison of marginal cost pricing and the service-related costs concept. The court considered marginal cost pricing inappropriate for two reasons. First, the court pointed out that the Postal Service was a regulated monopoly, with increasing returns to scale. As a result, application of the marginal cost approach could not produce a financially viable firm as it would in a competitive market. Second, the court argued that Congress specifically intended that marginal cost pricing not be applied to postal rate-making. The court concluded that the PRA's main objective was "not so much the regulation of demand for postal service, as the prevention of discrimination among the mail classes."[26] The court held further that the service-related costs concept, unlike marginal cost pricing, was consistent with the act. It argued that the concept is "reasoned, nonarbitrary, and congruent with the legislative objective."[27]

The USPS and the PRC Split over the Three-Tier Approach

But when the Postal Service, in April 1980, requested its fifth general rate increase, its submission to the rate commission rejected the concept of service-related costs as an unsound overreaction to Judge Bazelon's initial ruling in *NAGCP* I. The Postal Service was reasoning at this time that the assignment of costs as service related was artificial because mail volumes and political constraints (see Chapter 3) made a three-day delivery schedule entirely infeasible. These costs would remain the same regardless of whether there were expedited standards for some classes.

The Postal Rate Commission severely criticized the Postal Service for its alleged failure to apply correct cost allocation methods. The PRC went through a detailed analysis of the Postal Service's initial request and challenged each portion. Its most significant revision to this request was its reduction of the Postal Service's proposed first-class rate from 20 cents for the first ounce to 18 cents, and from 17 cents for each additional ounce to 16 cents. The rate commission was intent on a strict application of Judge Bazelon's three-tier cost allocation scheme in order to maximize attribution of costs to mail classes. Attributable costs, which were measured at 59 percent of the total by the Postal Service, were increased to 64 percent by the PRC. In addition, the PRC found about 9 percent of the total were "reasonably assignable" costs.

For the first time since the rate proceedings had begun in 1971, the Postal Service Board of Governors refused to accept the PRC's recommended decision, forcing the Postal Rate Commission to reevaluate while the Postal Service's proposed new rates were implemented on a temporary basis. After the governors sent the rate request back to the commission for reevaluation following the PRC's initial recommended decision, the PRC simply returned a second recommendation that was virtually identical to its first. At this point, the Board of Governors exercised its authority under section 3625(d) of the PRA by unanimously voting to modify the PRC's recommendation. Thus, the rate structure as originally proposed by the Postal Service was implemented on November 1, 1981.

The Second Circuit Court Casts Doubt

Coincidentally, it was also in November 1981 that the Second Circuit Court of Appeals held, in a case brought by magazine publishers who believed their businesses were being burdened by increases in second-class rates, that the Congress intended a more discretionary approach to costing and rate-making.[28]

The petitioners in this case had brought their action before the Second Circuit Court of Appeals, although most preceding legal challenges to postal rates had been decided by the D.C. Court of Appeals. (The petitioners had a right to bring their action before the court of any jurisdiction in which the Postal Service did business—that is, any state in the country.) Knowing that the D.C. Circuit would not reject the three-tier approach established by its own Judge Bazelon, the petitioners brought their appeal to another court (a "second opinion," so to speak). The Second Circuit Court reasoned that the rate-making process was supposed to be the responsibility of the Postal Service and the Postal Rate Commission. The courts had always abided by the principle that an agency's interpretation of its enabling act must be given deference.[29] The Second Circuit Court believed that postal rate-making should be handled no differently and that the D.C. Circuit had violated this basic tenet by mandating a specific interpretation of section 3622(b) of the act. The Second Circuit Court concluded that this interpretation "placed unwarranted and unintended restraints upon the discretionary authority of the PRC and the Board of Governors in setting postal rates and fees." Consequently, the D.C. Circuit was said to have "failed to give sufficient deference to the agency's own interpretation of the statute, misread the plain language of section 3622(b) and misconstrued the legislative history of the section."[30] The Second Circuit also noted that the concept of service-related costs had been adopted in response to what it regarded as an "incorrect" reading by Judge Bazelon of subsection 3622(b)(3). It argued that the subsection was not a *requirement;* it was simply one of many factors to consider. Since the D.C. Circuit had misread the subsection, the Second Circuit did not foresee a need to apply the service-related costs concept in the future.

The *Newsweek* case gave the petitioners reason to expect more favorable rate decisions in the future. The problem was that the Second Circuit's decision was a complete repudiation of the D.C. Circuit's decisions in the earlier *Greeting Card* cases. In order to resolve the dispute between the two courts, the U.S. Supreme Court agreed to review the *Newsweek* decision, on an appeal brought by the greeting card publishers and by United Parcel Service, both of which argued that the decision improperly granted rate-makers too much discretion and thereby created the opportunity for cross-subsidization. Both organizations favored the D.C. Circuit's "cost of service" approach, which would result in lower first-class rates (good for the greeting card industry) and higher Postal Service parcel post rates (good for UPS, the Postal Service's major competitor in the package delivery business). The Postal Service long had wanted more flexibility in rate-setting and favored the Second Circuit's approach. Nonetheless, it urged the Supreme Court to take the case, saying that the "great uncertainty" resulting from the appellate conflict needed to be resolved.

The 1983 Supreme Court Decision

In an important decision handed down on June 22, 1983, the Supreme Court resolved the dispute between the two appellate courts in favor of the Postal Service's position. The Court ruled that it is not mandatory that each class of mail pay its own way down to the last penny. The justices sided with the Second Circuit view that the actual costs of delivering a letter, magazine, or package should form the base for postal rates, but that the Postal Rate Commission should have flexibility to decide how to distribute other costs. The Supreme Court's ruling, written by Justice Harry Blackmun, was a defeat for the NAGCP and UPS, who claimed that users of first-class mail for too long had paid too high a rate, while fees for other classes of mail had been artificially low.

The Supreme Court examined the language of the statute and the legislative history of the Postal Reorganization Act and concluded that Congress had fully intended that professional discretion be applied to distribute those costs of the Postal Service that are not traceable to any one particular class of mail. The Court concluded that Congress had indeed intended to get politics out of the rate-making process, but that it had intended to do so by taking rate-making out of the political arena, where Congress itself had set the rates, and by placing it in the hands of experts trained to undertake the highly technical tasks involved in apportioning costs and determining prices. Congress had not intended to eliminate discretion on the part of rate-setters. The Court also agreed with the Second Circuit Court's opinion in the *Newsweek* case that an agency should be accorded great discretion in interpreting its own enabling legislation. The Court reasoned that if the interpretation does not frustrate Congress's policy objectives or contradict the statutory mandate, it must be upheld. The Court suggested that it was precisely to facilitate the exercise of such expert discretion that Congress had created the independent Postal Rate Commission. Therefore, the Court rejected the reasoning of the earlier court of appeals decision upon which UPS and NAGCP had based their appeal, and instead, as urged by the Postal Service, affirmed the Second Circuit's decision in the *Newsweek* case.[31]

Specifically, the Court interpreted the language of section 3622(b)(3) of the Postal Reorganization Act to require a two-tier, as opposed to three-tier, cost allocation process. All parties agreed that, as a first tier, certain costs of the Postal Service are either directly or indirectly traceable to the provision of one particular class of service, and hence are, in the language of the statute, "attributable" to that class. Similarly, all parties agreed that, as a second tier, certain other costs of the Postal Service cannot be causally linked with any particular class of service, and hence are considered "institutional" costs. However, the D.C. Circuit Court had interpreted the statute also to establish an intermediate, third tier of costs (termed "reasonably assignable costs") which, although not as surely identifiable as having been caused by particular mail classes as attributable costs, could nonetheless be allocated on the basis of more tenuous and speculative cost-of-service accounting principles. The Postal Service and the Postal Rate Commission disputed the three-tier interpretation of section 3622(b)(3), and the Supreme Court agreed that attributable costs and institutional costs were the only two types of costs contemplated by the statute.

The Court also sought to clarify the intended scope of "attributable" costs. Rejecting attempts to rigidly define procedures by which costs can be attributed, the Court held that any costing procedure that reliably establishes a causal link between particular costs and particular classes of service is appropriate. According to the Court, it is the Postal Rate Commission, with the aid of the Postal Service, that must identify the costs that are the result of providing the various classes of service. However, while declining to limit the concept of attributable costs, the Court did specifically endorse utilization of the economic concept of long-term variability within the attribution process, which has been consistently used by the Postal Service and the commission in the last three general rate cases. The Court also affirmed the Postal Service's and the commission's consistent position that the extended use of cost-of-service principles without an established causal basis is arbitrary and uninformative and not required by the act. Both UPS and NAGCP had argued that such extended attribution was necessary to avoid cross-subsidization and was an unfair burden on first-class mailers, but the Court squarely rejected these arguments and identified other measures written into the act that have served to prevent cross-subsidies and to protect first-class mailers.

As a result of their positions having prevailed in this appeal, the Postal Service and the Postal Rate Commission are free to formulate rate proposals based on the interpretation of the act that both agencies had employed in the first three general rate proceedings, before the D.C. Circuit Court announced its interpretation in the first greeting card case in 1976. Moreover, the door was left open for further development of costing and pricing approaches by the two agencies in subsequent commission proceedings.

In sum: the courts have felt free to intervene in technical postal matters to an extraordinary degree—even to the point of designing the structure of the cost system to be used. For the time being, the Supreme Court has resolved this issue by ruling that the PRC should have deference in technical matters. Nevertheless, given the legalistic and litigious context of the rate process, there is always the potential for other judicial surprises.

Subsequent Rate Cases

On November 10, 1983, the USPS requested its sixth general rate increase. This was the first request to be affected by the Supreme Court's decision. Hence, the Postal Service's submission to the PRC was based on a two-tier cost structure: volume-variable attributable costs and institutional costs. Revenue required was estimated at $29.3 billion, an increase of $3.7 billion.

In its recommendation, the PRC accepted the Postal Service's rejection of service-related costs, but held open the possibility of attributable costs based on mail characteristics other than volume variability. There were none such in this hearing, however. The PRC estimated a slightly higher revenue requirement ($29.7 billion) than did the Postal Service, based on a higher estimated volume. Attributable costs, which were estimated at 60 percent by the Postal Service, were increased to 64 percent. Recommended rates were 22 cents for first-class letters (instead of the 23 cents the Postal Service requested) and 14 cents for postcards (instead of the 15 cents the Postal Service requested). Recommended rate increases for most other classes ranged from 11 to 15 percent.

The recommendation of the PRC was issued on September 7, 1984 (just under the ten-month time limit for rate increase proceedings), but was not implemented by the Board of Governors until February 17, 1985.

On May 7, 1987, the Postal Service filed a request for its seventh general rate increase, proposing hikes averaging 16 percent for all classes of mail. The proposed rate increase was in anticipation of an estimated $5.1 billion deficit in fiscal 1989. Sixty-two intervenors and the PRC's Officer of the Commission participated in the case (see Exhibit 5-2), which included three rounds of hearings during which 116 witnesses presented testimony. The record in this case encompassed about 41,000 pages.

In early March 1988, the Postal Rate Commission issued its recommended decision. Partly because of the Postal Service's production of new data on both city carrier street time and purchased transportation, total attributable costs in this case reached 67 percent of Postal Service costs. On average, attributable costs rose 19 percent over the 1984 rate case.

The PRC's recommendations, approved by the Board of Governors on March 22 and implemented on April 3, led to an increase in first-class postage to 25 cents for the first ounce from 22 cents, and to 20 cents from 17 cents for each additional ounce. The cost of postal cards increased to 15 cents from 14 cents. Advertising mailers were hardest hit by this rate increase, as the rates for third-class bulk-advertising mail went up 25 percent.

Rate increases are a fact of life for the Postal Service and its customers, since costs in this labor-intensive industry are constantly rising and the Postal Service has a mandate from Congress to cover its costs. But like any business, the Postal Service has to worry about the consequences of increases in the price of its products or services. When the Postal Rate Commission announced its recommended rates in 1988, the president of the Third Class Mail Association reported that the news left advertising mailers "pessimistic, depressed, and flabbergasted."[32] Subsequent news reports indicated that many direct-mail advertisers believed they would have to cut back on the frequency of their mailings and the number of pieces mailed.[33] Many magazine publishers, hit less hard than direct-mail advertisers but still facing an 18 percent increase, also indicated in the wake of the rate hike that they would be investigating private delivery services in the hope that they might find cheaper ways to deliver their magazines.[34] Such reactions are a reminder to the Postal Service that, as the next chapter shows, it operates in an increasingly competitive environment.

Endnotes

1. President's Commission on Postal Organization, Report of the Commission, *Towards Postal Excellence* (Washington: U.S. Government Printing Office, 1968), Annex, vol. 2, chap. 1, pp. 2, 3.
2. Comptroller General of the United States, *Opportunities to Improve the Postal Rate-Making Process*, report to the Congress (Washington: General Accounting Office, April 23, 1984), No. GGD-84-10, pp. 11–12, 14.
3. *United States Code*, Title 39, sec. 3624(a).
4. The following description of the rate-making process draws on government documents and discussions with the principals.
5. 39 C.F.R. 3000.755-501.
6. 39 C.F.R. 3000.735-310.
7. U.S., Congress, House, Committee on Post Office and Civil Service, *Oversight on Operation of United States Postal Service, Joint hearings*, 99th Cong., 2d Sess., 1985, pp. 163–64.
8. Kathleen Conkey, *The Postal Precipice: Can the U.S. Postal Service Be Saved?* (Washington: Center for Study of Responsive Law, 1983), p. 212.
9. *United States Code*, Title 39, sec. 3622(b)(3).
10. "Chief Administrative Law Judge's Initial Decision," in United States Postal Service, *Action of the Governors under 39 U.S.C., Section 3625, and Supporting Record in the Matter of Postal Rate and Fee Increases, 1974: Docket*

No. *R74-1 before the Postal Rate Commission* (Washington: U.S. Government Printing Office, 1975), vol. 1, p. 3, col. 2.

11. See, for example, Alfred E. Kahn, *The Economics of Regulation*, 2 vols. (New York: Wiley & Sons, 1970), vol. 1, chap. 4.

12. For postal economists' explanation of their use of the inverse elasticity rule, see Postal Rate Commission, *Postal Rate and Fee Increases*, Docket R76-1, vol. 1, *Opinion and Recommended Decision* (Washington: Postal Rate Commission, 1977), pp. 123–25, 138.

13. Ibid.

14. Kahn, *Economics of Regulation*, vol. 1, p. 144.

15. Ibid., pp. 142–50.

16. Arthur Eden, in direct testimony before the Postal Rate Commission, in *Postal Rate and Fee Increases*, Docket R74-1, vol. 3, p. 37, col. 1; p. 32, col. 3.

17. Postal Rate Commission, *Chief Examiner's Initial Decision on Postal Rate and Fee Increases*, Docket R71-1, February 3, 1972, p. 98.

18. *Association of American Publishers, Inc.* v. *The Governors of The United States Postal Service*, 485 F.2d 768 (1973), pp. 777–79.

19. "Chief Administrative Law Judge's Initial Decision," in *Postal Rate and Fee Increases*, Docket R74-1, vol. 1, p. 4.

20. "Opinion and Recommended Decision of the Postal Rate Commission," in *Postal Rate and Fee Increases*, Docket R74-1, vol. 1, pp. 612–14.

21. *National Association of Greeting Card Publishers* v. *United States Postal Service (NAGCP I)*, 569 F.2d 570, 584 (D.C. Cir. 1976), *vacated on other grounds*, 434 U.S. 884 (1977).

22. See, for example, *American Commercial Lines, Inc.* v. *Louisville & N.R.*, 392 U.S. 571 (1968); *Wisconsin* v. *FPC*, 373 U.S. 294 (1963); *Colorado Interstate Gas Co.* v. *FPC*, 373 U.S. 581 (1945); *Trans World Airlines, Inc.* v. *CAB*, 385 F.2d 648 (D.C. Cir. 1967), *cert. denied*, 390 U.S. 944 (1968).

23. U.S., Senate, Committee on Post Office and Civil Service, *Postal Reorganization*, S. Report No. 91-912, 91st Cong., 2d Sess., June 3, 1970, p. 17.

24. Postal Rate Commission, *Opinion and Recommended Decision*, Docket R77-1, May 12, 1978, p. 9.

25. *National Association of Greeting Card Publishers* v. *United States Postal Service (NAGCP III)*, 607 F.2d 392 (D.C. Cir. 1979), *cert. denied*, 444 U.S. 1025 (1980).

26. Ibid., at 403.

27. Ibid., at 404.

28. *Newsweek, Inc.*, v. *United States Postal Service*, 663 F.2d 1186 (2d Cir. 1981).

29. Ibid., at 1196.

30. Ibid.

31. *National Association of Greeting Card Publishers* v. *United States Postal Service*, 103 U.S. 2717 (1983).

32. *Wall Street Journal*, March 7, 1988, p. 24.

33. *Boston Globe*, March 29, 1988, p. 29.

34. *Wall Street Journal*, March 23, 1988, p. 32.

Chapter 6

POSTAL MARKETS: CUSTOMERS AND COMPETITION

Perhaps the most extraordinary aspect of the postal system's operation and performance in the 1980s is the steady growth of its business even in the face of increased competition. Contrary to what many people seem to think, marketplace rivalry is nothing new to the postal system. It has faced competition for years—for example, from private firms in the conveyance of small parcels, from newspapers and the broadcast media for advertisers' business, and from the telephone, which became a readily available substitute for many kinds of mail communication. But in recent years, one of the most important developments in the Postal Service's managerial environment has been the rapidly stiffening pressure in many of its service classes or product lines from competitors who would like a piece of the multi-billion dollar mail business. Some competition is direct, as other carriers seek to transport and deliver various kinds of mail in their current physical form. Some is indirect, as competitors in the communications industry are trying to transform what is currently in the mailstream so it can be carried by other means, usually electronic. Because of the availability of physical and electronic transmission delivery services, no class of mail is entirely free of competition.

In the early- to mid-1970s, various forecasters and prognosticators offered the most dire predictions for the postal system. At the time, mail volume showed little or no growth and even declined in 1975. Moreover, the changes then occurring in the electronic communications marketplace seemed likely to divert mail business elsewhere, causing significant declines in mail volume, with serious consequences for the future operation and financing of the

postal system. But all such forecasts were wrong. Neither competitive physical delivery systems nor electronic communications
systems now seem likely to put the Postal Service out of business—
or even lead to declining volumes. In fact, mail volume has been
growing rapidly and is expected to continue to do so (see Exhibit
6-1). In the past few years, total mail volume has been growing
steadily by about 6 percent, with much higher increases in some
years (up 10.2 percent, or 12 billion pieces, in 1984, for example).
And volume is expected to continue to grow at a rate averaging a
little above 5 percent, bringing mail volume to a level of 165 to 175
billion pieces by 1990.[1]

The reasons are many and varied for the postal system's business
growth in the face of such dire predictions for its future. To
understand what has happened in the postal marketplace in the
past decade, it is necessary to examine specific postal markets or
services to see who the customers are, what are the sources and

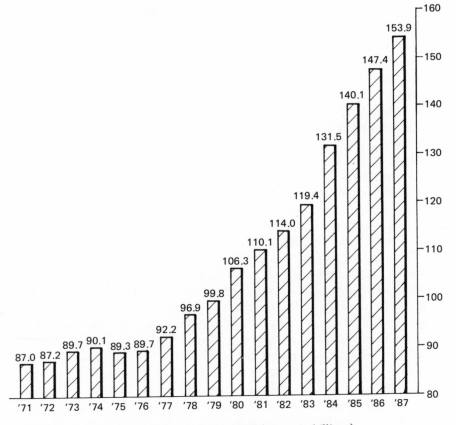

Exhibit 6-1   Total Mail Volume, 1971-1987 (pieces in billions).

types of competition, and what the Postal Service has been doing to try to retain and strengthen its business. For purposes of analysis, this chapter divides the Postal Service's market into five segments. The largest, both in volume and revenue, is its first-class service category in which the Postal Service provides traditional delivery services for correspondence and transactions of all sorts. The second largest part of the postal market is its role as an advertising channel, principally for third-class mail. Third, the postal system is a distributor of publications of all sorts, principally magazines and newspapers. A fourth market function of the postal system is as a deliverer of parcels. Finally, the Postal Service is a competitor in the expedited delivery market, where its competitive efforts to hold onto its small market share have been especially conspicuous and controversial.

First-Class Mail:
Mainstream (Business) Communications

First-class mail is the dominant mail category. A little over half (51 percent) of the 154 billion pieces of mail handled by the system in 1987 were first-class mail items. The composition of first-class mail includes letter, post and postal cards, sealed parcels, and almost all mailings that contain written or typewritten materials. An estimated 80 percent of first-class mail consists of business-related items—invoices, bills, payments, statements of account, purchase orders, financial papers, and business letters. Christmas and other greeting cards make up more than half of the remaining 20 percent, while personal letter correspondence comprises only about 3 percent of all first-class mail. In short, although first-class mail is the service most commonly used by householders, the business community is by far the dominant user of first-class mail.

Imaginative applications of fast-changing electronic technologies provide new modes of information transmission in the business world and thus pose a competitive threat to first-class mail volumes. In particular, electronic funds transfer (EFT) and electronic mail together would seem to have the ability to meet much of the "mail" needs of the business community. Because of the transmission and information-storage capacities of contemporary electronic-communications technologies (including microprocessors, glass fiber optics, facsimile systems, broadband satellite connections, microwave transmissions, sophisticated video-display instruments, and high-speed printers), it is technologically possible to transmit by electronic means well over half of what is currently in the first-class mailstream.

Electronic Funds Transfer

As a consequence of the confluence of a number of important trends in the American financial community—deregulation, the advent of new technologies, growing public demands for convenience, and financial institutions' own struggles to increase productivity (and, thereby, profitability)—financial institutions have been turning more and more to paperless (that is, computer-based) systems. In other words, they are increasingly substituting an electronic transfer of funds for conventional payment systems—substituting an electronic impulse for checks or cash.

The developments in EFT not only are contributing to the emergence of what has come to be known as the checkless society, but also have implications for the diversion of first-class mail volume. Although it is difficult even for industry analysts to be very precise about the impact, the potential loss comes into sharp relief when one considers the potential number of pieces of mail associated with a traditional check payment: (1) the bill or invoice sent by the firm requiring payment; (2) the mailing of the check from the payer to the recipient; (3) the mailing of the check by the recipient to the bank for deposit; and (4) the various mailings from the bank such as receipts, notices, and new mail-deposit envelopes.[2]

Electronic systems for transferring funds encompass a broad range of systems for recording financial transactions. But there are two principal applications where electronic systems can be used in lieu of first-class mail to transfer funds: (1) direct electronic deposit of payments—wages or salary, retirement benefits, dividends, Social Security and other government benefits; and (2) payment of bills and premiums through pre-authorized debits, automated teller machines, point-of-sale terminals, and two-way interactive electronic systems that typically involve the use of personal computers.

Under direct-deposit programs, large corporations and government agencies offer employees or other payees the convenience of having their regular payments deposited directly in a bank. The employer or government agency either supplies financial institutions directly with lists or magnetic computer tapes indicating names and accounts to be credited or it transfers the funds electronically through the 31 interconnected automated clearinghouses (ACH) organized in the early 1970s by the American

Bankers Association for the purpose of such transfers. Particularly worrisome from the Postal Service's standpoint are the diversions in first-class mail resulting from the direct-deposit programs of other government agencies. In 1974 the U.S. Treasury Department began direct deposits of Social Security payments. This service was subsequently expanded to include payment of benefits for a host of federal retirement programs (railroad and civil service workers and most of the armed services), veterans' benefits, and active duty pay for the Air Force and Marines. At the end of September 1985, the federal government's direct-deposit programs via EFT involved over 20 million payments monthly (an annual rate of over 242 million). That number is likely to expand, since only 44 percent of federal-payment recipients eligible for this service are now participating, and both the Treasury Department and financial institutions are vigorously promoting direct deposit.[3]

Although not a particularly new development, another common application of EFT is the pre-authorized payment, by which consumers authorize future debits to their checking accounts. Many consumers arrange to have fixed, recurring bills such as life and health insurance premiums and home mortgage payments automatically paid from their bank accounts. In the past, it was common practice for, say, an insurance company to mail banks regular statements debiting each payer's checking account and, in many cases, also to send a statement to the customer confirming the transaction. But it is now increasingly common for computers simply to transfer the funds electronically from one account to another through automated clearinghouses. Insurance companies and mortgage lending institutions are among the leaders in the use of such systems. For example, the Equitable Life Assurance Society collects over 490,000 premiums each month via EFT, and the New York Life Insurance Company processes about 950,000 monthly premiums via EFT. Such arrangements, of course, eliminate a substantial portion of billing expense for these firms. But the Postal Service loses the first-class mail volume that was formerly carried in the billing of and payment by the participating policyholders.

Another type of funds transfer is by automated teller machines (ATM)—the computer-based devices owned by financial institutions and operated, by definition, without teller intervention. ATMs can provide a variety of consumer financial services such as check dispensing, deposit acceptance, funds transfer between checking and savings accounts, balance inquiries, and bill payment. Of the 2.6 billion ATM transactions in 1985, 52 million were for bill payments that for the most part used to be sent as first-class mail.[4]

When first introduced in the early 1970s, ATMs were installed almost exclusively on financial institutions' premises with access outside the office area so that service could be available twenty-four hours a day. A combination of increasing consumer acceptance, banking deregulation, and financial institutions' business interests (i.e., reducing labor costs, increasing market share, creating an image of being innovative) led to a proliferation of ATM installations, including off-site locations, especially at supermarkets and convenience stores. In the mid-1980s, about 60 percent of those financial institutions having deposits of over $25 million had ATMs. This translated into about 57,000 ATMs installed nationwide. Moreover, in a number of regions, many financial institutions have either formed or joined shared networks, which in some areas operate in more than one state, and a few operate nationwide. As ATMs thus become more widespread, they promise to divert even more first-class mail volume.

Point-of-sale (POS) systems are an associated EFT development posing a potential future, but as yet insignificant, threat to first-class mail volume. Owned and operated by retailers, such systems are primarily used at this time for electronic verification of checks and credit cards. But such systems already in place in many stores permit immediate electronic transfer of funds at the time of sale. Sales clerks operating the POS terminals simply enter the customer's personal identification number and data relevant to the transaction (retailer's identification number, price, date, and so forth), making an immediate electronic transfer from the customer's bank account to the account of the retailer. Depending on consumer and retailer acceptance, such systems could eventually replace millions of pieces of first-class mail now generated through billings, deposits, physical transmission of bankcard sales slips, and the like.[5]

In many cities, banks already provide customers with the opportunity for paying bills (utility, department store, and the like) or transferring funds between accounts over their telephones. Users of traditional rotary-dial telephones need the assistance of an operator at the bank. But customers with Touch-Tone® telephones simply use them as computer terminals, calling a special number at the bank, keying in an identification number, and then, with the help of recorded instructions, entering other information needed to complete bill payments. Payments are electronically deducted from customer accounts and routed to the accounts of the parties being paid; it is all done without checks and without postage.

From the projected growth of telephone bill-paying services nationwide and from the transaction volumes handled by banks when offering such services, the Postal Service in 1979 estimated that telephone payment systems could mean the loss of anywhere from 625 million to 2.5 billion pieces of first-class mail each year, depending on consumer acceptance of the new system. But the roughly 450 telephone bill-paying systems in operation nationwide in 1982 declined to about 215 systems in 1986, a drop of over 50 percent, with the greatest decline coming from the commercial banks. The reasons for this decline appear to be economic. Both the introduction of new financial products and the harnessing of more powerful computer-based systems give financial institutions more profitable ways to expend their efforts and resources. Even so, a telephone system is less costly to install and operate than an ATM system, so telephone bill-payment systems are likely to continue to have appeal to thrift institutions that generally do not have the resources of commercial banks.[6]

Yet another possible threat to first-class mail volume comes from two-way interactive electronic systems that use computer technology to provide a variety of services—home banking and shopping, electronic mail, entertainment, and the like. Two such systems—one offered by Knight Ridder Newspapers in southern Florida and the other by Times-Mirror in southern California—went out of business in 1986 because of lack of consumer support.

But other financial giants see market potential in the service. For example, Chemical Bank of New York offers a videotex banking service employing personal computers. Its "Pronto" system is available under a licensing arrangement to other financial institutions and permits funds transfers and bill paying. These kinds of systems are viable and proliferating. In fact, Chemical Bank announced in 1985 that it was joining with AT&T, Bank of America, and Time, Inc., to form a new corporation, COVIDEA Corp., to develop, produce, and market videotex services nationwide to consumers and small businesses. The 44,000 customers of Chemical Bank's Pronto system and Bank of America's home banking services were to make up the initial customer base. Within a few months a similar project was launched by Hearst, ABC, CitiCorp, and NYNEX.

Electronic Mail

Paralleling the clear threat to the Postal Service's first-class mail revenues from EFTs is the rapid development of new telecommunications and computer technologies that seem capable of changing fundamentally some of the nation's habits of communicating. The 1970s and 1980s brought exciting new developments in integrated circuitry, including powerful microprocessors that enable enormous reductions in the costs of message storage and retrieval. In systems for transmitting information, we now have highly sophisticated communications satellites, fiber optics, microwave relays, and enhanced coaxial cables. All these foundation stones of new telecommunications systems go far beyond the traditional telephone or even the now-familiar TWX/Telex systems provided by Western Union. Along with new, low-cost video display terminals, software packages, and high-speed printers, these developments are contributing to revolutionary changes in the business world's communications systems and hold the potential for diverting volume from the postal system.

The communications services based on these technological inventions are many and varied. One system with great potential for being a direct substitute for first-class mail is the facsimile system—machines that function much like ordinary office copying machines but scan a document and transmit it electronically to a receiving terminal, where an exact photographic image of it is reproduced.

Facsimile systems are not new nor is the concern they cause postal officials. As long ago as 1872, Postmaster General Jonathan Creswell noted in the Post Office Department's annual report:[7]

> *The probable simplification of the facsimile system by Caselli, by which an exact copy of anything that can be drawn or written may be instantaneously made to appear at a distance of hundreds of miles from the original; and the countless other applications of electricity to the transmission of intelligence yet to be made—must sooner or later interfere with the transportation of letters by the slower means of the post.*

The technology has existed for some time. But as with many telecommunications systems, the problem has been in making the technology economically feasible and developing a market for it. In the past two decades, communications and business-machine companies have refined both the technology and the economics of facsimile systems. The "fax machines" now manufactured and marketed largely by Sharp, Ricoh, Canon, and Pitney Bowes are able to transmit high-quality reproductions in seconds; they use state-of-the-art digital scanning equipment and cost-effective transmission methods such as microwave relays and satellites. As a consequence of the refinements in the technology, there has been a rapid acceleration in the number of facsimile units in use by businesses throughout the United States. There were roughly 200,000 facsimile units in place in the United States in 1980. By 1985, there were an estimated 580,000 facsimile machines in place around the country, generating an annual volume of about 565 million pages. But more than 417,000 fax machines were shipped in the United States in 1987, and nearly twice that number were expected to be sold in 1988. Most of this market growth has come from low-priced fax machines, listing at between $1,500 and $2,000. Although fax machines' threat to first-class mail volume is uncertain at this point, the machines already have acquired a stronghold in the business community, where they appear at least to pose a serious threat to the overnight document delivery business held by companies like Federal Express and United Parcel Service.[8]

The extraordinary developments in the 1980s in computer technology also promise great changes in the way businesses communicate with one another. The most obvious application is computer-based message systems or "electronic mail" systems— communications services that permit the transmission and storage of messages by electronic means. These computer mailbox services have been offered by a handful of large companies, among them General Electric, ITT, and GTE. Under such systems, a sender, using his own keyboard-type terminal (or personal computer or communicating word processor), enters messages or data, which are then stored in the memory of a computer at a remote location. Then the receiver, at his convenience, connects with the computer via his own terminal and draws off the information onto either a printer or a video display screen. These systems generally operate with electronic mailboxes in a store and forward mode. Each designated user has an electronic mailbox, which can be accessed using unique codes. A significant advantage is that such systems operate independent of both time and place, and thus the users do not have to be in simultaneous contact.

There is little in the way of reliable quantitative data on current electronic message volumes, but Link Resources, a New York-based research and consulting firm, has estimated that the U.S. computer-based and electronic message services had a market size of about $300 million in 1985 and an expected size of $1.5 billion by 1990. In the same time frame, electronic mail message volume was expected to increase from about 140 million messages in 1985 to over 800 million messages by 1990.[9]

In the mid-1980s, two of the most aggressive mass marketers in the United States moved into electronic mail in a big way. MCI

Communications, the long-distance phone company, and Federal Express, the leader in the overnight shipping market, launched electronic mail programs backed by heavy spending for development, advertising, and promotion.

MCI started its electronic mail system in late 1983 with an initial investment of about $40 million. "MCI-Mail" is a standard computer mailbox service, subscription to which is free but the use of which is limited to those with the necessary electronic equipment—a modem (telecommunications device) and either a computer, word processor, telex machine, or electronic typewriter (with a memory). To send a message, a subscriber uses his equipment to communicate with MCI's computer over telephone lines.

MCI Mail offers a variety of services. It provides three types of delivery at different prices. A subscriber to MCI Mail can simply use it as a computer-mailbox service and send instantaneous messages to other subscribers. The price for this service in early 1988 was $1 for what MCI, perhaps in a gesture to postal tradition, calls an "ounce"—7,500 characters, or the equivalent of about five double-spaced typewritten pages. There is a charge for each additional "ounce." For very short messages (up to 500 characters), MCI charges only forty-five cents per "instant mail" message.

But an MCI Mail subscriber may want to send a hard-copy message. If so, the subscriber creates the letter in the same way, using a personal computer, word processor or other communicating device, and then chooses between two paper mail delivery options that offer different speeds of delivery. If the subscriber is willing to wait a day or two for delivery, the message is transmitted electronically to an MCI Mail postal center near the recipient, laser-printed on white bond paper, enclosed in MCI Mail's distinctive envelope and placed in the U.S. mail stream. The charge for this service in early 1988 was $2 for the first three pages and $1 for each additional three pages. If the sender wants faster delivery, guaranteed overnight delivery by noon of the following business day is available at a price (in 1988) of $9 for up to six pages and $1 for each additional three pages. Any of these delivery options also can be used to send multiple copies of a single document, such as memos going out to the many local offices of some national organization.

In short, MCI staked out a broad range of electronic mail services, from instant on-screen delivery to conventional paper delivery, and the company positioned itself so that it could readily shift its emphasis as the market develops. MCI's entry into the electronic mail market was a logical offshoot of its basic long-distance telephone business, and the company by the late 1980s seemed well-positioned to benefit from any boom that may occur in electronic mail.

Federal Express, by contrast, launched its electronic mail program (called ZapMail) not so much because it was a logical extension of its business but because the firm was concerned about the potential impact of electronic mail and facsimile transmissions on its principal business—the overnight delivery of urgent letters and documents. In exploring ways to counter the threat, the company decided to offer an even speedier alternative to its existing services. Federal Express spent three years and hundreds of millions of dollars trying to make this diversification effort work, but finally closed down the service in September 1986.[10]

The technology used by Federal Express in its ZapMail service was radically different from that used by MCI. To use ZapMail, neither the sender nor the recipient needed electronic equipment. Someone who wanted to send a letter or document by ZapMail merely had to call Federal Express, which dispatched a courier to pick it up and took it to one of the company's nearby offices. There it was transmitted by facsimile machine to the Federal Express office nearest the ultimate destination. A courier at the receiving end then transported the facsimile copy the rest of the way. The charge for this service was $35 to send documents of up to five pages, plus a dollar for each additional page. Federal Express offered a money-back guarantee if it failed to deliver the letter or document within two hours after the sender called for a pickup. (Senders who brought the material to a Federal Express office paid $10 less—and delivery was guaranteed within *one* hour.)[11]

The distinctive character of ZapMail (and the feature Federal Express thought would give it an edge over the competition) was that its use of facsimile technology offered the advantages of photographic reproduction, thus permitting the transmission of charts, graphs, and illustrations. MCI, by contrast, can transmit only text, not images.

The entry into this market by MCI and Federal Express came at roughly the same time that the Postal Service was ending its own foray into the electronic mail market. Begun in 1982, the Postal Service's E-COM (Electronic Computer Originated Mail) system was so poorly designed and marketed that the service's Board of Governors finally voted in 1984 to discontinue the service.

To many observers, the E-COM system seemed doomed from the start. E-COM afforded mailers, either directly or through an intermediary, the opportunity to transmit the text of letters (a minimum of two hundred per transmission) over telephone lines to computers in any of twenty-five specially equipped post offices located around the continental United States. The text was then printed and placed in an envelope bearing the blue and white E-COM logo. From that point on, E-COM letters were treated as regular first-class mail, except that there was an assurance of two-day delivery if the text was transmitted to the specially equipped post office closest to the ultimate destination of the letter. The cost of the service in 1983 was 26 cents for a one-page message and 31 cents for a two-page message.

From the sender's standpoint, however, the system had serious drawbacks. Not least was the requirement that letters be sent in batches of two hundred or more. This completely closed the service out of the market for smaller mailings. Moreover, E-COM's printers did not use color and could not reproduce corporate logos, making it less attractive than MCI Mail, which can do so. Finally, the E-COM system was unable to support the inclusion of additional items (advertisements, return envelopes, or other "stuffers"), again making it relatively less attractive to customers such as credit card companies, which wanted such features.

As a consequence of its many design flaws, the high-volume mailing customers the E-COM service was supposed to attract never materialized. At its peak, only about 950 companies, many of them direct-mail advertisers, used the service. Volume in fiscal 1984 ran at an annual pace of approximately 23 million pieces, less than half of projected volumes.[12]

Ironically, the demise of E-COM may have improved the market for electronic mail that is delivered in hard copy form. Because E-COM was subsidized so heavily—it charged 26 cents to send a letter, which by a rough congressional estimate in 1983 was about one dollar less than Postal Service costs—other providers were reluctant to enter the field.[13] That has changed since the Postal Service left it.

Whither the Decline in First-Class Mail Volume?

Between 1974 and 1975, first-class mail volume declined by roughly 222 million pieces. Analysts believed that the downturn in volume reflected the inroads of electronic communications and funds transfer systems and that these developing technologies would find such widespread use in the business community as to spell a continuing decline in first-class mail. But first-class mail volume turned around and since 1982 has increased at unprecedented rates (see Exhibit 6-2). The Postal Service handled almost 79 billion pieces of first-class mail in 1987 (an increase of 5.2

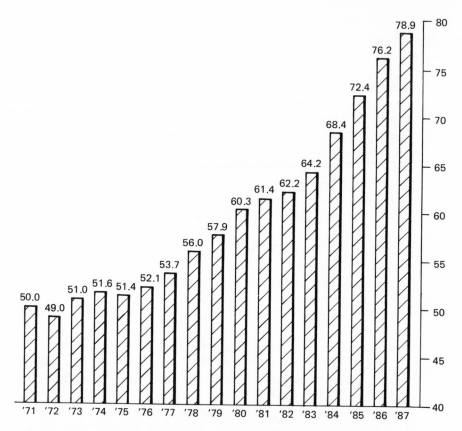

Exhibit 6-2   First-Class Mail Volume, 1971-1987 (pieces in billions).

percent over the previous year), and was expecting 85 billion pieces by 1990.

Predictions of the devastation of the Postal Service's first-class mail business were clearly wrong. Why? Developing a reliable forecast of either the rate of increase in electronic messaging or its potential for mailstream diversion has been complicated by the evolutionary nature both of the technologies and of the applications and also by the absence of reliable data about their use. Moreover, predicting human behavior is chancy. The public simply has not been as quick to embrace new technologies as informed experts thought. Many people are understandably reluctant to entrust their paychecks or their mortgage payments to electronic transmission systems that they do not understand.

Another reason the impact has been less devastating than expected is that first-class mail volume has grown tremendously as a result of the overall growth of the economy. Mail volume is heavily

influenced by the level of economic activity. All messages, transactions, and merchandise volumes increase in a growing economy.
In particular, the growth of the communications and service sectors of the economy has greatly expanded the total number of
messages in all forms. In addition, deregulation in the communications and financial services businesses has profoundly affected
the way these businesses interact, generating multiple new message opportunities. Moreover, economic analysis of the demand
for three information distribution modes (telecommunications,
postal services, and advertising) suggests that decreases in the
price of telecommunications, such as have occurred in recent
years, lead to an increase in the use of both telecommunications
and postal services. The sectors of the economy for which this
appears to be most true are telecommunications itself, banking,
insurance, professional services and nonprofit organizations, and
periodicals and book publishing.[14]

Moreover, economic research performed for the Postal Service
has indicated that as household income increases, more mail is
sent to that household. In fact, households earning $35,000 or
more in 1976 dollars received over twice as much mail as those in
the $10,000 to $15,000 bracket. And the number of households in
the middle- to upper-level income categories has been increasing
proportionately more than the overall increase in households.[15]

But the continuing health of first-class mail volume is not solely
a consequence of larger economic forces; the Postal Service also
has nurtured this sector of its business through the initiation of a
discount for presorted first-class mail. The discount is intended to
motivate large-scale mailers to prepare their mailings in ways that
permit the Postal Service to handle them more quickly and economically. The program takes advantage of the fact that those
preparing large mailings can perform certain sorting and bundling
operations easier and more cheaply than can the Postal Service.
By making the most efficient use of the capabilities of the mailers,
the presort program benefits not only them but also the postal
system as a whole. The program has improved the attractiveness
of the postal system as compared to alternative forms of delivery.

Since the introduction of a first-class mail presort discount in
July 1976, the volume of mail in this category has grown tremendously. During the first full fiscal year, 2.2 billion pieces were
presorted, only 4 percent of first-class mail volume. By fiscal year
1987, presorted first-class mail exceeded 21 billion pieces, over 28
percent of total first-class mail volume. In addition, the Postal
Service embarked on a major new program in 1984—the ZIP + 4
program. The volume of mail that qualifies for the ZIP + 4

discount has not been as strong as the Postal Service hoped (for reasons discussed in Chapter 3), but reached 4.7 billion pieces in 1987, an increase of 1.2 billion pieces or 35.6 percent over fiscal 1986.

Although overall first-class mail volume has shown a steady increase since 1983, the percentage of total mail volume constituted by first-class mail has been gradually decreasing since 1982. First-class mail comprised 55 percent of the total mail volume in 1982; by 1987 that composition had dropped to 51 percent. In other words, first-class mail volume, while rapidly increasing, is not increasing relative to total mail volume.

The Postal Service as an Advertising Channel

The second biggest segment of the contemporary postal market is the advertising business. In fiscal year 1985, nearly 56 billion pieces of advertising mail were delivered by the Postal Service, including about 50 billion pieces of third-class mail. Third-class comprises advertising and printed promotional materials as well as parcels that weigh less than 16 ounces. Third-class is technically referred to as Bulk Business Mail or, more casually, advertising mail (still more casually, as "junk mail"). This mail category is used by a wide variety of organizations and causes and by businesses large and small. As just about any mail recipient can attest, bulk regular rate mail is the fastest growing mail category. Its volume has more than doubled just since 1980. The principal reason for this is that it is an extremely flexible advertising medium. Specific geographic areas can be saturated or specific constituencies can be reached throughout the nation. Using one of many available mailing lists, broadly or narrowly defined demographic groups can be targeted for receipt of a sales or fund-raising pitch.

Third-class mail offers an effective way for candidates running for office to seek ballot support and financial contributors. Organized interest groups of all sorts use third-class mail to solicit funds, to persuade people of the worthiness of their cause, to mobilize support and to influence opinions. Charitable organizations of various sorts—medical, scientific, and religious groups, as well as cultural institutions—also use third-class mail to reach their constituencies and maintain their financial bases. Most conspicuously, of course, third-class mail is used to sell products and services—everything from packaged goods and consumer products to financial services.

Because it is an effective advertising vehicle for so many elements of the American business community, third-class mail has grown at a rate much greater than other classes of mail. Third-class mail increased its percentage share of the total number of pieces in the mailstream from 26 percent in 1977 to 39 percent in 1987. Thus, over that decade, third class-mail increased its percentage share of total mail pieces by about 50 percent (see Exhibit 6-3). By contrast, first-class mail, though growing substantially in volume, declined in its percentage share of the whole, from 58 percent in 1977 to 51.2 percent in 1987.

In actual numbers, there were 24 billion pieces of third-class mail in 1977, compared with 59.3 billion pieces in 1987—a difference of 35.3 billion pieces over the ten-year span (see Exhibit 6-4). This means that in a decade the annual volume of third-class mail more than doubled—an overall growth rate of 147 percent. Meanwhile, first-class mail grew by 25 billion pieces over those ten years, from 53.6 billion to 78.9 billion.

Third-class volume has grown more than twice as fast as total mail volume in the past decade. That is, while third-class mail experienced a 147 percent growth rate in the past decade, the growth rate for all mail in the same ten years was 66 percent. The 154 billion pieces of mail delivered by the Postal Service in fiscal 1987 represented a 4.4 percent increase over the previous year. Within that period, third-class grew by 8.5 percent; first-class grew by 3.5 percent.

A number of factors account for the growth in third-class mail, but changing life-styles and modern technologies must figure

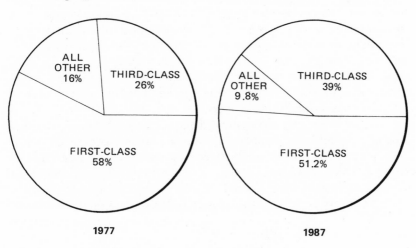

1977   1987

Exhibit 6-3   Percentage Share of Total Mail Volume.

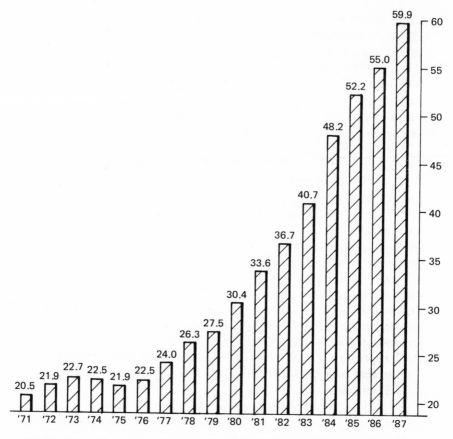

Exhibit 6-4   Third-Class Mail Volume, 1971–1987 (pieces in billions).
prominently in any explanation. More and more women have
exchanged housework for a full- or part-time job outside the home,
and consequently have little time to go to stores to shop. Mail
order permits them to make purchases at any time, day or night,
and from almost any location. The spread of sophisticated computers also has contributed to the growth of direct mail. These
computers store vast databanks of names and addresses, and can
sort mail by address, enabling the sender to take advantage of rate
discounts for presorted mail. Moreover, computers allow sophisticated analysis of marketing data, enabling mailers to pinpoint the
precise audiences they want to reach. These computerized marketing lists are central to the growth of third-class mail.

   Finally, the discounts for presorted mail also have contributed
greatly to the extraordinary volume increases in third-class bulk
mail. Throughout the 1970s the growth rate in the volume of
pieces handled by the Postal Service was fairly constant. But when

the Postal Service began in 1978 to offer third-class presort dis-counts (that is, lower rates for those mailers who presort their bulk business mail according to its destination), volume began a dra-matic and steady rise. In fact, more than 65 percent of third-class mail now consists of carrier-route and five-digit presorted pieces.

It is also the case, however, that many postal officials now worry about the system's ability to absorb the continuing increases in third-class volume, especially since the growth rate in *non-pre-sorted* third-class mail has been increasing over the past five years, and presorted third-class mail, while still showing volume growth, has been increasing less rapidly. What this means is that the actual work load represented by third-class mail has been increasing rapidly over the past five years and is expected to continue to grow in the future.[16]

While the Postal Service obviously has a strong market in its third-class mail business, direct mail is not the only option for advertisers interested in generating orders and contributions di-rectly from the recipients of their pitch. For example, many retailers and other firms use newspapers to deliver their advertis-ing inserts. The Newspaper Advertising Bureau has estimated that in 1985 there were 45.4 billion advertising inserts accompanying daily and Sunday newspapers. This is an 89 percent increase over the 24 billion delivered in 1978 and more than six times greater than the 7.1 billion delivered in 1970.[17] Theoretically, these bil-lions of inserts could have been delivered by the Postal Service.

Another example of the use of alternative media to direct mail is the distribution of "cents-off" coupons. The A. C. Neilsen Com-pany has estimated that in 1975 there were 35.7 billion coupons distributed; by 1985, the total increased to nearly 180 billion.[18] In 1975, direct mail was used to distribute about 4.2 percent of the total, and in 1985 the volume was 4.4 percent. Newspapers carry over three-quarters of all cents-off coupons. But the response rate to coupons distributed by direct mail is 7 percent as compared to less than 4 percent for all methods of distribution.[19]

Third-class advertising mail also faces competition from media such as radio, television, print, telephone (telemarketing), and other electronic means. Radio and broadcast television are used primarily for "message" advertising that promotes goods and ser-vices that can be obtained from retail outlets. But television increasingly carries direct response ads that include "800" toll-free numbers, soliciting mail and telephone orders directly from the audience. And cable television is attracting great interest on the part of direct marketers.

The proliferation of direct response methods suggests that there will be a reallocation of advertising dollars among more media. But that does not necessarily mean a decline in the use of direct mail advertising. Indeed, it is possible that advertising mail might experience increased volume when used for direct response and as a supporting supplement to emerging electronic direct response advertising techniques. It is also possible that as direct response advertising develops further, increased mail volumes will result from the increase in transactions and shipping of merchandise.

Publication Delivery Service

The Postal Service is the principal delivery service in the United States for magazines, newspapers, and other periodical publications, chiefly through second-class mail. On a national level, large publications such as *Reader's Digest, Time,* and *Newsweek* are an important part of the Postal Service's business. And on a local level, smaller newspapers are important to the communities served by individual post offices. The Postal Service tries to accommodate the needs of publishers by, for example, altering mail processing and transportation schedules to facilitate the movement of specific publications.

The rate structures associated with the various subclasses of second-class mail are generally the most complex of all major mail categories. The rates charged a particular piece of second-class mail may depend on a variety of factors: the nature of the publication, the ratio of editorial to advertising content, the number of pieces mailed, the weight of the mailing, the distance from sender to receiver, and the degree of mailer preparation (presorting and entry in the mailstream at destination processing facilities).

Although complicated, second-class regular rates generally are low relative to other classes of mail. This has been a feature of American public policy for many decades. Initially, preferential rates for periodical publications were designed to foster the widespread dissemination of public information and the encouragement of a strong local press. There even was a period starting in the mid-1800s when publications sent locally, or in the county of publication, were carried free. For some copies, free carriage lasted until 1951.

But when Congress passed the Postal Reorganization Act in 1970, it decided (as discussed in the previous chapter) that rates for all classes of mail should recover the direct and indirect costs that could be attributed to that class. Over time this change in policy has brought sharp increases in the rates for second-class mail.

Faced with increased postage costs, a number of large magazine publishers, national newspapers, advertisers, and book and record clubs commenced experimenting in the late 1970s with private delivery firms that typically limit their activities to densely populated metropolitan areas. For example, the *Wall Street Journal* for years relied primarily on the postal system for same-day delivery of that newspaper, but the *Journal* now has hundreds of thousands of copies delivered each day by private carriers in locations around the country. Other big publications that have turned to private delivery firms at various times in recent years include *Good Housekeeping, Better Homes and Gardens, Ladies' Home Journal, McCall's, Newsweek, Time, Sports Illustrated,* and *U.S. News and World Report.* Large book and record firms such as Book-of-the-Month Club, Reader's Digest Books, Time-Life Books, Columbia House, and RCA Record Clubs have used private delivery systems.

Private delivery firms typically are in a position to offer services at a price lower than what the Postal Service charges, in part because their carrier forces usually consist of part-time workers (for example, retired persons, homemakers, students, moonlighters) who want supplementary income. Thus, although these firms tend to operate in a highly labor-intensive environment, the capital outlays required for entry to the market are modest, and compensation costs for employees in this so-called secondary labor force are much lower than those shouldered by the Postal Service for its full-time, unionized employees.[20]

Another way in which private delivery services lower the costs for publishers is by delivering advertisements along with the publications—a practice popularly known as "piggybacking." This brings a publisher's delivery cost below what the Postal Service charges. Consider a monthly publication where the basic private delivery charge would be 15 cents a copy. Each piggyback advertisement delivered with the publication would reduce the publisher's cost by 2 cents. Thus, with two piggyback advertisements, the publisher would pay 11 cents a copy for delivery.

Although reliable data are not available, the amount of mail volume diverted by private delivery systems is still fairly small. In the late 1970s, a number of large firms (ARA Services, Harte-Hanks Communications, H & R Block, and Warner Communications) began offering delivery services, primarily for magazines, but most later withdrew from the market, in part because they experienced quality control problems that their customers could not tolerate. Private firms delivered over 35 billion pieces of mail in 1984, the latest year for which data are available.[21]

The Postal Service was extremely concerned about the gradual decline in its second-class mail volumes in the 1970s, but second-class volumes stabilized and, in fact, grew in 1985 and 1986. Even so, the Postal Service continues to worry that private delivery firms will win business away from the mail system by offering services at a lower price.

Parcel Delivery Service

For years, the postal system was the carrier of first resort for small-parcel shipments, parcels or packages weighing up to 50 pounds. But over the years many private firms in the United States have entered the surface parcel and air parcel markets. Parcel shippers have virtually deserted the Postal Service and taken their business to the competition.

Parcel post volume has declined steadily since 1971 (the year in which the Postal Service began operation in accordance with the Postal Reorganization Act). Volume declined from 536 million pieces in 1971 to 143 million pieces in 1987, a decrease of 73 percent (see Exhibit 6-5). During the 1971–1986 period, the average annual rate of decline was 8.1 percent. Big decreases (those exceeding 10 percent) occurred in 1976, 1978, 1979 and 1981 and appear to be correlated with rate hikes implemented in those years. Parcel post contributed only 0.1 percent of all mail class volumes in 1986, compared with 0.6 percent in 1971.

The Postal Service has lost this parcel business in spite of its expenditure in the 1970s of $1 billion for the development of a national network of bulk mail processing centers. In years past, parcels and bulk mail had always been processed in post offices along with letter mail. But in 1971, arguing that processing both letters and bulk mail in the same facilities was "like trying to manufacture tractors and sports cars on the same assembly line," Postmaster General Winton Blount announced plans to build a separate network of twenty-one huge facilities for processing bulk mail.[22]

The hope at the time was that these bulk mail centers would improve the handling of parcels and bulk mail enough to stem the flow of parcel-delivery business away from the postal system. The centers were to use modern sorting equipment designed to reduce handling time and also to keep damage to a minimum; they were to be located outside congested urban centers but near main

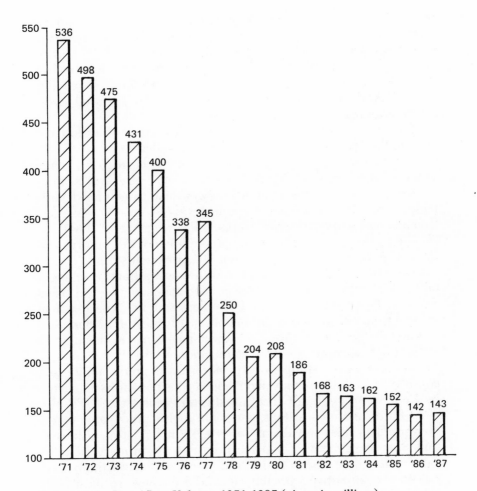

Exhibit 6-5   Parcel Post Volume, 1971-1987 (pieces in millions).

transportation lines. The concentration of bulk mail processing operations at these twenty-one highly automated facilities would presumably let the Postal Service achieve economies of scale in processing and also lead to more efficient and economical use of transportation. These benefits were expected to derive from the reduction in the number of shipping points from 73 to 21, and the Postal Service could then move greater volumes of mail over fewer routes.[23]

Few of the expected benefits of the National Bulk Mail System came to pass. When the system was first put into operation, faulty building layouts and equipment designs led to the damage of millions of packages a year, crushed by the conveyor systems and sorting machinery used in the facilities.[24] Another problem with the bulk mail system had to do with high percentages of "misdirected mail," or mail mistakenly sent to the wrong destination—errors resulting in delivery delays and in increased processing costs.[25] Although the Postal Service made progress by the late 1970s in reducing the rates of damaged and misdirected parcels, the new system was not enough to stem the diversion of parcel business away from the Postal Service.

Most of the parcel business that the Postal Service has lost has gone to the United Parcel Service (UPS). The development of UPS into a seriously competitive common carrier occurred over many years. From its inception in 1907 as a messenger service in Seattle, the company moved into retail delivery of small parcels for department stores. It then began its common carrier service in earnest for industrial and commercial shippers following World War II, as retailing patterns shifted with the proliferation of the suburbs and the declining importance of downtown department stores.

In recent years, UPS has captured the most attractive segment of the small-parcel shipment market once dominated by the Postal Service. From 1967 to 1985, UPS increased its surface parcel volume from 404 million to 1.9 billion, nearly a five-fold increase.

Many factors help explain the diversion of parcel business to UPS. First, market research conducted by the Postal Service reveals that parcel shippers care more about predictability and consistency of delivery than about speed. Business firms contacted by General Accounting Office investigators report that UPS provides faster, more consistent, and more highly predictable parcel delivery than does the Postal Service.[26] But for most businesses that ship large volumes of parcels, cost is the primary factor in determining how to ship them. And parcel post rates simply have not been competitive with the rates UPS charges, so most large shippers take their business there especially since it also beats the Postal Service in speed and predictability of service.

The Postal Service has been consistently losing its parcel business in part because its competitors are unusually aggressive, well-managed, efficient firms. But perhaps more important, the political demands on the government's parcel post operation prevent it from being an effective competitor. For example, unlike UPS, which is free to accept only what it wants (and it wants only what it can handle efficiently), the Postal Service must handle a wide variety of shipments from occasional customers as well as from regular shippers. UPS deals largely with business firms. At the end of 1985, UPS had more than 700,000 customers receiving daily pick-up service for a nominal service charge of $3.25 a week. These business customers generated more than 93 percent of

UPS's total package volume in 1985. The advantages to UPS of dealing primarily with business customers on a contract basis are considerable: the parcels it handles usually come well packaged, a substantial amount of its volume involves highly concentrated business-to-business and city-to-city traffic, and the company can devise the most efficient pickup routes for its drivers well in advance. Moreover, unlike the Postal Service, which is required by political demands to maintain almost 40,000 facilities for accepting parcels and other mail, UPS maintains a lean network of approximately 1,000 facilities. The sites of most post offices are chosen for the convenience of patrons. UPS, on the other hand, is under no compulsion to choose its sites for the convenience of the shipper. Although UPS will accept packages over the counter, its facilities consist mostly of distribution points and truck terminals for its own fleet, so convenience to business and residential areas is not a key factor in its choice of facility locations. Moreover, unlike the Postal Service, UPS can close a facility without prompting congressional intervention to stop the move, and if it chooses, it can deliver to certain neighborhoods on alternate days—again without incurring the wrath of politicians.

United Parcel Service's competitive strength is evident in the impressive financial results it records each year. Net profits for 1986 climbed 18 percent—from $568 million to $669 million— largely because of a substantial growth in parcel volume (up to 2.3 billion pieces in 1986) and the famed success of UPS in controlling its labor costs. (While UPS's total labor costs were only 59 percent of revenue in 1986, the Postal Service has never in recent years managed to get its wage and benefit costs below 82 percent.) Few major American companies keep pace with UPS's 27 percent return on equity. (Even Federal Express had a return of "only" 16 percent in 1986.) UPS reportedly is reinvesting much of its profits in its own rapidly growing air services business (more on its express delivery services below), a truck leasing subsidiary, and the acquisition of technologies for computer-assisted vehicle routing.[27]

UPS, however, is beginning to face stiffer competition from Roadway Express, a subsidiary of Roadway Services, Inc. The distinguishing characteristics of the Roadway Package Service (RPS) are: the service is designed for business-to-business users on a contract basis; package size and rates are identical to those of UPS except that volume discounts are given; a state-of-the-art bar code label is affixed to each package to identify, sort, trace, and invoice automatically; the weight limit is 100 pounds as compared to 70 pounds for UPS and parcel post; and several payment options are offered. Additionally, RPS offers daily pickup; three delivery attempts; return of undeliverables, insurance, acknowledgment of delivery; address correction and centralized customer services. RPS contracts with local companies for pickup and delivery. The disadvantage of this arrangement is that it inherently limits total management control of shipments from pickup through delivery (historically the strong suit of UPS). Still, market analysts expect Roadway to take a chunk of the market from UPS.[28]

Despite the tremendous decline in its parcel post volumes in the face of such stiff competition, the Postal Service insists that it has not given up the fight for the parcel business. Postal officials privately acknowledge that there is little the Postal Service can do at this point to reestablish itself as a strong competitor in the market. But the Postal Service nevertheless continues to try to improve its parcel business. For example, in 1985 it implemented a system for color coding parcels according to the required day of delivery. The Postal Service also has implemented a new program that reduces shippers' operating costs by eliminating the need to apply postage to each piece of mail. Postage is paid through a centralized advance deposit account, which is especially conven- ient for drop shippers using multiple entry points. The Postal Service claims that many large shippers have returned to using parcel post because of this new program. The USPS also is explor- ing parcel bar coding and laser scanning to expedite sorting of parcels.

Despite its efforts, the Postal Service faces a difficult cycle of cumulative deterioration of its parcel business. Declining parcel post volumes result in higher processing costs for each parcel. These higher unit costs in turn lead to higher parcel post rates. But as the rates increase and become even less competitive with alternative delivery systems, still more parcel business is driven away from the Postal Service, leading to the further deterioration of that service line.

Overnight Delivery Service

In view of what has happened to the Postal Service's position in the parcel market, there are justifiable concerns over its ability to compete effectively in the even more rough-and-tumble overnight delivery market. A competitor in the overnight market must provide an extremely reliable and consistent service, convenient acceptance and delivery procedures, and a competitive price. These are the minimum attributes a mailer requires from an overnight carrier. As services become more and more similar, prices become of increasing relative importance to customers and, of course, to carriers in order to maintain market share. The Postal Service was the market pioneer in providing urgent mail service, with the introduction in 1971 of its Express Mail Service. But the Postal Service now has a number of major competitors engaged in a fierce battle for a share of this $6 billion market.

The leader in this market now is Federal Express, the company largely responsible for creating the express delivery market as we know it today. Federal Express entered the overnight delivery market about two years after the Postal Service first introduced its Express Mail service. What was novel about Federal Express's operation at the time was that it operated its own fleet of aircraft and trucks and established a central sorting hub in Memphis. Packages are flown into Memphis, sorted, and flown out to destination cities for delivery all in the same night. Thus, Federal retains total control of packages from pickup to delivery. But the greater reasons for the primacy of Federal Express in this market are its creative pricing strategies, volume discounting, innovative services such as early morning delivery, parcel tracking, convenience centers, and a strong advertising campaign, targeted at executives and secretaries rather than at mailroom or office managers. Although Federal Express is facing challenges to its grip on overnight delivery, it is by far the dominant force, enjoying roughly 58 percent of the market.[29]

Other firms competing in this market include Airborne Express, Emery/Purolator, DHL Worldwide Express, and, most recently, United Parcel Service, which entered this market in 1985 with a next-day letter service that carried the lowest published price ($8.50) of all the expedited delivery companies. United Parcel's overnight service had a 35 percent growth rate in 1986, with volume reaching 35 million pieces. However, other companies, like Emery/Purolator, are experiencing hard times as a consequence of increasing turbulence in this market that has led to a fresh round of price cutting and a sudden slowdown in sales growth. The Postal Service's troubles with its Express Mail service are especially severe.

Express Mail experienced continuous and rapid growth during the 1970s, despite the increasing competition from Federal Express and others. In 1979, following suspension of the Private Express Statute (PES) for extremely urgent letters, Federal Express assumed the leadership position in the market. Nonetheless, Express Mail unit revenue remained much the same, and volume continued to grow at a slowing but still significant (30 percent) rate of annual growth. However, by late 1982, when the Postal Service was starting to prepare the omnibus rate case that resulted in the new rates of February 1985, its market share had peaked at 26 percent. (This was expected in light of the 1979 PES suspension.) While the Postal Service was aware that its competitors were offering enhanced service (on-demand pickup, rapid shipment tracing, dedicated transportation), its 1983 rate filing did not propose to follow suit. The Postal Service was, as it saw itself to be, the low-cost provider to the mass market, and, under pricing regulations, it could not follow competitive moves that required significant front-end investment.

Following several banner years in which Express Mail volume grew by 19 percent (1982), 29.4 percent (1983), and 19.2 percent (1984), the rate of increase fell dramatically to 2.6 percent in 1985, and volume actually declined by 8.7 percent in 1986 to 40.1 million pieces, the first annual decline ever experienced in Express Mail volumes. A number of reasons help explain the dramatic reversal of volume growth.

First, in addition to facing more innovative competition, the USPS in 1981 started to experience erosion in its on-time delivery performance for Express Mail. From 1981 to 1985 it fell from appproximately 95 to 91 percent. This caused great difficulty with—and mass exits by—volume mailers who prize reliability. When Postal Service executives try to explain this decline in service reliability and performance, one thing they consistently point to is the deregulation of the airline industry, which led to a significant decline in the number of scheduled nighttime airline flights and the cessation of freighter operations by many airlines. When the CAB closed its doors on January 1, 1985, airlines no longer had to carry the mail, so contracts had to be negotiated with them for the service. But even with contracts for guaranteed flights, the Postal Service experienced a dramatic decline in service performance levels in midyear largely as a consequence of the suspension of late night flights by major carriers and constant fluctuations in air transportation schedules. Its competitors (UPS and Federal Express) were at an advantage at this time because they had their own fleet of planes and did not have to rely on private air carriers as did the Postal Service.

Second, coincident with service problems, the Postal Service in February 1985 implemented the Postal Rate Commission's recommended 15 percent increase in the rate for the basic Express Mail Two-Pound Pack, which went from $9.35 to $10.75. At about the same time, competitors cut prices for light-weight pieces by offering letter rates. And UPS entered the market and introduced an

$8.50 overnight letter rate, which it proceeded to market aggressively.

Third, the competitive pace quickened overall. For example, Federal Express countered UPS's new service with heavy discounts for volume mailers, separate pricing strategies for next-morning and next-afternoon delivery, and reduced rates for drop-off.

Whatever the reasons for the Postal Service's fumbling of Express Mail in 1985, the importance of the reversal cannot be overstated. The Postal Service lost many customers to its competitors and is unlikely to regain them because of the nature of this market: customers care most about reliability and speed, and have little reason to return to the Postal Service when other companies are meeting those criteria well. In this business, a company has to do its job right the first time. A customer burned does not return.

The Postal Service faces substantial hurdles in trying to increase its share of this market. Perhaps its greatest handicap is that it cannot follow suit when its competitors offer innovative services, volume discounts, or lower prices. Its competitors are free to change services and prices at will. But because all postal service and rate changes must be approved in advance by the Postal Rate Commission (a process that, as the previous chapter showed, takes up to ten months once a rate case has been submitted to the commission), the Postal Service is not able to adjust prices or services in response to the marketplace. The Postal Service finds it especially difficult to compete against the volume discounts offered by competitors such as Federal Express. For example, Federal will offer an entire office building a special rate if everyone in the building uses its service. Federal also gives a variety of other dramatic discounts to their high-volume users, and they price selectively, charging what the market will bear. This pricing strategy has been highly successful in taking business away from the Postal Service.

But the Postal Service has tried to elbow its way back into the fight in this market. In 1986 management awarded a contract for night freighter service to provide needed airlift during critical time frames within a network of fifteen cities. Helicopters are employed to transport mail to and from airports and downtown mail processing centers. This form of transportation has been invaluable in areas where heavy traffic congestion and other impediments would normally delay motor vehicles. Also, some long-distance service routes have been created in heavy traffic corridors, such as the "Eagle Express Run" between the New York area and the Washington, D.C., area.

In addition, the USPS embarked both on an internal organizational campaign to reemphasize the time-critical nature of Express Mail services and an external campaign to make Express Mail service more attractive to customer needs. These latter actions, stressed in ambitious new advertising and promotion programs, included improved proof of delivery using a computerized system for entering complete delivery receipt data; introduction of three new shipping containers (an Overnighter box, an Overnighter tube, and a new letter envelope); the deployment of 10,000 new Express Mail outdoor collection boxes in strategic locations near office buildings, in industrial parks and other convenient locations and another 3,600 indoor collection boxes in high-rise office buildings; the growing use of mobile Express Mail acceptance vans; and the inauguration of the Express Mail Corporate Account, a centralized, nationwide advance deposit account that permits customers to mail at any acceptance location by simply using an account number.

In 1986, the Postal Service launched other initiatives designed to keep its Express Mail service competitive. It began testing a before-noon delivery service for Express Mail in thirty cities. At five other sites, USPS began testing the acceptance of credit cards for use with Express Mail purchases—a significant departure from traditional cash-on-the-line payment methods typically associated with postal transactions.

In 1988 the Postal Service received the acceptance of the Postal Rate Commission for various proposals designed to increase the competitiveness of Express Mail service. Although the rate commission did not accept the Postal Service's proposal for volume discounts (since there was inadequate evidence that such discounts would be based on any cost avoidance), it did recommend a new "letter rate" of $8.75 for overnight Express Mail items weighing eight ounces or less. Approval of the letter rate was important since the Postal Service was the only major competitor without letter rates, at a time when they had become a major advertising theme in the overall market. The rate commission also approved a new second-day service for locations off the network for next day service; accepted a proposal for flexible pickup service; and permitted the Postal Service to set earlier guaranteed delivery times in cities it selects.

In one of its more ambitious (and, some say, silly) efforts to compete with Federal Express, the Postal Service in 1987 began testing an electronic tracking system to monitor the delivery status of Express Mail shipments. Federal Express has made much of its guarantees to its customers that it can track down the location of their packages within half an hour. The Postal Service was eager to equip itself with a similar capacity, believing that its inability to provide precise tracking information might have been contributing to a feeling on the part of customers that the Postal Service is unreliable and is operating Express Mail as a loose, hit-or-miss service. (Postal executives acknowledge that very few customers really "need" tracking information, but that the simple inability to offer it may be a competitive handicap.)

Yet another ambitious move by the Postal Service is its effort, begun in 1987, to mimic the hub-and-spokes distribution concept pioneered by Federal Express and later adopted also by Airborne, Emery/Purolator, and DHL. The Postal Service created a new air transportation network linking major metropolitan areas in the United States. The cities initially included in the network are Atlanta, Baltimore-Washington, Boston, Charlotte, Chicago, Cincinnati, Cleveland, Dallas-Ft. Worth, Denver, Detroit, Houston, Los Angeles, Miami, Minneapolis-St. Paul, Nashville, New York (Newark Airport), Orlando, Philadelphia, Pittsburgh, St. Louis, San Francisco, and Seattle. Another fourteen cities could be added to this network.

Started on June 8, 1987, and using the Terre Haute, Indiana, airport as the "hub" for the network, the new system aims to augment existing nighttime commercial air transportation being used to move Express and Priority mail and to give the Postal Service greater flexibility and control of its transportation of mail. One of the nation's largest cargo airlines, Evergreen International Aviation, Inc., of McMinnville, Oregon, won the two-year, $136 million contract from the Postal Service to establish the hub air network. The system's aircraft include 727s, DC9s, L188 propjets, and Convair 580s. Except for flights from the West Coast, the planes depart the origin cities about 10 P.M. After exchanging cargo in Terre Haute, the planes arrive in the destination areas by 7 A.M.

Many people in Postal Service headquarters believe that too much emphasis is being placed on Express Mail by top management in view of the fact that the $498 million in revenue from Express Mail in 1987 was a mere 1.6 percent of total Postal Service revenues and the 41.5 million pieces of Express Mail accounted for a mere .02 percent of total mail volume.

It may be that the Postal Service is making a mistake in trying to compete so vigorously in the overnight delivery market. It seems clear that the Postal Service lacks the resources to compete head to head with Federal Express and UPS in this market. It might instead simply focus its attention on providing express services that can be piggybacked on existing services and that can provide customers with relatively cheap and reliably speedy service (not necessarily "overnight"). In any case, it seems clear in light of this chapter's analysis of the Postal Service's business areas that postal management should be putting its greatest emphasis where its real business is—in first- and third-class mail, where volumes are increasing at rates that the Postal Service finds alarming.

Endnotes

1. U.S. Postal Service, *Strategic Business Plan, Fiscal 1986–1990* (June 1985), p. 7.
2. Commission on Postal Service, *Report of the Commission on Postal Service* (Washington: U.S. Government Printing Office, 1977), vol. 1, p. 22.
3. U.S., Postal Service, Marketing Department, *Competitors and Competition of the U.S. Postal Service,* vol. 18 (Washington: U.S. Postal Service, June 1986), pp. 41–42.
4. Ibid., p. 39.
5. Henry Geller and Stuart Brotman, "Electronic Alternatives to Postal Service," in *Communications for Tomorrow,* ed. Glen O. Robinson (New York: Praeger Publishers, 1978), p. 323.
6. U.S. Postal Service, *Competitors and Competition,* p. 41.
7. U.S., Post Office Department, *Annual Report of the Postmaster General, 1972,* p. 30.
8. Postal Service, *Customers and Competition,* p. 32; *New York Times,* May 6, 1988, pp. A1, D5.
9. Ibid., p. 31.
10. See *Wall Street Journal,* January 8, 1988, p. 10.
11. See Arthur Louis, "The Great Electronic Mail Shootout," *Fortune,* August 20, 1984, pp. 167–72; and *Newsweek,* August 20, 1984, p. 64.
12. U.S. Postal Service, *Comprehensive Statement on Postal Operations,* 1984, p. 26.
13. See U.S., Congress, House, Committee on Government Operations, *Postal Service Electronic Mail: The Price Still Isn't Right,* 98th Cong., 1st Sess., 1983, House Report No. 98-552, p. 3.
14. Stanley Feldman et al., "Estimating the Use of Telecommunications Services, Postal Services, and Advertising by Industry" (Paper prepared for presentation at the Conference on Telecommunications Demand Modeling: An Integrated View, New Orleans, October 23–25, 1985).
15. Postal Service, *Strategic Business Plan, 1986–1990,* p. 6.
16. I am grateful to Charles E. Guy, Director of the Postal Service's Office of Economic Analysis, for making me aware of this point.
17. Postal Service, *Customers and Competition,* p. 4.
18. Ibid., p. 50.

19. Ibid.
20. See testimony in U.S., Congress, House, Committee on Post Office and Civil Service, *Private Express Statutes, Hearings before a Subcommittee of the Committee on Post Office and Civil Service*, 96th Cong., 1st Sess., 1979, Serial No. 96-39, p. 81.
21. Postal Service, *Customers and Competition*, p. 4.
22. Quoted in *Washington Post*, June 12, 1974, p. A8.
23. U.S., Congress, House, Committee on Appropriations, *Treasury, Postal Service, and General Government Appropriations for Fiscal Year 1973, Hearings before a Subcommittee of the Committee on Appropriations*, 92nd Cong., 2d Sess., 1973, p. 29.
24. See Comptroller General of the United States, *Problems of the New National Bulk Mail System*, report to the Congress (Washington: General Accounting Office, December 10, 1976), No. GGD-76-100, p. 19; U.S., Congress, House, Committee on Post Office and Civil Service, *National Bulk Mail System, Hearings before a Subcommittee of the Committee on Post Office and Civil Service*, 94th Cong., 2d Sess., 1976, pp. 11, 18, 54, 58.
25. Comptroller General, *Problems of the New National Bulk Mail System*, p. 15.
26. Comptroller General of the United States, *Grim Outlook for the United States Postal Service's National Bulk Mail System*, report to the Congress (Washington: General Accounting Office, May 16, 1978), No. GGD-78-59, pp. 14–15, 20, 43.
27. *Business Mailers Review*, June 29, 1987, p. 2.
28. Postal Service, *Competitors and Competition*, p. 27.
29. *Wall Street Journal*, January 8, 1988, p. 1.

Chapter 7

CONCLUSIONS ON MAINTAINING A STRONG POSTAL SYSTEM

Although the United States Postal Service is an easy target for critics of all sorts—journalists and cartoonists inclined to cheap shots, self-styled "public interest" advocates, opportunistic legislators and their ambitious aides, and knee-jerk free-market ideologues—this is a governmental organization that works, and works well. Since its corporate transformation nearly two decades ago, the Postal Service has dramatically altered its internal organizational culture, changing from a stodgy, constipated old bureaucracy to a relatively aggressive organization that operates about as much like a business as any organization can in a governmental context. It has devised a more streamlined and effective management structure, decentralizing internal decision-making authority as much as possible without compromising the need for certain centralized controls in such an interdependent system. It has conspicuously improved its emphasis on marketing and on meeting customer needs. Despite some disappointing setbacks, the Postal Service has notably modernized the physical plant of the postal system, making particular progress in the automation of mail processing. And although the rising costs of operating the vast mail system have driven postal rates up sharply in the past two decades, the Postal Service nevertheless maintains postage rates significantly below those of most other industrialized nations (see Exhibit 7-1). Finally, the Postal Service has substantially accomplished the break-even objective Congress gave it: over the ten-year period from 1978 to 1987, its revenues and expenditures were essentially in balance.

On the other hand, it is true that the Postal Service has had the

Country	Rate for first Unit of Domestic Letter Postage (National Currency)	Postage Converted to U.S. Cents*
1. Italy	600.00 Lira	48.0
2. Germany (Fed. Rep.)	.80 Mark	47.2
3. Japan	60.00 Yen	46.5
4. Norway	2.70 Krona	42.3
5. Austria	5.00 Schilling	42.0
6. Netherlands	.75 Guilder	39.4
7. France	2.20 Franc	38.3
8. Belgium	13.00 B. Franc	36.4
9. Sweden	2.20 Krona	36.5
10. Switzerland	.50 S. Franc	35.6
11. United Kingdom	.18 Pound	31.8
12. Canada	.37 C$	29.5
13. Australia	.37 A$	26.8
14. U.S.A.	.25 US$	25.0

*Foreign exchange rates prevailing on March 3, 1988.

Exhibit 7-1   Selected Foreign Postal Rates Compared With United States Rate.

normal share of defeats and misadventures, as the continued decline of its parcel business and the failure of its E-COM program attest. And many of its efforts to economize and to increase the efficiency and productivity of its operations have fallen short of their objectives—in some cases because of managerial bungling but usually because threatened or inconvenienced constituencies have successfully importuned Congress to intervene on their behalf. Such experiences have shown postal executives that the full measure of managerial autonomy that was supposed to be accorded to the Postal Service in its corporate transformation nearly two decades ago does not really extend to many important areas of postal policy. Postal executives have learned that their continuing efforts to rationalize the mail system are likely to arouse vociferous resistance from citizens who believe there is something sacrosanct about long-established postal policies. Top management also has learned to expect that its efforts at cost control will inspire opposition from members of Congress who are ever-ready to intervene at the urging of powerful organized interests.

In short, despite the obstacles in its path, the Postal Service has done remarkably well at improving the performance of the American mail system in most every dimension—finances, technological innovation, productivity, and service delivery.

Toward a Stronger Postal System

Postal policy and administration are obviously not free of continuing problems. And as with any large enterprise, there are many ways in which the effectiveness of the postal system could be improved. Most of them have been tried but stopped aborning by congressional intervention or aborted at conception by postal executives who anticipate it. Three matters, however, cannot be ignored in any summary discussion of American postal policy. They have to do with (1) eliminating senseless financial obstacles to the attraction of the best possible managers; (2) investing more money in technological solutions to the most pressing problem in the postal system's future—crushing increases in mail volume; and (3) ridding an otherwise creditable rate-making process of some obvious flaws in institutional and legal design.

Attracting Managerial Talent

A common criticism of the Postal Service is that postal employees are paid too much. People hear of postal clerks and letter carriers earning roughly $30,000 a year and may believe such wages to be excessive. Surely it is true that postal workers have done well financially since 1970 through the collective bargaining process. Of course, "doing well financially" is a highly subjective notion, and there is no rigid standard by which the adequacy or excessiveness of compensation can be measured. Thus, it seems pointless to rail against "those overpaid postal workers."

But a serious pay compression problem *inside* the Postal Service needs fixing. It is caused by the cap on the postmaster general's salary, which is the top level of pay in the postal system. The Postal Reorganization Act of 1970 directs the Postal Service to "achieve and maintain compensation for its officers and employees comparable to the rates and types of compensation paid in the private sector of the economy of the United States." And while plenty of attention has been paid to meeting that objective on behalf of rank-and-file postal workers, the salaries of Postal Service officers and high-level managers fall far short of this goal. This is one of the largest and most complicated enterprises in the world, yet its top executives and managers earn salaries that are substantially below what most of them would be making in positions of comparable responsibility in the private sector. In order for the Postal Service to attract and retain highly qualified persons to its top management positions, the Board of Governors, empowered by law to set the pay of the postmaster general, should lift the cap on the postmaster general's salary. Maintaining this artificial ceiling makes little sense, since it has little practical use other than to avoid damaging the egos of legislators.

The pay compression problem is most serious at the top, but there also is a wholly inadequate differential between the wages in the top carrier and clerk grades and those of supervisors and postmasters. The pay of supervisors and postmasters gets squeezed from both ends. Above them are many layers in the managerial hierarchy, where an effort is made to maintain some differential, however slight, up to the postmaster general. Beneath them are the craft employees whose pay keeps getting pushed up against theirs because the craft employees benefit from collective bargaining privileges that supervisors and postmasters lack. The unfortunate consequence is that it is often hard to persuade good people to accept positions as postal supervisors because their doing so would mean that their level of compensation would drop below what they were earning as a clerk or a carrier.

Spending on Technology to Handle Growth in Mail Volume

The U.S. Postal Service is the largest mail system in the world. In fiscal year 1987, it handled over 154 billion pieces of mail. In the past ten years, mail volume has increased by 58 percent. This mail volume is likely to continue to grow because of favorable economic and demographic factors. That is, mail volume is influenced principally by two things, the level of economic activity and changes in household demographics. Postal planners expect economic growth to continue, and those sectors of the economy that are the largest users of postal services are expected to be among the most rapidly growing sectors. Three demographic factors also point toward continuing sharp increases in mail volume. First, increases in population and in the formation of households affect mail volume. Data Resources, Inc., has estimated that there will be approximately 15 million new households formed in the United States from 1986 to 1995, at an average increase per year of approximately 1.5 million new households. Second, the American population is aging, and research conducted for the Postal Service indicates that older people receive more mail than younger people. Third, previous research also indicates that as household income increases, that household tends to receive more mail. In fact, households earning $35,000 or more in 1976 dollars received over twice as much mail as those in the $10,000 to $15,000 bracket. Postal planners in 1985 forecasted that income per household will increase in real terms at least through the start of the next decade, and that this will cause a proportionately larger increase to occur in the number of households in the mid-level and upper-level income categories, where mail volume is heaviest. In view of all these trends, postal planners expect total mail volume to be 165 to 175 billion pieces by 1991. At current rates of increase, volume could grow to 240 billion pieces by the year 2000.[1]

The Postal Service has dealt with past increases in mail volume largely by improving worker productivity through training and mechanization, increasing customer work sharing, implementing stronger management controls, and improving management information and control systems. However, applications of technology must be accelerated, and new and innovative ways of handling mail will need to be developed if the Postal Service is to sustain its goal of providing high-quality services while maintaining reasonable rates.

Progress is clearly being made in this regard. In 1976 the Postal Service devoted only one-tenth of 1 percent of its budget to spending on new technology. Ten years later, in fiscal 1986, its capital spending for new equipment was $600 million, almost 2 percent of its $31 billion budget. Another $700 million was spent in 1986 on investments in physical plant. This total capital spending of $1.3 billion in 1986 was two and a half times the amount spent the previous year, but still left total capital spending by the Postal Service far below the spending of other delivery organizations when compared on a gross, per-employee basis. For example, the Postal Service's capital investment per employee in 1985 was less than $2,000, compared with $5,700 by United Parcel Service and $13,500 by Federal Express.[2]

The Postal Service is also seriously underinvested (in terms of assets per employee) when compared with other large service organizations. For example, in 1985 the assets per employee of Federal Express were about $70,000; UPS, about $27,000; McDonalds, about $34,000; and the Postal Service, about $12,700. Although even the experts agree that it makes little sense for the Postal Service to try to catch up to some industry "norm" on technology-related spending, it is clear that, in light of the extraordinary growth in mail volume and the crippling labor-intensity of current postal operations, the Postal Service must substantially increase its investment in new operating processes and equipment if it is to reach its goals of increased efficiency and higher-quality service. Although the Postal Service is focusing more attention and more dollars on one of its most labor-intensive operations—carriers' early morning preparation of the day's mail for delivery—still

greater emphasis should be given to the mechanization or automation of these tasks.[3]

Empowering the Postal Rate Commission

As the analysis in Chapter 6 showed, the current process for
setting postal rates is a far cry from the pre-1970 days when rates
were artificially depressed by legislative rate-making in which
political considerations were more highly valued than economic
ones. In those days, rates were set by Congress and the president
through routine legislative processes that were relatively informal,
embarrassingly amateurish and perfunctory, and highly politicized, affording powerful special mailing interests opportunities to
shape postal rate structures in their own best interests.

By contrast, the postal rate-making process of today is much
more formal, rigorous, and professional. Congress made it quite
clear when it created the Postal Rate Commission that this was to
be a professional body that would utilize its expertise to apply
technical costing and important policy criteria to reach independent recommendations on postal rate and classification matters.
The commission is required to make detailed findings of fact based
on the evidence of record. It must affirmatively evaluate many
statutory factors. And it is charged with balancing the goal of a
healthy postal service with the needs and rights of individuals and
businesses.

For the postal rate-making process to work in accordance with
Congress's intentions, there is a required partnership between the
Postal Service and the Postal Rate Commission. From the beginning of this arrangement in the early 1970s, there has been a
certain degree of tension between the two agencies, which is
probably inevitable in view of the nature of the commission's
function. For the first half of the 1970s, the PRC acted as little
more than a rubber stamp for the Postal Service's rate requests,
but it slowly developed analytic strength and a spirit of independence and grew to be respected for its rigor and professionalism.
Working side by side, if not together, the Postal Service and the
rate commission managed to craft a creditable rate-making system.
But by the late 1970s and early 1980s, the flaws in this institutional
arrangement were increasingly apparent as the commission and
the Postal Service came to serious loggerheads on a variety of
fronts—proper cost allocation methods, the implementation of a
controversial new electronic mail service, and the unwillingness of
the Postal Service to provide the commission with needed information and data.

The single most important defect in the institutional arrangement for postal rate-making is that the Postal Rate Commission
does not have final authority over rates. The commissioners (with
the assistance of lawyers and economists) hold months of hearings,
take testimony from all sides, and labor over thousands of pages of
interrogatories, examination and cross-examination. But their final
decision is subject to the approval of the Postal Service's Board of
Governors who can either accept the PRC's decision or send it
back for further consideration. And even after the commission has
reconsidered, the governors, by a unanimous vote, can still reject
its recommendations. That is precisely what happened in 1980
when the commission, having sharply criticized the Postal Service
for what it regarded as the Service's failure to apply correct cost
allocation methods, recommended against the proposed increase
to 20 cents for a first-class stamp and proposed an 18-cent rate
instead. Following a lengthy interagency battle, the Postal Service's Board of Governors simply turned down the commission's
recommended rates and adopted the 20-cent stamp.

It hardly seems an acceptable situation that a government agency
enjoying a monopoly over certain of its services has the ultimate
power to put into effect whatever rates it chooses, irrespective of
the recommendations of the independent Postal Rate Commission,
and irrespective of the factual record established in a ten-month
long formal proceeding. Worse yet that this power is vested in a
part-time Board of Governors that meets once a month and consists
of people who are not only generally untutored in the intricacies
of postal economics but who, however able, obviously lack the
time to master the commission's recommended decisions, much
less the tens of thousands of pages of information in the hearing
records. A far better, and certainly more streamlined, arrangement
would be to give final authority to the Postal Rate Commission.
The expert and highly technical review it makes of Postal Service
rate requests is more than adequate. And its carefully reasoned
and detailed decisions constitute an ample and professional record,
open to public and judicial review. (The institutional capacities of
the Postal Rate Commission improved conspicuously throughout
the 1980s under the skillful and steady direction of its chairman,
Janet Steiger, and her top staff.)

Congress should amend the Postal Reorganization Act to give
the PRC the genuine regulatory powers it should have been given
in the first place. That is, the recommendations of the Postal Rate
Commission should not be subject to a dispositional decision by
the Board of Governors of the Postal Service. Rather, the decisions
of the PRC should be final, but subject, before any question of

judicial review arises, to the governors' right to return them to the PRC for reconsideration, accompanied by a statement of their objections. The PRC should be required then to consider and make findings on the governors' objections. And having acted on this remand from the governors, the commission's decisions should be final, subject only to judicial review.

Regardless of what Congress does to remedy that institutional flaw, it should at least better equip the Postal Rate Commission to discharge its responsibilities by giving it specific authority to subpoena relevant information and documents during its proceedings. Like any regulatory body with authority to set rates, the Postal Rate Commission runs on information, and—while progress is being made—data are too often available too late or in too sketchy a form to be fully satisfactory. Moreover, as it stands now, there is no satisfactory remedy when data of a controversial nature are withheld. As noted in Chapter 5, this has become an especially serious problem as more and more analyses and forecasts are computerized. Although the use of computer models holds out the promise of shorter regulatory proceedings and more enlightening analysis, a fair proceeding requires that testimony resting on computer studies be accepted only when accompanied by documentation and program materials (along with the computer-based evidence) sufficient to let other parties to the case replicate and test those studies.

Subpoena authority would not subject the Postal Service to additional or burdensome data requests (since the commission would probably invoke the authority rarely, if ever), but it would allow the commission to enforce reasonable requests for informative materials addressed to any party in the commission's formal proceedings, and thereby promote expeditious, informed decision-making.

None of these observations or recommendations is especially new or fresh; others attentive to U.S. postal policy over the years have advocated similar steps. But compelling needs are facing the postal system in the last decade of this century that render these policy suggestions especially timely and deserving of action—the need for skilled and committed executives and managers, the need for technological assistance in reducing the system's labor intensivity in view of the rising tide of mail, and the need for a postal rate-making process that is efficient, predictable, and unambiguously based on expert judgments. Fortunately, with respect to each of these matters there are unusually clear opportunities for improving the system, and it makes no sense for decision-makers to continue to ignore them.

The balance of this concluding chapter examines two fundamental and important issues that intermittently attract the attention of those attentive to American postal policy: (1) whether the Postal Service's statutory monopoly on letter mail delivery should be dropped in the hope that "privatization" is the formula for achieving postal excellence; and (2) whether the current institutional arrangements governing postal policy and operations guarantee sufficient responsiveness and accountability to the American people and their elected representatives.

Privatization: A Questionable Approach to Postal Policy

One of the more fervently advanced prescriptions for American postal policy is the repeal of the private express statutes, the body of laws that prohibit private carriage of letters. Free-market economists long have called for such a move and in recent years have advanced this nostrum with increased assuredness. The proposal received a conspicuous boost early in 1988 when the President's Commission on Privatization released its report calling for the "privatization"of assorted government activities ranging from the operation of military commissaries to the operation of air traffic control facilities. Elimination of the Postal Service's monopoly on letter delivery figured prominently in the commission's formulary of prescriptions.

On the surface the arguments for repeal of the monopoly seem appealing. The primary contention of the free-market advocates is that repealing the Postal Service's monopoly on letter mail delivery would allow a more efficient allocation of economic resources. Proponents of this move tend to be quite sanguine about the benefits to be gained in terms of quality of service, and economic efficiency. As the presidential commission put it:[4]

> *Although a competitive market for mail services, left entirely unregulated, might lead to higher prices for some services, such as rural delivery, advocates of lifting the private express statutes believe that the overall cost savings to society from competitive mail service would outweigh the cost of directly subsidizing any "losers," so that everyone would ultimately gain.*

There is nothing particularly new about this argument. Free-market advocates long have been saying that competition would have assorted salutary effects. But the likely negative effects seem equally clear and, in my view, sufficiently deleterious to argue against.changing a system that has worked well for two centuries.

If the monopoly were repealed, the most likely event (as even the advocates admit) is that the profit motive would lead private entrepreneurs to serve only the most lucrative portions of the market for letter mail delivery. This process of identifying and then serving only the more profitable (lower-cost) markets is known as "cream-skimming." The most lucrative of all the "cream" in today's postal system is the first-class mail that is mass produced by computers: this category includes bank statements, bills for bank charge cards, bills from utility companies and department stores, and the like. It is very easy in the computer age for this kind of mail to be carefully and efficiently presorted.

Computer-produced mail is therefore relatively inexpensive to handle. This is why a handful of utilities around the country have taken to using their regular, full-time employees for delivering bills by hand in concentrated areas of the larger cities they serve. The law permits this particular practice, but removing the broader private express restrictions would compound the Postal Service losses of this desirable local mail volume. Entrepreneurs in every large metropolitan area would cash in on the profit opportunity inherent in relatively easy and inexpensive local delivery of monthly bills and financial statements for local companies.

As cream skimmers expanded their operations to handle, say, billings from large oil companies, and as large-volume mailers sought out these cheaper, more specialized services, the resulting diversion of volume and revenues away from the Postal Service would be substantial. Just as the cream-skimming by UPS eventually left the government's duty-bound parcel post operation in a shambles, so too the inevitable cream-skimming of first-class letter mail would leave the Postal Service with only the most expensive, least productive segment of the letter-delivery market—such as Aunt Susie's occasional birthday cards to her nephew and niece in Sandy, Utah. The increasing unit costs of handling this remaining mail would force postal rates up very rapidly unless Congress chose to step in with massive subsidies to the Postal Service.

Just as in the case of its parcel post operation, the Postal Service could not compete effectively after repeal of the monopoly unless it were free to adjust service and rates to reflect market conditions, not political and social demands. For instance, Congress would have to drop its requirement that the Postal Service charge uniform postage on first-class letters regardless of the distance sent or the circumstances of their origin or destination. That is, the Service would have to be free to set its rates to reflect the differences in unit costs occasioned by delivery to and from remote rural areas and maybe even the cost differences between delivery to single-family houses in the suburbs and large apartment buildings in the city. (One need only reflect on the inevitable administrative complexity of such a rate structure to understand why such a move is unlikely.)

Moreover, the Postal Service would have to be free to alter its service structure by, for example, pruning its network of uneconomical rural post offices or reducing deliveries to three days a week. If the Postal Service were not freed from the political demands and statutory constraints that prohibit it from taking these and similar steps, free-market competition in letter mail delivery would, in one observer's words, be "less competition than cannibalism."[5] The only alternative, after all, would offer only very short-term survival; the Postal Service could continue to increase postage rates for its remaining customers, but these price hikes would quickly induce the same cycle of cumulative deterioration in mail volume that the Postal Service has witnessed in its parcel business.

Either way, the central policy question (though inadequately considered by the advocates of the monopoly's repeal) seems to be who should pay the increased costs on low-volume letter mail, and through what method. The economists have produced one answer: to be fair, the costs should be borne by the users, and rates should be based on costs. So, simply identify the marginal costs of the services and increase the rates accordingly.

However, this answer fails to indicate a clear financing solution for two reasons. First, setting costs at marginal prices does not cover the system's costs; it leaves a substantial, unrecovered "fixed," or institutional, cost. Second, economists are concerned not only with basing rates on costs, but also with eliminating cross-subsidization between or within services. To say that "users" of mail services should pay the charges is to overlook another element of cross-subsidization in the postal system that is less obvious than cross-class subsidies. That is, the current method of postal financing assumes that the *users* of the system are the *senders* of mail and that the method of paying for the system's fixed costs should be through charges exacted from them. Yet it is clear that a significant portion of the fixed costs of the Postal Service involves maintaining a delivery network to all households and businesses. Most of these costs are incurred regardless of the volume of mail handled. Thus, if the free-market economists' call for cost-based charges is to be met, these customer network charges should be borne, at least partly, by *recipients* of the mail and not just the senders.[6]

By these considerations, there appear to be several methods of financing high-cost, low-volume services besides simply raising rates so high that Aunt Susie pays more for the stamp than for the birthday card.

First, delivery network costs could be charged directly to mail recipients through a fixed annual delivery charge to all addresses. This approach would entail several conspicuous problems of equity and efficiency. Devising a fair charge would not be easy. The fee could be based, for example, on the statistical relation between the total number of addresses and total delivery network costs. But this approach would be unfair since it would charge all addresses a uniform fee even though a uniform fee would not reflect variations either in cost per address or in the value received by different recipients. There are, after all, significant cost differences among delivery to a post office box, an apartment house mailbox, a suburban residence, and a mountain cabin. Apart from these "topographical" inequities inherent in a uniform fee, it is also clear that not all residents have the same ability to pay a uniform fee for mail delivery.

There are also efficiency considerations related to the cost of collecting such a fee. If the Postal Service tried to collect billions of dollars in delivery network costs each year from its 96 million or so addresses, the cost of recordkeeping, billing, and collecting would amount to so much that any gain from the fee would be obviated, particularly since over 20 percent of all household addresses change each year.

An alternative financing method would be to help defray the higher cost of providing low-volume delivery (especially the rural delivery) through general tax support. That is, Congress could simply appropriate to the Postal Service the total amount of network delivery costs, in effect providing an open, direct subsidy for the maintenance of a universal delivery capacity and the provision of high-cost services in rural areas. Though this tax-financed method would entail none of the high administrative costs of a direct fee, the substantial economic and redistributive effect of such a subsidy would require careful consideration.

Still other alternative methods of financing the postal system's fixed costs include establishing a special fund from the taxes paid by private delivery firms. Alternatively, the costs could be internalized within a subsidiary "delivery agency" that would be supported either by general tax revenues or by a special fund. The Postal Service could then serve exclusively as a collecting and sorting agency, turning the mails over to the subsidiary at the local post office of the addressee for ultimate delivery.

The point here is merely to emphasize that the basic issue over possible repeal of the letter monopoly is not whether it would lower costs or improve service. Clearly this would be the result for some elements of the business community that use the mails heavily. Rather, the basic issues are who would pay the increased costs for low-volume letter mail services, how might those costs be paid, and what might be the distributional effects of alternative financing solutions. Unfortunately, these are questions that even the economists who advocate repeal of the monopoly have examined inadequately.

In any event, these questions, and their answers, remain largely moot, since many factors make repeal of the postal monopoly very unlikely. First, the Postal Service is already demonstrably meeting two of the key objectives of those who advocate increased competition—innovation and responsiveness to market needs. For example, the Postal Service has developed a vigorous (and, in view of the constraints under which it operates, reasonably successful) guaranteed overnight delivery service. Moreover, the Postal Service responded in the late 1970s to growing market demand for express delivery of letters by giving up part of its letter monopoly to allow private carriers to delivery letters that have to be delivered very quickly. In addition, the Postal Service has instituted rate discounts for presorted first-class mail and third-class mail that has been sorted by carrier route; the attractiveness of the postal system has thereby been improved, compared with alternative forms of delivery.

Second, the political incentives for such a dramatic shift in public policy do not currently exist. Strong opposition would come from the postal unions that are so expert in lobbying Congress. Many users of first-class mail would be opposed to the move, fearful that service would decline, that costs would rise, and that alternative delivery firms would be uninterested in their business. And the users of other classes of mail would fight the monopoly's repeal out of fear that their pocketbooks would be hurt, since inevitable losses in the volume of first-class mail would force higher rates on them. On the other side, there are no strong groups, and only a few headstrong libertarians and free-market economists, favoring the monopoly's repeal.

Third, Congress over the years has shaped a postal system that serves a wide array of social and political objectives, and repealing the monopoly would mean that some or all of these goals would have to be abandoned. The political costs of this would be politically formidable, especially since the benefits of such a move are uncertain. Thus, the political consequences of repeal make it unattractive to elected officials, who would have to answer to the general mailing public.

But the political obstacles to such a change are not forbidding enough to stifle the enthusiasm of those who believe in the likely benefits of privatization. Indeed, some of the proposals recently advanced toward that end are much more ambitious. For example, Douglas Adie, a professor of economics at Ohio University, has proposed that the Postal Service be broken up (in the manner of American Telephone & Telegraph Co.) into five regional companies, plus a parcel-post company and a support services firm. The five regional operating companies would then be sold via stock offerings to the public, interested businesses, and postal employees (the last of whom would be offered stock at a 15 percent to 20 percent discount to encourage their support of privatization).[7] Though interesting as an economist's exercise in speculation, such a proposal bears little relation to what is possible in the real world. Political support for such a sweeping change in the system would be virtually non-existent.

Remarkable enough for the naivete that informs them, such proposals are even more noteworthy for the way in which they seem to embrace unthinkingly the view that private enterprise is inherently more efficient or more desirable than governmental enterprise. As Paul Starr has observed, such a view is the product of "heroically selective attention":[8]

> *Given the American experience with defense production, construction projects, and health care—all mostly produced privately with public dollars—it is remarkable that anyone could see a path toward budgetary salvation simply by shifting the locus of service production from the public sector to the private sector.*
>
> *Advocates of privatization show an undue tenderness toward private contractors and an undue hostility toward public employees. They indulge private contractors their history of cost over-runs; they rebuke public employees for their history of wage increases.*

Of course, free-market advocates are not alone in their suspicion of governmental enterprises. Even persons without ideological axes to grind may find themselves worried about the way governmental organizations provide services and make decisions. With respect to the Postal Service, for example, concern over public accountability of the nation's largest public enterprise has been an enduring theme in policy discussions in the past two decades.

The Instruments of Public Accountability in Postal Policy

The dust surrounding the shake-up of the nation's postal system in 1971 had barely settled before concerns began to emerge from various corners that the corporate transformation had yielded an organization more given to "blind budget worship" (as one union leader charged in 1973) than to concerns for providing service to the public. By 1976 and 1977 the chief criticism had changed; the concern by this point was that the decision-makers in the Postal Service (the Board of Governors and the postmaster general) were not responsive to the public or to the concerns of elected officials. Washington even buzzed for a while with proposals to make the postmaster general a presidential appointee again and to reclaim greater congressional control over postal rates and services.

The concern about the public accountability and responsiveness of the Postal Service has persisted over time and has had a wide assortment of exponents. Not surprisingly, members of the House Post Office and Civil Service Committee have been particularly tendentious. In late 1981 and early 1982, members of two subcommittees held joint hearings committed in part to addressing the "prevailing view" that Postal Service management was becoming "increasingly insulated from public, congressional, and administration opinion."[9] Consumer advocates also have been critical of the Postal Service. For example, in 1981 Ralph Nader charged that "the Postal Service is no longer accountable to anyone—not to the Postal Rate Commission, not to the President, not to Congress and certainly not to the American people."[10]

Journalists have added to the din. For example, writing in 1984 for the *Washington Monthly*, Richard Meyer criticized the Postal Service as being run by "a small group of executives who are unaccountable to the public."[11]

One need not be overly cynical to refuse to be whipped into hysteria by any of these sources. Legislators on the postal subcommittees are in the congressional equivalent of Siberia and do not like the thought that everyone knows it. Moreover, "public interest" advocacy is not always as selfless as it appears. Ralph Nader's diatribes against the Postal Service in the early 1980s typically ended with a self-serving argument that what was really needed in postal policy was an organizational mechanism to articulate the interests of first-class mail users—a "Post Office Consumer Action Group" that would become part of his Washington empire of consumer action groups.[12] Finally, journalists and free-lance writers also live in a world crowded with motives. When writing about the Postal Service, for example, a writer knows in advance that an "all is well in postal land" approach will find little favor among editors and publishers who think a good story is one that makes the reader's blood boil; far better, then, to find an angle that will be sure to attract the eye of editors-in-chief already known by their penchant for printing cheap shots.

Still, it is obviously true that, as the congressional panel contended, the Postal Service during the 1970s had become "increasingly insulated from public, congressional, and administration opinion." That was, after all, the whole point of the 1971 reorganization of the postal system. The architects of the change hoped to "take politics out of the post office," and make the management and operation of the mail system more effective and efficient than it had become under many decades of control by elected officials.

But the critics have a point. The Postal Service has made enemies for itself over the years in the press and elsewhere by being extraordinarily tight-fisted with information about its operations. This seems unnecessary in view of the nature of the organization's operations (these are hardly sensitive national security issues) and is unfortunate inasmuch as it only magnifies the Service's reputation for being insulated and unaccountable. Moreover, the institutional arrangements for ensuring public accountability and responsiveness on the part of the Postal Service—while far more substantial and effective than the critics would allow—are not without flaw. For example, the usefulness and vigor of the Board of Governors seem to depend very much both on the mix of personalities on the board at any given time and on the dynamics of the board's relationship with top management. And, as the discussion earlier made clear, the Postal Rate Commission, though consistently professional and effective, is nevertheless handicapped by an insufficiency of formal authority.

The important question, however, is whether the public's representatives in the United States Congress have sufficient control over the postal enterprise—whether the Postal Service is accountable and responsive to the national legislature or disregarding of congressional will and public opinion. I clearly incline to the former view. In fact, on the basis of the evidence presented in the preceding chapters, one could easily argue that the most serious problem for the long-term integrity of the postal system is not an insufficiency of congressional input and control, but an excess of it—not too little managerial autonomy, but still not enough of it. However, before examining in greater detail the nature of Congress's continuing role, it seems worthwhile to comment briefly on several other governmental institutions involved in postal affairs that have varying roles in ensuring public accountability in postal affairs: the Postal Service's Board of Governors, the Postal Rate Commission, and the General Accounting Office.

The Board of Governors

Congress placed the exercise of the powers of the Postal Service at the direction of an eleven-member Board of Governors. Nine of the board's members are appointed by the President with the advice and consent of the Senate; these nine appoint the postmaster general and deputy postmaster general, both of whom also serve on the board. Upon first inspection, such a board, akin to the board of directors of a private corporation, might seem well suited to the fostering of public accountability in the Postal Service. But in fact its record is spotty and suggests that the role of the board is likely to be highly idiosyncratic over time.

One way in which the board appears to be a channel of accountability is by virtue of the presidential appointment of its members. But any influence the President might enjoy in postal affairs as a consequence of this power of appointment is reduced by the fact that the governors' appointments are for fixed terms, with normally only one term expiring each year. Thus, the mark a President can make on the board through this appointment power works very slowly, if at all.

With nine appointed members, the board also would appear to be a good vehicle for creating representational opportunities for broad "public" interests such as those of consumers. But Presidents have not used their appointment power to that effect: indeed, the board has been heavily dominated over the years by persons with executive experience in big business (for example, Crocker Nevin, chief executive officer of CF&I Steel Corporation; M. A. Wright, chairman and chief executive of Exxon, U.S.A.; and David Babcock, chairman of May Department Stores), with occasional persons having executive backgrounds in academic administration (such as Robert Hardesty, vice chancellor of administration for the University of Texas system, and Andrew Holt, president emeritus of the University of Tennessee). There has not been a single board member representing consumer or labor interests, and only several with any postal experience or knowledge at all.

But the real opportunity for enhancing public accountability would seem to rest in the board's formal responsibility for determining how the affairs of the Postal Service are to be managed. The board performs a variety of roles which give it an opportunity to have a say in a wide range of postal affairs. For example, the board serves as the final authority for making postal rate and mail classification changes, subject to court review, after receiving recommendations from the Postal Rate Commission. The board also directs and controls expenditures by the Service and reviews its practices and policies. This general mandate of overall policy direction thus involves the board in strategic planning, allocation of resources, and policies concerning employee pay and performance.

One problem with the multiple roles played by the board is that they may conflict with one another from the standpoint of protecting the "public interest." For example, when the governors approve policies that promote the well-being or financial stability of the Postal Service, they do so, presumably, because it is in the public interest to maintain the sound condition of the Postal Service. But the governors also are supposed to act in the public interest when they approve and implement rates. If they accept low rates that are in the public interest, they may harm the short-term interests of the enterprise they are also responsible for as managers. This is another reason for the recommendation made earlier that the governors should not have a dispositional decision on postal rates.

Although postal reformers vested responsibility and authority for the system in the hands of the governors, it was never the intention or expectation that the board would attempt to "micromanage" the operations of the Postal Service on a day-to-day basis. Except for authority it specifically vested in the presidentially appointed governors, the Postal Reorganization Act expressly authorized the board to delegate all or any part of its authority to the postmaster general. The architects of the reconstituted Postal Service believed that the board could discharge its responsibilities most effectively by selecting a postmaster general in whom it had confidence, giving him broad authority to manage the enterprise, receiving periodic reports on his stewardship, and securing the services of another postmaster general if his performance did not live up to expectations.

For most of the first decade after the reconstitution of the postal service, the board of governors amounted to little more than a rubber stamp, deferring most key decisions to Postal Service officials and leaving the postmaster general relatively free in running the day-to-day operations of the service. The governors' low profile seemed consistent with the aims of postal reformers, who never really contemplated that the board would attempt to manage the operations of the Postal Service on a day-to-day basis.

But the board assumed a much more aggressive role in the 1980s. The increase in the board's activism was engineered initially by Robert Hardesty, who was first appointed to the board in 1976 and elected board chairman in 1980. In order to "get the members of the board more involved in postal affairs," Mr. Hardesty insti-

tuted an expanded committee system for the board, providing it
for the first time with the institutionalized capacity to explore new
policy initiatives and to evaluate more systematically what the
governors were hearing from postal executives and from outside
sources. To the three already existing board committees (Audit,
Finance and Compensation, and Postal Rates), Hardesty's plan
added committees on Electronic Communications; Corporate Responsibility; Technology, Research and Development; and Worker
Health and Safety.[13]

The board's transformation from a largely passive group began
partly out of reaction to increasing pressure from Congress for the
Postal Service to earn its own way and partly in response to
growing criticism that the board was detached, inattentive, inex-
perienced, and uninformed. Whatever the precise sources of the
board's increased activism in the 1980s, the evidence of it was
clear in many areas of postal policy and management, but not
really publicly manifest until the spring of 1983 when, in a widely
publicized dispute, the board rejected a request by William F.
Bolger, then the postmaster general, for raising first-class postage
to 23 cents, from 20 cents, and put off any decision until later that
year. From that point on, the board gradually took on a conspicuously more assertive role in Postal Service operations.

But the vigor of the board's entry into operational management
dissipated in 1986 with the revelation of the scandal involving
board member Peter Voss (see Chapter 3) and the realization on
the part of others in the postal community that membership on
the Board of Governors held the potential for promoting not only
the public's interest but the members' own interests as well. It
seems unlikely that the board will exercise much influence in the
Postal Service over the next decade or so.

The Postal Rate Commission

Although there has been much criticism over the years of the
Postal Service's cost attributions, of the role of the Board of
Governors in turning down the rate commission's recommended
decisions, and of the rate-making process in general, the Postal
Rate Commission enjoys widespread respect and acclaim from
private parties to the rate-making process.[14] From the standpoint
of assuring public accountability, the commission also must receive
high marks, for two principal reasons.

First, the architects of the postal system's corporate transformation in 1971 anticipated that among other proclivities, a more
independent Postal Service might be inclined to try to push an

unfair portion of the cost burden onto first-class mailers. The Senate Post Office and Civil Service Committee, for example, explicitly acknowledged that "the temptation to resolve the financial problems of the Post Office by charging the lion's share of all operating costs to first-class mail is strong; that's where the big money is."[15] With an eye toward trying to prevent that imposition on first-class mailers, Congress included in the Postal Reorganization Act a requirement that the Postal Rate Commission should appoint an Officer of the Commission (OOC) "to represent the interests of the general public" in proceedings before the commission.[16] The Officer of the Commission staff have available to them the extensive resources of the Postal Rate Commission in pursuing that task.

Second, the commission itself is strictly accountable to several bodies, and its actions are subject to several types of review. It is accountable to the courts, since its recommended decisions are prepared and issued in accordance with a detailed substantive statute and strict procedural requirements. The commission is also accountable to the Congress and to its auxiliary arm, the General Accounting Office. Perhaps most important, the whole of the commission's activities is by nature subject to scrutiny. Its decisions are made on the basis of a formal record, developed through public hearings, participation in which is available to anyone with a legitimate interest. Its decisions are required to have, and do have, an exhaustively detailed basis in findings of fact and conclusions of law.

The General Accounting Office

Although persons outside the Washington beltway may seldom hear of the General Accounting Office (GAO), national policymakers pay attention to the investigative reports of this establishment of the federal government that serves as Congress's principal field investigator, auditor, and program evaluator.

Before the Postal Reorganization Act became effective, the General Accounting Office had statutory authority to disallow expenditures of appropriated funds by the Post Office Department when GAO concluded that such expenditures were not authorized by law. This power was lost under the Reorganization Act. In addition, the Postal Service obtained authority, under the act, to settle various types of claims without going through the General Accounting Office, as the Post Office Department was previously required to do. The reorganization act also took away GAO's power to prescribe accounting principles and standards for the Postal Service.

However, the Postal Reorganization Act expressly provided that "the accounts and operations of the Postal Service shall be audited by the Comptroller General and reports thereon made to the Congress to the extent and at such times as he may determine."[17] The comptroller general has long had statutory authority to investigate all matters relating to the application of public funds, and he is authorized to make recommendations to Congress "looking to greater economy and efficiency in public expenditures."[18] In authorizing GAO audits of the operations of the Postal Service, Congress undoubtedly expected that the GAO would continue to review postal operations and report to Congress whenever it found room for program improvement or greater economy.

In the years since the reconstitution of the postal system, the GAO frequently has taken a critical look at postal operations with a view to offering constructive suggestions for increasing efficiency or otherwise improving the practices of the Postal Service. The GAO has investigated postal affairs on matters ranging from the rate-making process to the implementation of the ZIP + 4 automation program. It is not uncommon for a major GAO report to send shockwaves through the postal community, as has happened with reports on subjects such as the benefits of closing thousands of small rural post offices and the need for changes in the bulk mail system.

The U.S. Congress

Article I, section 1 of the Constitution provides that "all legislative Powers herein granted shall be vested in a Congress. . . ." Among the legislative powers granted to Congress in section 8 is the power "to establish Post Offices and post roads." When Congress passed the Postal Reorganization Act in 1970, the legislators were mindful that this statute represented the most significant exercise in many years of the legislative power "to establish Post Offices and post roads." Thus, Congress went out of its way, in the opening words of the act, to emphasize the continuing "governmental" nature of the new Postal Service as a creature of Congress established under the postal power of the Constitution. In the words of the Act:[19]

> *The United States Postal Service shall be operated as a basic and fundamental service provided to the people by the Government of the United States, authorized by the Constitution, created by Act of Congress, and supported by the people.*

Moreover, Congress rather conspicuously retained the power to step back into the picture, or to revise the structure of the Postal Service, if public pressure and/or other factors resulted in sufficient congressional unhappiness over the way the Postal Service operates. Section 208 of the enabling statute expressly reserves to Congress the power to "alter, amend, or repeal any or all" of its provisions.

In order to keep themselves informed on the operations of the Postal Service and the desirability of changes in the laws under which the Postal Service operates, the legislative committees of the Congress routinely hold hearings, just as they did prior to reorganization. Members question the postmaster general and other officers (and, sometimes, the chairmen of the Board of Governors and the Postal Rate Commission), about postal operations generally or about specific programs or policies such as mechanization efforts, moves toward greater centralization of delivery modes, or safety problems in large mail processing facilities.

Moreover, the Senate has the authority to advise and consent on presidential appointments to the board and the Postal Rate Commission. Although these confirmation hearings are frequently rather perfunctory, they at least provide senators with an opportunity to express themselves on whatever aspects of postal policy may be concerning them at the moment and may from time to time give the Senate a degree of leverage that it would not otherwise have. (This, presumably, is what the framers of the Constitution had in mind when they provided that the power of the President to appoint officers of the United States should be exercised with the advice and consent of the Senate.)[20]

The Appropriations Committees of both houses also have had an opportunity to make themselves heard by the Postal Service. While the Reorganization Act contained a permanent appropriation to the Postal Service of all revenues received by the Service, the act also authorized the Postal Service to receive three additional categories of annual appropriations: "public service" appropriations to reimburse the Postal Service for providing postal services nationwide (in communities where post offices may not be deemed cost-effective); transitional appropriations to pay for unfunded workers' compensation and annual leave liabilities of the former Post Office Department; and "revenue foregone" appropriations which act to reduce the rates for certain categories of mailings, such as those for nonprofit organizations, library rate mail, and free mail for the blind and visually handicapped. Although there has been no "public service" appropriation since 1981 and the transitional appropriations have been irregular and sporadic in the 1980s, the annual appropriations acts have afforded a convenient vehicle for legislators to express their will with respect to the way in which the funds of the Postal Service are expended. It is not uncommon in appropriations measures for Congress to attach statutory provisos or limitations, frequently called riders, to control matters of policy or administrative performance. For example, tucked away in the language of the government wide appropriations bill for 1988 is the usual array of provisions, including an order that the Postal Service keep open and remodel a post office in downtown Holly Springs, Mississippi. That is in the district of Representative Jamie L. Whitten (D-Miss.), the chairman of the House Appropriations Committee. The Postal Service had been considering relocation to a suburban facility, and Whitten wanted to make sure that it would not do so. Moreover, Appropriations subcommittees use their hearings to raise problems and reach understandings with executive officials, and then use the committee reports to tie down the legislators' most important intentions by issuing guidance, advice, warnings, and recommendations to the agency.

The Postal Service also is required by law to submit to Congress each year both an annual report and a comprehensive statement on its operations (mail volume, productivity, speed and reliability of service for various classes and types of mail), policies, plans, procedures, finances (expenditures and obligations). This requirement symbolizes, in a sense, the interest that members have in the Postal Service, and serves as a reminder that in the final analysis, the people can always change the postal system, through their representatives, if they are dissatisfied with the way it conducts its business.

Congress has more than enough power—and certainly more than enough political incentive—to oversee the policies and programs of the Postal Service and to change them when that seems desirable. Congress has the authority to step in at any time and stay the hand of postal management or to revise policies that are not to legislators' liking. This is a more than adequate guarantee of postal management's accountability to the people through their elected representatives.

*   *   *

Perhaps it is inevitable that postal policy debates in the late 1980s focus on such issues as the possible merits of privatization and the appropriate measure of political control of the postal system. After all, the Postal Service was created in 1970 out of the ribs of the old Post Office Department precisely because policy-makers believed that the mail delivery system was essentially a business operation that could be managed more efficiently and effectively if it were converted from an old-line cabinet agency to a government corporation. The former organizational arrange-ments appeared to restrict managerial flexibility, stifle innovation, discourage cost-consciousness, and cater to the demands of special interests.

What is often overlooked about the U.S. Postal Service—both in popular discourse and in the deliberations of policymakers—is what a remarkable accomplishment it represents. That is, for all its many failings, real and imagined, the postal system is in vastly better shape than it was a mere twenty years ago when the President's Commission on Postal Organization pronounced the postal system a failure.

Today, the Postal Service can proudly and accurately claim that it provides a range of dependable services, at fair prices, in a manner fully responsive to the public's needs and accountable to the public's representatives; that it is soundly financed and self-supporting; that it has made great progress in automating postal operations; that its rates are determined through professional and rigorous deliberations; and that it has improved the working con-ditions and career opportunities for the nation's largest nonmilitary work force. These are significant accomplishments.

Endnotes

1. U.S. Postal Service, *Strategic Business Plan, 1986–1990* (Washington: U.S. Postal Service, June 1985), pp. 5–7.
2. U.S., Congress, Senate, Committee on Governmental Affairs, *Annual Report of the Postmaster General, Hearing before the Subcommittee on Federal Services, Post Office, and Civil Service of the Committee on Governmental Affairs*, 100th Cong., 1st Sess., 1987, pp. 169–74.
3. Ibid.
4. President's Commission on Privatization, Report of the Commission, *Privati-zation: Toward More Effective Government*, Washington, D.C., March 1988, p. 116.
5. U.S., Congress, House, Committee on Post Office and Civil Service, *Postal Service Staff Study*, "Necessity for Change," 94th Cong., 2d Sess., 1976, Committee Print No. 94-26, p. 28. The author of this excellent staff study was John F. McLaughlin.
6. Commission on Postal Service, *Report of the Commission on Postal Service* (Washington: U.S. Government Printing Office, 1977), vol. 2, pp. 700–01.
7. See Douglas Adie, "Privatization Would Work," *Wall Street Journal*, March 31, 1988, p. 20.

8. Paul Starr, "The Limits of Privatization," in *Prospects for Privatization*, ed. Steve H. Hanke (New York: Proceedings of the Academy of Political Science, 1987), vol. 36, no. 3, p. 128.

9. U.S., Congress, House, Committee on Post Office and Civil Service, *Effectiveness of the Postal Reorganization Act of 1970, Joint Hearings before the Subcommittee on Postal Operations and Services and the Subcommittee on Postal Personnel and Modernization*, Part I, 97th Cong., 1st Sess., 1981, p. 2.

10. Ralph Nader, "Price Fixing by the Postal Service," *The Nation*, December 12, 1981.

11. Richard Meyer, "Care for a Spin in My Chateau, Postmaster?" *Washington Monthly* 16 (February 1984): 54.

12. Some of Nader's articles are gathered together in one place in U.S., Congress, House, *Effectiveness of the Postal Reorganization Act of 1970*, Part 2, pp. 364–74. Nader even had the audacity to propose that, in order to assist this new citizens' group, "a simple Federal law be passed requiring the Postal Service once or twice a year to deliver letters to every residence and business inviting all first-class users to join. Members of the group would pay modest annual dues, which would be used to retain a full-time national and regional staff of advocates" (p. 369).

13. U.S., Congress, House, *Effectiveness of the Postal Reorganization Act*, Part 1, p. 17.

14. Comptroller General of the United States, *Opportunities to Improve the Postal Ratemaking Process*, report to the Congress (Washington: General Accounting Office, April 23, 1984), Report No. GGD-84-10, pp. 70–73.

15. U.S., Congress, Senate, Committee on Post Office and Civil Service, *Postal Reorganization*, S. Rept. No. 91-912, 91st Cong., 2d Sess., 1970, p. 13.

16. *United States Code*, Title 39, sec. 3624(a).

17. Ibid., sec. 2008(a).

18. 39 C.F.R. 53.

19. *United States Code*, Title 39, sec. 101(a).

20. On the general purposes of the Senate's confirmation process, see Arthur Maass, *Congress and the Common Good* (New York: Basic Books, 1983), pp. 181–88; and Calvin G. MacKenzie, *The Politics of Presidential Appointments* (New York: The Free Press, 1981).

INDEX

THE U.S. POSTAL SERVICE

Status and Prospects of a Public Enterprise

John T. Tierney, *Boston College*

The U.S. postal system is the nation's oldest and largest public enterprise, with almost 800,000 employees and an annual budget of over $31 billion. This highly complex organization holds rich insights for anyone wishing to understand the difficulties that confront those who try to supply services under governmental auspices. Yet surprisingly little scholarly attention has focused on the complex elements and issues of postal policy and administration. *The U.S. Postal Service*, based on careful research and analysis, offers a current, fair-minded, and instructive view of the Postal Service and, by extension, of other public enterprises.

This fresh and interesting examination debunks the conventionally negative perspectives on the Postal Service that are largely the product of journalistic excess or ideological fervor. Although noting the continuing problems of the nation's mail service, this balanced study finds creditable and praise-worthy accomplishments as well. Comprehensive in its scope, the book focuses on such important topics as the reorganization of "the Post Office" as a public enterprise; the problems of managing a cost-effective mail delivery system in the face of congressional constraints and political and social demands; the controversial process of setting postal rates; labor relations, collective bargaining, compensation levels, and workers' commitment; and the impact of new